Exercise Tiger

Richard T Bass

TOMMIES GUIDES

"I heard Ensign Brown shout, "abandon ship" and saw guys started over the side in droves. Many landed on top of one another with a thud. Many soldiers, who for some reason were dressed for battle, pitched forward in the water with legs up and faces down. They were top heavy and struggled unsuccessfully to overcome it, even though I could see they were wearing lifebelts. It was unbelievable. Those who survived the jump swam towards the raft.

I looked to where Dailey had been standing – he was gone. Rutherford wasted no time. Said he'd see me later and took off. I threw down my helmet and started over when I heard someone frantically calling my name. I turned and saw another corpsman standing there shaking with fear. I took his hand and led him to the railing and told him we would jump together, but for God's sake don't grab onto me, to rely on his lifebelt for support. I had to keep reassuring him that we would be OK. Then we slowly climbed over the railing together and before he had time to hesitate I grabbed his hand and jumped, pulling him down.

We hit the water together, our grasp broken as we sank deep into the freezing English Channel. It seemed an eternity before we reached the surface. I stayed where I was, holding on and treading water, getting my breath. After a few minutes I tried heading for the raft which surprisingly was still in sight, lit up by the burning 507. The 507 was sinking slowly at the stern and I knew there wasn't much time left, and without a lifebelt I wasn't sure I could make it to the raft if I delayed any longer.

I made it to the raft and strangely enough there were only a handful of men clinging to the side. I thought by now it would be overcrowded. I guess a lot of guys floundered and died before they even got started. When I got their Star was kneeling alone on the top. I found an open space on the side and took hold. It wasn't long before we were swarmed by men who quickly filled the other open spaces along the sides. Those who didn't make it to an open space had to hold onto those who did. It was made clear that only one guy was allowed on top. It wasn't challenged – yet. But the extreme cold and hysteria were already taking their toll. Guys without lifebelts and waterlogged clothing were in a constant struggle to stay afloat, holding on to guys with belts or Mae West's. Even those with *preservers were struggling because of the freezing water and the desperate situation we were in. Men were dying all around in those first few minutes of trying to settle into our perilous predicament. It puzzled me how young healthy men could give up and die so easily. It still does."*

There were about 75 of us now, jammed around and about the raft holding onto each other as before. Guys came and guys went. It was hard to keep count. Across from me were six other corpsmen clinging to the side including Rutherford who had one of them hanging on piggyback. One of the doctors was to the left of me at one end holding up a soldier who kept moaning that his leg was broken. The other doctor was opposite with the corpsmen. Dailey wasn't there. Neither was Lewis. We were so packed in that the raft was arm length under water from the sheer weight of us so we had to extend our arms to keep our heads above water. It was agonizing.

Guys were dying off all around us. Those without life preservers just let go, struggled a bit, then disappeared. Dead weight made it impossible to do much of anything to help them. One of the first to go was a corpsman who was only 19 years old, married and the father of a 4-month-old son. He wasn't wearing a lifebelt and had been holding on next to Rutherford. Suddenly and without warning he was struggling in the water, screaming for help. Star couldn't reach him and Rutherford (who was still holding up the other corpsman) threw him his leg to grab onto. He managed to get hold of the foot but slid off and sank beneath the surface. We waited for him to pop up, but he never did. In a twinkling he was gone. We were dumbfounded and devastated and prayed for him. That's all we could do. But no sooner was he gone when the boy on Rutherford's back let go and started sliding down. Rutherford reached back to try and hold him up but he was too heavy and wet and kept going straight down. Star tried to help but it was too late. He never said a word and never tried to stop himself. Just quietly disappeared beneath the surface and never came up. It happened to be his 19th birthday."

Also by Richard T Bass

Spirits of the Sand (1992)
Precious Cargo (1993)
The Brigades of Neptune (1994)
Clear the Way (1996)
Spirits of the Sand – field edition (2005)

Tommies Guides
Menin House
13 Hunloke Avenue
Eastbourne
East Sussex
BN22 8UL

www.tommiesguides.co.uk

Published by Tommies Guides 2008

ISBN 978-0-9555698-2-1

Cover design by: Tommies Guides
Typeset by: Graham Hales, Derby
Printed by: CPI Antony Rowe

Contents

Foreword 9

Part One – Background
Chapter One   Establishment of U.S. forces in the U.K. and Protocols 10
Chapter Two   Need for rehearsals and Army and Navy planning 19
Chapter Three   Fabius series 23

Part Two – Tiger
Chapter Four   Army and Navy planning for Exercise Tiger 28
Chapter Five   Operation Order 38
Chapter Six   Loading 40
Chapter Seven   The landings 46

Part Three – E-Boat attack
Chapter Eight   German view 53
Chapter Nine   American view 60
Chapter Ten   British view 79

Part Four – Survivors, bodies and burials
Chapter Eleven   Survivors 85
Chapter Twelve   Bodies and wreckage 91
Chapter Thirteen Portland 98
Chapter Fourteen Brookwood burials 110
Chapter Fifteen First reports 117
Chapter Sixteen Threats and bribes 127

Part Five – Reports
Chapter Seventeen Reports 139
Chapter Eighteen Fabius 143
Chapter Nineteen Aftermath 146
Chapter Twenty   D-Day 158

Part Six – Appendices 162

Appendices

1. Battalion Landing Teams 162
2. Plymouth Command War Orders: Control of Forces escorting and covering U.S. task forces during amphibious exercises. 164
3. Map of Slapton and Slapton Sands Battle Area 166
4. First United States Army order initiating Exercise Tiger 167
5. Training Schedule for Exercise Tiger 170
6. Admiral Moon's war diary 171
7. Field Order No 1 177
8. Army LST landing table 181
9. SHAEF instructions for Exercise Tiger 182
10. Troop list (Annex No 2 to Field Order No 1) 183
11. Landing diagram 4th Division 187
12. Boat Assignment table 188
13. APA Boat Assignment table 193
14. Ship sheet Dickman 194
15. Ship sheet Barnett 195
16. Ship sheet Gauntlet 196
17. APA road or rail movement sheet 23rd April 1944 197
18. Unit Furnishing Co Troops and TQM 198
19. LST 508 loading sheet 199
20. Annex Fox 200
21. Appendix 3 to Annex Fox to Operation Order: Sailing Directions 206
22. LST loading order 209
23. Vessels involved in Exercise Tiger 210
24. Slapton beach defence map 224
25. LCVPs involved in "Green" beach 225
26. LCVPs involved in "Red" beach 226
27. Medical Plan for Handling and Disposing of Simulated Casualties 227
28. List of survivors picked up by the Oslow on 28th April 1944 228
29. Medical plan for Actual Casualties 229
30. U.S. Army Brookwood cemetery burial list 231
31. LST 531 survivor list 232
32. Memo from Headquarters VII Corps ordering silence on Exercise Tiger ...238
33. Letter from 1st Engineer Special Brigade awarding medals for the night of 27th- 28th April 1944 239
34. Rules for awarding a "Purple Heart" 240

35. 33rd Chemical Decon Co Morning report for 28th April 242
36. Headquarters 462 Amphibian Truck Co report 1st May 1944 243
37. Headquarters 478 Amphibian Truck Co report 1st may 1944 244
38. H.M.S. Saladin report on E-Boat Attack on Convoy T-4 – Exercise Tiger . .245
39. Commanding Officer LST 531: Report on the loss of LST 531 247
40. LST 515 deck log for 28th April 1944 250
41. H.M.S. Azalea report on E-Boat Attack on Convoy T-4 on the night
    of 27th – 28th April 1944 252
42. Letter from Colonel Caffey in 1951, refuting claims made by
    General Omar Bradley 254
43. Murdock Interview 256
44. Battle casualties sustained by VII Corps 6th June to 1st July 1944 258
45. The types of craft involved in Exercise Tiger and their abbreviated names . .259

Acknowledgement

Many of the first hand accounts quoted in this
book have been extracted from letters, diaries
and personal accounts from eye-witnesses and
survivors obtained by Dale Rodman from
California, USA in his meticulous research into
the truth behind Exercise Tiger. It is with his
kind permission and loan of these documents
that extracts have been reproduced

Richard T Bass
Exeter
December 2007

Foreword

EXERCISE "TIGER" was a necessary rehearsal for D-Day that for many reasons developed into a tragic disaster of such proportions that a high level cover up became immediately necessary.

This study proves that a cover up took place, which was so convoluted and devious in its conception and execution that an accurate figure of casualties cannot honestly be given. Over the years many calculations have been made concerning these casualties, but all theories have to return to the official number of 749 being unable to prove this is incorrect or produce a firm alternative, until now.

Much has been written and discussed about Exercise "Tiger". Television companies have attempted "in depth" documentaries, the occasional appearance of an "eye-witness" prompts a brief flurry of interest in the local press, and the Internet has several websites devoted to it.

For decades no new information has been officially released, so any investigation could only re-hash what is already in the public domain by merely repeating and unwittingly perpetuate the official version of events, for which the U.S. government and military must be grateful.

The number of survivors of the disaster is rapidly dwindling and the passing years cloud their memories which become tainted by what they have recently seen and heard reported, but by careful questioning and cross evidencing their testimony, accurate accounts of their ordeal have emerged.

This investigation has benefitted from access to many documents not publicly available, and matched with circumstantial, hearsay and corroborative evidence produces comprehensive and accurate conclusions that discredit many available documents as being false or altered.

All this is compounded by the suicide of the one man who may have known the whole truth. Perhaps he wasn't told the true circumstances and had been deliberately misled to believe he was responsible for the disaster. Perhaps he did know the whole true story, and it wasn't suicide.

One

Establishment of U.S. forces in the UK and Protocols

E VER since U.S. Army units moved to the western counties of England, they had been training, practicing and rehearsing their individual and unit skills in preparation for the invasion of northwestern Europe. As the invasion time frame approached, so the intensity, frequency and scale of those exercises and rehearsals increased. From company and battalion-sized training, the tempo and size of maneuvers increased from December 1943 as a formalized work-up timetable started the final countdown to D-Day.

Saunton Beach – U.S. Assault Training Centre.

From September 1943 combat troops who would spearhead the beach assault had all attended three-week training courses at the U.S. Assault Training Center in North Devon to learn and practice the novel doctrine of an amphibious assault upon a heavily defended coastline. This doctrine had been conceived from scratch in the absence of any U.S. Army Field Manual directions or suggestions of tactics, and was developed in a matter of weeks. Drawing on the experiences of the British at Dieppe, the latest weapon developments and intelligence of German defenses it was refined by two restricting factors. The topography of the landing beaches allocated to American forces, neither of which would allow the conventional use of tanks in the assault, left the task of neutralizing enemy defenses entirely with the infantry. Secondly, the only suitable craft available in sufficient quantity to convey the assaulting troops to the enemy shore were LCVPs with a capacity of thirty combat troops.

Assault Section.

Consequently the basis of the whole assault doctrine revolved around 30-man "Assault Sections" of *"engineer-like infantry"* each capable of neutralizing an enemy pillbox or position. At the Assault Training Center, the 1st, 4th and 29th Infantry Divisions were reorganized in accordance with that doctrine to form Regimental Combat Teams, seen as the most efficient way to successfully overcome the German defenses on the Normandy beaches. Consequently many organic units, vehicles and weapons of these conventional divisions became superfluous to the assault effort and were to be left on the "near shore" when the assault upon Europe was made.[1]

1 See Appendix 1 – "Battalion Landing Team"

By the early spring of 1944 the U.S. Army were fully trained for the invasion, it only remained for detailed briefings of their objectives, assignments and tasks to be revealed and allocated once they had moved to their secure marshalling areas only a few days before embarking for Normandy.

The U.S. Navy's mission was equally complicated. From the very earliest stages of planning their task for the invasion of Europe in 1944 was to provide the necessary lift for the Army, conveying the troops, vehicles and supplies to the assault beaches in combat order, and then maintain a re-supply programme in accordance with the army's requirements.

The U.S. Navy's 11th Amphibious Force was to provide this armada and in December 1943 when planning by the commander began in earnest; Operation "Overlord" was a three-division assault with the US Navy committed to supply one assault force under the command of Admiral Hall. The follow-up component was to comprise of three divisions of

Admirals Kirk, Hall and Wilkes.

combat loaded transports under the command of Commodore Edgar who already had gained experience in this role during the invasion of North Africa. But in March 1944 the assault scale was increased from three assaulting divisions to five. Now the U.S. Navy was required to provide vessels for a second assault force, and due to this increased commitment the U.S. Navy rearranged their command structure by creating four components. Force "O" would be commanded by Admiral Hall, and convey the army's V Corps to "Omaha". Force "U" would be commanded by Admiral Moon and take the army's VII Corps to "Utah". Force "B" was for follow-up formations, with shore based facilities and formations supporting all three forces. Admiral H.R. Stark was Commander US Naval Forces in Europe (COMNAVEU); Rear Admiral A.G. Kirk became Commander of Task Force 122 (CTF 122) with responsibility for all U.S. Navy forces within Operation "Overlord". Rear Admiral John L. Hall remained commander of 11th Amphibious Force (COM 11th Phib) having assumed command on 11th November 1943 with just 235 landing vessels, which by 1st June 1944 had increased to 2,458 ships and craft.

Their base and maintenance organization, LANCRABEU (Landing

Craft and Bases, Europe) remained unchanged although accumulated new pressures of demand upon their facilities. Commanding was Rear Admiral John Wilkes as he had done since 1st August 1943 with a Chief of Staff that he had particularly requested, Captain Virgil Eben Korns. Included in LANCRABEU's responsibilities were the protection of ships and ship movements from enemy air and naval action, and experimental stations and training areas. Whilst Admiral Wilkes was the named commander, he knew little of the intricate detail within those responsibilities, leaving them to his Chief of Staff who had the power and authority to influence all exercises and rehearsals without supervision or hindrance.

Admiral Don P. Moon.

The vast influx of American army and naval forces with their equipment and vessels to the United Kingdom placed great pressures upon existing British armed forces home command structures, most particularly the Royal Navy Plymouth Command. This was a consequence of broad principles that had been agreed at the very highest level some years earlier whereby combat forces for Operation "Overlord", the invasion of Europe, would concentrate and embark from ports along the south coast of England. U.S. forces would concentrate in the west of England, the British forces in the south and east.

Just as American land forces were settling throughout the southwestern shires of England, more and more U.S. Navy vessels were arriving in the southwestern ports to take their place in the great invasion armada, creating a shortage of anchorages and crowding other Allied ships and craft in the small picturesque harbors. It was a problem of huge proportions that Plymouth Command were well aware of as they had been making plans for a cross Channel invasion since an Admiralty survey published on 16th July 1942 stated that naval shore facilities in southern England were totally inadequate for mounting an invasion, specifically highlighting a lack of docks and wharves.

This was resolved by a huge construction programme of "hards" which were completed by the end of November 1943. Hards were quick, easy and cheap to build and rapidly solved the lack of vessel loading facilities, described by the U.S. Navy as ...

"hard surfaced sloping causeways leading from road ashore down to the beach to a point well below the low water mark

and so arranged that a landing vessel could run its bows onto the hard at any stage of the tide, open its ramp and load or unload vehicles by the simple process of driving them on or off."

By the end of the construction programme Falmouth and Fowey in Cornwall had moorings for 34 LSTs and 163 major landing craft. The Devon ports of Plymouth, Salcombe, Dartmouth, Brixham and Torquay had moorings for 49 LSTs and 290 major landing craft. All these ships and more were required for the invasion itself, and there had to be amphibious landing rehearsals for them all, together with the army assault units they were to transport, and that meant they would be maneuvering off the Devon and Cornwall shore, requiring protection by the Royal Navy's Plymouth Command.

Liaison at all levels between American and British armed forces was essential for co-operation in the build-up and execution of Operation "Overlord" and the intensity was increasing as the proposed D-Day approached. This was all in addition to existing commitments of the Royal Navy, Plymouth Command, who were responsible for all naval defensive and offensive matters around the southwest peninsula of England. It had always been under pressure to maintain a high level of activity in both types of operation, now their responsibilities multiplied and co-ordination of Allied vessels within their waters became more complex as liaison and co-operation with the U.S. Navy became a necessity.

For centuries the English Channel had successfully deterred or defeated European nations with ambitions of invasion and conquest of the United Kingdom. It was a natural obstacle that Great Britain through the ages considered their home waters, knowing just how vital it was to maintain control of that narrow stretch of sea. Not only for the nation's security by preserving it as a frontier, but also in times of conflict to blockade trade routes around the north western ports of Europe.

Since the outbreak of the Second World War in September 1939 the English Channel had kept Nazi armies at arm's length, and apart from one serious threat of invasion in 1940, the narrow seas appeared to be effectively isolating the nation from German imperial aspirations. The Royal Navy was far from complacent in protecting the southern coastline of England from sea borne aggressors particularly with vessels of the German navy only a few sea miles away. The English Channel had been a battleground where Allied and German navies daily confronted each other in an escalating and deadly game of "tit-for-tat". Each laid mines in their enemy's shipping lanes, hunted down convoys of escorted merchant ships that nervously hugged the coast, hopping from port to port, and both aggressively patrolled right up to their enemy's shore in hopeful anticipation of provoking an encounter and an opportunity for a fight. Both sides were helped in seeking out their prey by patrolling aircraft and shore radio and radar installations, all of which were capable of directing ships to intercept their targets. The British had a chain of coastal radar stations and the Germans an efficient radio direction finding network that would triangulate radio signals. Both had coastal radio listening stations, intercepting enemy transmissions, decoding and extracting items of useful intelligence. There were defensive commitments as well, enemy mines had constantly to be swept, convoys required escorts, and ports had to be guarded.

Most offensive operations were undertaken during the hours of darkness by groups of destroyers or small, fast craft, lightly armed and reliant upon their speed and agility to infiltrate enemy waters, carry out an attack then withdraw at high speed. The main protagonists in these hit and run operations were Allied Motor Torpedo Boats, Motor Gun Boats, and German Schnellboots, known to the Allies as "E-Boats". Allied destroyers also played their part in patrolling home waters; they were swift, maneuverable and ideally suited for engaging high-speed craft and submarines, although many were of Great War vintage.

The Germans knew from increasing Allied radio traffic and their own sea and air reconnaissance that ship numbers in south coast harbors were growing, correctly reasoning they were for an impending Allied assault upon Europe, but they needed to know more, especially the Allies' destination and timing. So they increased their probing patrols, ranging further afield, pushing ever closer to British ports, sometimes taking prisoners from ships they sank to interrogate them for any useful intelligence.

By early 1944 two of the most successful German E-Boat flotillas were the 5th and 9th. Both were based at Cherbourg and had routinely worked together since their arrival in 1942. Their standard S-Boats were capable of reaching a top speed of 42 knots, mounting two torpedo tubes and recently modified armament, their 20mm guns being replaced by 40mm versions. On the 7th of July 1942 they took the British by complete surprise when they attacked a convoy in Lyme Bay and sank six ships. To counter this threat the British moved their 8th MGB Flotilla to Dartmouth, Devon, and had almost instant success by sinking several German merchant vessels and in August sank two E-Boats in a twelve-minute action off Cherbourg.

But the E-Boats continued to harry Allied shipping in the Channel, attacking slow moving freight convoys escorted by Royal Navy Patrol Service trawlers that were poorly armed to put up much of a fight, and while relatively slow moving, had the advantage of presenting small targets to the fast and highly maneuverable E-Boats. But the Germans weren't averse to attacking larger warships. On 3rd December 1942 they attacked convoy PW 257 and sank the escort destroyer "Penylan".

Their war diaries for the first quarter of 1944 illustrate how fierce the Channel battles were becoming. During the night of 5th January the 5th Flotilla attacked British convoy WP 457, firing twenty-three torpedoes and sinking three freighters, "Polperro", "Underwood" and "Solstad" as well as an escorting trawler "Wallasea". There followed a period of failure as during the night of 16th January, convoy escorts drove off 5th Flotilla vessels as they made an unsuccessful attack off the Lizard, Cornwall. Again on 20th January, Allied Beaufighters attacked them while making a sortie to Start Point, Devon, and one E-Boat suffered slight damage. Destroyers, MGBs and MTBs were deployed to intercept, but failed to locate them. On 31st January the 5th Flotilla had a turn of fortune when they attacked convoy CW 243 off Beachy Head, sinking freighters "Emerald" and "Caleb Sprague" as well as an escorting trawler "Pine". Two more convoy attacks were thwarted, the first on 14th February when the E-Boats were located by coastal radar and withdrew, the second on the night of 15th March as they attacked convoy WP 492 north of Land's End, Cornwall, detected by Allied air reconnaissance they were driven off by escorts including the corvette HMS "Azalea".

The 5th and 9th Flotillas began operating together again from mid-March 1944, but their initial sorties had to be broken off as they were twice detected by coastal radar, first off the Lizard, Cornwall and then at Weymouth, Dorset. After switching to mine-laying escort duties for a week, they returned to attacking Allied coastal convoys, twice being driven off by escorting destroyers until 23rd April when 5th Flotilla sank the Allied tug "Roode Zee" off Dungeness, Kent, while 9th Flotilla decoyed escorting destroyers away. On the night of 25th April 1944 both flotillas were deployed against shipping that had been located by air reconnaissance near Selsey Bill where they were engaged by destroyers and lost one E-Boat.

Defending the increased number of Allied vessels in the English Channel put great strain on the Royal Navy's resources, and the first American rehearsal at the end of December 1943 prompted Admiral Leatham of Plymouth Command to write a letter dated 1st January 1944 to the

American Admiral Hall unofficially setting out his interpretation of the responsibilities of American and British naval forces during invasion exercises. It was his view that ... *"from the time of leaving Falmouth you are in tactical control of your forces, including the British vessels forming the close escort."* He would however ... *"retain full control of the covering forces throughout the operation. "* And retain overriding control ... *"should there arise circumstances which render it strategically necessary for me to cancel or curtail the exercise. I cannot at present see any likelihood of such circumstances arising.* "Should he have ... *"any information of enemy attack by E-Boat, submarine or air, it will be passed to you to take such action as you may think fit. "* This unofficial approach was later formalized as a section of "Plymouth Command War Orders". [2]

Slapton Sands.

The time had come that Allied forces needed to put their invasion plans to the test, and to practice large scale, live fire amphibious assaults in the build-up to D-Day the American army and navy required a vast tract of land with a sheltered coastline in the south west of England. The location was important as the army was billeted throughout the counties of Devon, Cornwall and Somerset, and the navy had most of their vessels for the invasion harbored in ports along the southern coastline. The coastline almost identical to "Omaha" beach was in north Devon at Slapton and Woolacombe where the U.S. Assault Training Center was firmly established but the beaches were not quite large enough to accommodate assault exercises of the scale required, so an alternative had to be found. The area finally selected was at Slapton Sands. It became available in November 1943 when the British government authorized the Admiralty to

Woolacombe Sands – U.S. Assault Training Centre.

requisition the land. This necessitated the total evacuation of the population, their crops, livestock and worldly possessions from an area five miles square, as the land would be used for live ammunition firing and naval bombardment from Lyme Bay. The Admiralty delegated administration of the area to C in C, Plymouth Command, Royal Navy. As it was to be used principally by American forces, a U.S. Army colonel was appointed range commandant with a range party for maintenance, and a Royal Navy liaison officer. While the Commanding General, First U.S. Army, directly controlled the range, responsibility was delegated to the corps commander of whoever was using it at the time.[3]

4 – See Appendix 3 – "Slapton battle area map"

Two

The need for rehearsals and planning

IN THE face of rising German interest and hostile activity in British waters, the Allies had reached the stage where they crucially needed to test and rehearse their final plans for the invasion of Europe. With American armies billeted throughout the south west of England, it was logical for them to use their closest available training area which was the recently acquired Slapton Firing Range on the western shore of Lyme Bay in Devon.

Slapton Sands was almost large enough to accommodate a full-sized task force simulating an amphibious landing and their establishment of a beachhead, but the topography of the beach was unlike either of the two intended American D-Day beaches and presented unique problems. Facts highlighted by a secret intelligence appreciation of the beach characteristics which ...

Tank negotiating Slapton shingle.

"have a composition of shingle and gravel, with little or no sand which will not support any concentrated weight. There are small pebbles from low to high water levels, and a certain amount of large flat stones from high water level to the back of the beach. Tracked vehicles, when unloaded, can negotiate the

surface of the beach if they proceed slowly in low gear and cross the beach in a straight line. Wheeled vehicles with the exception of DUKWS carrying a tire pressure of about 5 pounds cannot negotiate the beach under their own power. "

Additionally, the beach profile and tide range were quite different to the intended invasion beaches, so any rehearsals would be for the benefit of the command and control of large numbers of vessels and troop units, rather than for the troops themselves facing a physically realistic beach assault. A fact confirmed even before the last villagers had left their homes within the Slapton Firing Range area when, on the 19th November 1943 the U.S. V Corps had issued a planning directive *"to conduct exercises in Slapton Sands area to train units and staffs in embarkation, landing on hostile shores, and in seizing and holding a beachhead to cover the landing of follow-up forces."*

Planning for the first Slapton exercise codenamed "Duck" had actually started on 11th November involving V Corps, the U.S. Navy, the U.S. Army Service of Supply, and the U.S. Air Force. Their headquarters and bases were so widely spread across the west of England that much time was lost by their representatives traveling to planning meetings. This was later identified as one element that adversely affected many important meetings inevitably leading to delays in producing essential, individual sub-plans that built the overall outline plan.

V Corps Planning Group had earlier listed those sub-plans, and decided in which order they needed to be progressed, but in the event none were completed in the correct order to deadline, and when the Embarkation plan was late. It ... *"threw all the other plans out of step and it was with difficulty that recovery from this upset was accomplished."* Lessons were already being learned, especially that delays caused ... *"the plans to be issued in fragmentary form."* Planning for "Duck" was a tough experience yet despite identifying weaknesses and mistakes in the planning procedure, they were to be repeated in every subsequent exercise.

Army and navy had to fully co-operate and co-ordinate their planning that had different priorities, and a certain element of rivalry becomes evident, each trying to promote their needs as being of paramount importance requiring precedence over the other. Where both clashed on paper was at the vessel loading stage of the operation. The army had been advised which vessels were available, and exercised their right to dictate priority of units required to be delivered to the far shore according to their tactical timetable. In doing so they created troop and equipment loads the navy could not always accommodate, nevertheless the army pushed ahead with their planning, creating documents for troop movements and vessel loads.

It was vital for the assault upon the enemy held beaches that craft of the first waves carrying the assault troops were loaded with the correct mix of infantry and engineer skills as dictated by the assault doctrine. For their landing would trigger an unstoppable timetable of men, equipment and supplies, all of which had to beach at the time it was needed by the army.

To achieve this prioritized arrival for the invasion itself and all rehearsals, including Exercise "Tiger", the army divided the operation into four phases, assault, follow-up, build-up, and normal reinforcement. In all four phases of "Tiger", more than 25,000 troops and 2,750 vehicles would flow through concentration, marshalling and embarkation areas in the sequence dictated by priority tables set out by VII Corps planners.

There was an established procedure for achieving this schedule and was the result of co-operation between the British Movements Director and US theatre chief of transportation. Published on 10th January 1944 entitled "Preparation for Overseas Movement-Short Sea Voyage" (ETO-POM-SSV), it included procedures for stripping units of overhead personnel and excess equipment, leaving only those elements necessary for the Regimental Combat Teams. The document detailed the loading of unit vehicles with organization equipment, and the preparation of the necessary embarkation documentation and went into great detail of the procedures to be followed by U.S. and British movement control personnel.

U.S. Army and U.S. Navy responsibilities for loading were divided. Movement of personnel, vehicles and supplies for the landing force to the ports, and embarkation itself was the army's responsibility, principally their Service of Supply. Allocation of units to ships and craft was again for the army to decide in consultation with the navy to ensure that they were discharged from the ships in the correct priority. Thereafter, once boarded, the navy took responsibility for all movements of vessels.

The principle of any overseas movement of U.S. Army units started with the production of a standard format "Boat Assignment Table". These assigned a "serial" number to each group of troops and vehicles they required to be transported and delivered as a complete unit, each dovetailing into their master landing plan and timetable. Liaison with the U.S. Navy provided the next sequential document where the army serial numbers were matched with available LSTs producing the army's "LST Assignment Tables".

The U.S. Army was precise in moving troops to the marshalling areas through documents entitled "Road/Rail Movement" sheets, which were calculated by backward planning. These matched navy craft and vessels to troops, tanks, artillery and supplies to arrive on the far shore according to the assault timetable. Correct loading of units in homeports for the sea voyage required the marshalling of men, vehicles and supplies for embarkation, and their traveling from home stations marked the beginning of the entire plan.

These procedures were to be tested on a grand scale during a series of final rehearsals that had long been planned for the American, Canadian and British task forces under the collective code name of "Fabius", scheduled to run from April to the middle of May 1944.

There were many smaller build-up exercises prior to the Fabius series, each designed to test either individual units, or co-operation between two or more that were destined to fight alongside each other on D-Day. They all had the necessary amphibious assault element running through them, which also tested and practiced co-operation and co-ordination between the navy and army.

The first two exercises codenamed "Duck" were planned before the assignment of troops for Operation Neptune had been decided. Exercise "Duck I" was a three day exercise for the U.S. 29th Infantry Division at the end of December 1943 after they had completed their three week training course at the U.S. Assault Training Center at Woolacombe, North Devon. Exercise "Duck II" was a weeklong exercise starting on 7th February through to 15th February for the 1st Engineer Special Brigade who would land in support of the 4th Infantry Division on D-Day.

The next exercise at Slapton was for engineer and combat troops of

Exercise "Duck".

Force "O" who loaded at Portland and Weymouth onto APA's (passenger ships converted to troop transports) that were being used for the first time to participate in Exercise "Fox", a three day exercise starting on 4th March 1944. As the APAs stood off Slapton Sands, the beach was bombarded by gunfire from two cruisers and eight destroyers of the convoy escort prior to the troops landing. Just as soon as they had discharged their loads, the APAs were sent back to the Clyde to safeguard them from enemy air attack, so critical was shipping for the D-Day lift.

Only a few days later, on 11th March 1944, many Canadian units of Force "J" held their final three-day rehearsal at the Slapton Firing Range under the codename Exercise "Trousers".

Towards the end of March Force "U" assault troops held two separate exercises for the 12th Infantry Regiment. "Muskrat I" ran from 13th to 23rd March 1944 when troops embarked at Plymouth on three APAs and sailed immediately for the Clyde to practice ship to shore movement before sailing back to Slapton. Destroyers, corvettes and trawlers under the command of the Force "U" Task Force Commander, Captain Maynard, USN, escorted the convoy. "Muskrat II" was a continuation of the original exercise, this time at Slapton Sands. It opened with a beach bombardment by two cruisers before the 12th Regimental Combat Team made their assault landing and were joined by a detachment from the 1st Engineer Special Brigade. Admiral Moon watched all this from his flagship, the USS Bayfield. The Operation Order for "Muskrat II" which was for Force "U" troops had been written by officers lent from Force "O" and temporarily assigned to Moon's staff. The "Muskrat" series hadn't even concluded before those same officers were day and night preparing for Exercise "Beaver" that was imminent.

While the 12th RCT had been involved in "Muskrat I", the 3rd Battalion of the 8th Regimental Combat Team had their own exercise, loading at Dartmouth and using Slapton beach between the 15th and 18th of March for two daylight assaults codenamed "Otter 1". Following immediately was "Otter II", a duplicate of "Otter I", this time to exercise the 2nd Battalion of the 8th RCT. Running parallel in date and location to Exercise "Otter" were exercises "Mink I" and "Mink II", for the 1st and 2nd Battalions of the 22nd Regimental Combat Team. Mink I ran from 15th to 18th March and Mink II from 19th to 22nd March.

Exercise "Beaver" was for the 8th and 22nd Regimental Combat Teams, running from the 27th to the 30th March. They were joined by a detachment of the 1st Engineer Special Brigade, two companies of the 1106th Engineer Group, and the 502nd Parachute Infantry Regiment. XIX

District of the Southern Base Section mounted the operation, following the plan and facilities it used in the "Duck" exercises. Marshalling and embarkation areas were located in the Brixham-Plymouth district, and Slapton Sands was used as the assault area. Group 2 of the 11th Amphibious Force provided the lift, protected the assault convoy and supported the landing. All had embarked at Plymouth, Dartmouth and Brixham in Tank Landing Ships (LSTs) and LCI (L) s – (Landing Craft Infantry (Large). In order to make a good beach approach to Slapton the convoy took a circular route around the western half of Lyme Bay. This time two minesweeping flotillas swept the channels ahead of the convoy before two cruisers and four destroyers bombarded the beach before the infantry landed. The disembarkation and beach assault went according to plan with the assault units securing a beachhead and making rapid progress inland. The following day units were re-supplied and reorganized for extended operations and approximately 1,800 tons of supplies were unloaded from two coasters.

The last exercise at Slapton before the "Fabius" series began was for the US 203rd Engineer Combat Battalion who held their own logistical exercise, "Cargo 5" from the 1st to 7th of April.

Now the US VIIth Corps as part of Force "U" was scheduled to hold their final grand rehearsal at Slapton before handing over the area to Forces "O" and "B" for their last exercises in the "Fabius" series.

The U.S. Navy invasion armada grew as D-Day neared, and rehearsing the ships, their companies and commanders for their invasion role was imperative, but alongside the basic exercises was the need to become accustomed to co-operation with other allied navies. For Exercise "Tiger" the naval protecting force was to be British and Canadian forcing the implementation of a mutually acceptable command structure and policy to cater for any and every eventuality. This had been negotiated some months before, apportioning responsibility for the safety of the task force to the Royal Navy both en route to the exercise area, and also during the three-day landings, with the proviso that in dire situations the senior American naval officer present could take tactical command of Royal Navy ships assigned to his exercise.

For the next few weeks of Exercise "Fabius" rehearsals the Royal Navy Plymouth and Portsmouth Commands had a daunting task before them. With increasing commitments to provide more cover for the invasion ports sheltering the invasion armadas, the need to counter increasing enemy activity, and to continue offensive operations, they would be hard pressed to meet all demands.

Three

Fabius Series

FOLLOWING the relatively minor exercises and rehearsals run by individual units to date, it was time for exercises on a much grander scale, and the final opportunities to test the months of planning and organisation, running everything in parallel to Operation "Overlord". This last series of six exercises before D Day for four invasion assault groups and two major build-up forces were overall codenamed "Fabius", and were to run between the 3rd and 6th of May 1944.

The six Fabius exercises, which together constituted the greatest amphibious exercise in history, were to follow immediately after Exercise "Tiger", which was notionally included in the Fabius series although not assigned a number. "Tiger" concerned only Force "U", the units that were to assault Utah Beach.

"Fabius 1" was for Assault Force "O", the U.S. Army's 1st and 29th Infantry Divisions, the Provisional Engineer Special Brigade Group, and attached units destined for "Omaha" beach in Normandy. They loaded at Portland and Weymouth before making their assault landings on Slapton Sands. The transport convoys, escorts and bombarding force vessels including HMS "Glasgow" and the USS "Augusta" and nine U.S. destroyers were under the command of U.S. Navy Admiral Hall. All was progressing well until just prior to the landings taking place the weather deteriorated so badly that the rehearsal was postponed for twenty-four hours and smaller craft were forced to take shelter in Dartmouth and Brixham harbours. The amphibious landings went ahead a day late, umpires and observers noting several flaws in the operation, principally deficiencies in the operations of the beach engineers.

Traffic and Personnel: Personnel embarkation rosters were not picked up from incoming ships and their form reports of personnel passed across the beaches were not received. Military police were not loaded in time to control traffic, and there were not enough military police for all important posts. Signs to direct traffic were not available early enough, and military police had not been sufficiently briefed on the operation. Vehicles were allowed to bunch on the beach while awaiting their assignments, thus presenting profitable targets for enemy artillery and planes.

Supplies: Unloading tallies were not maintained and consequently accurate situation reports could not be maintained. DUKWS generally were loaded too light, loads averaging about two tons. While this was the rated capacity of the amphibians, trials had shown that they were capable of carrying up to five tons without difficulty. There were too many DUKWS for the number of coasters, and unloading of coasters was delayed because of failure to return cargo nets from the beach.

Signal: Telephone lines were put out of commission much of the time due to lack of care in laying wire. Signal personnel were not landed in time to perform their job. The communications section of one company did not come ashore until after the company had been operation for several hours.

Medical: Clearing station personnel of both brigades and the 5th Brigade's clearing station equipment were late in arriving, hampering both treatment and evacuation.

Dump Operations: Signs were posted very late, and there was little uniformity. Trucks thus had difficulty in locating the dumps. Dump reports generally were very poor.

"Fabius 2" was assigned to Assault Force "G", the British 50th Infantry Division due to assault "Gold" beach in Normandy, the troops embarking from Southampton and Lymington to land on Hayling Island.

"Fabius 3" rehearsed the Canadian 3rd Infantry Division of Assault Force "J", loading at Southampton and Gosport to land at Bracklesham Bay.

"Fabius 4" was for Assault force "S", elements of the British 3rd Division who would assault "Sword" beach; they embarked at Gosport and Portsmouth, landing near Littlehampton.

"Fabius 5" was a marshalling exercise for British units of the build-up forces that were destined to embark from the Thames estuary and east coast ports.

"Fabius 6" was another marshalling exercise held between 4th and 6th May 1944, for other British units in Force "B" using the south coast ports. The American buildup force used about half of marshalling area D and the ports of Portland and Weymouth. The British buildup force used about half of marshalling area C and the port of Southampton. For the Americans, "Fabius 6" was to test the organization for calling forward and marshalling buildup units. During this exercise about fifty per cent of the first three days buildup scheduled to move through Portland and Southampton were called to the loading hards, totaling approximately 35,000 men and 5,000 vehicles. However they weren't loaded onto vessels, instead returning to their home stations.

With D-Day only a month ahead, many of the combat units participating in the Fabius series returned directly to the their secure marshalling areas to await embarkation for the actual invasion. No matter what faults or shortcomings were identified, there was no time for any drastic revisions to the landing plans.

The last codenamed exercise before D-Day was "Pigeon". Held between 7th and 10th May 1944, this was a communications rehearsal for Utah beach operations and involved the 4th Infantry Division, 50th Signal Battalion, 1st Engineer Special Brigade, 90th Infantry Division, Ninth Air Force, and Group Two of the Navy's 11th Amphibious Force.

There was also to be a defence exercise on the 18th and 19th of May where build-up elements of Forces "S", "G" and "J" would assemble off the coast of Brighton on the assumption that a successful landing had taken place, and would then be subjected to attack by craft simulating E-Boats. A scenario the U.S. Navy knew of and was tempted to replicate in Lyme Bay.

Four

Army and Navy planning for Exercise 'Tiger'

WHILE other American and Allied units took advantage of the battlefield facilities offered by the Slapton Firing Range to run their own exercises early in 1944, U.S. Army VII Corps planning staff were concentrating their efforts and attention to their first and only test of a full scale rehearsal codenamed "Tiger". Scheduled to last from 22nd to 29th April 1944 it would rehearse and test the movement, marshalling and embarkation of troops and vehicles as well as the many interlocking facets of the beach assault and the follow-up units.

"Tiger" would enable the higher levels of American command to practice their control of a large number of vessels in a small, defined area and to a precise timetable of landings. It was a test to smooth out any unforeseen problems that may be encountered, although there was precious little time to rectify any major shortcomings that maybe highlighted.

The assaulting infantry destined for "Utah" beach had already rehearsed their tactics in Exercise "Beaver" at the end of March, so "Tiger" was to test Force "U" plans that were a blueprint for their actual landings on D-Day. This included the first critical test of Anglo-American co-operation under simulated combat conditions, as vessels actively participating in the exercise would be both American and British.

For exercise "Tiger" the Royal Navy were to shepherd several large, slow moving convoys of US vessels totaling 337 ships and landing craft from various ports in south Devon to the exercise area of Start Bay.

USS "Dickman".

Additionally, they were to provide an effective screen of warships, under Royal Navy control from Plymouth and Portland, well beyond the perimeter of the exercise area to guard against enemy attack by submarine or E-Boats. Plymouth Command had already promised the Americans that their convoys would be "screened" by at least four destroyers, three MTBs and 2 MGBs, plus other coastal forces that, they were assured, would be more than adequate for their protection.

The Royal Navy were also to provide a minesweeping force to sweep ahead of the convoys, clearing and marking a safe channel because for this exercise, to give a true taste of the invasion to come, the sea journeys were calculated to last as long as the actual voyages would take to reach "Utah" beach. This was to be the first exercise ...

> "in which searched channels were purposely extended and complicated in order better to simulate operational conflicts, and in which several "build-up" convoys were scheduled to follow the assault phase."

To move so many combat troops to the assault area was impossible by small craft, so large vessels capable of accommodating them and carrying smaller landing craft to ferry them ashore were used. These were classified as "APAs" and two such ships were used in "Tiger", USS Barnett and USS Dickman together with the USS Bayfield, which was constructed specifically as an attack transport, and HMS "Empire Gauntlet" a British converted passenger vessel.

LCI(L)s were a standard ship type that were capable of being mass produced and having already proved their worth in other amphibious operations, formed a large part of the U.S. Navy's armada for transporting troops to the far shore. With a complement of three officers and twenty-one men, an LCI (L) could carry 188 troops or 75 tons of cargo. LCI Flotilla 4 was a typical example and was to be used in Exercise "Tiger". It had been commissioned early in 1943 under the command of Captain Miles Imlay, and after training at Virginia Beach and Little Creek from the Naval operating base at Norfolk, Virginia, departed for French Morocco via Bermuda. Loading troops for the Sicily landings in July 1943, and again for the Salerno landings in September, Flotilla 4 returned to the south west of England in late October 1943. There it was redesignated 10 Flotilla and established their headquarters in Greenway House, Dartmouth, the home of the author Agatha Christie, while the flotilla ratings were billeted at nearby Maypool House.

Already code-named "Tiger" by the U.S., First Army on the 21st March it had sent a top secret memorandum to General Collins advising him of the event, so he had some pre-warning and used his time wisely in making early plans that placed his planning staff ahead of Admiral Moon's at every turn. They had to be swift because their tactical plan had to be submitted for approval to First Army headquarters by a seemingly impossible deadline of the 7th April. [4]

Combat engineers aboard an LCI.

Exercise "Tiger" featured on the First U. S. Army list of "Highlights of training for April 1944" published on 28th March 1944, listing each unit by Corps together with dates and locations of training together with any code names assigned to their exercises. [5]

On Tuesday 4th April, Admiral Moon and his staff went to Paignton, Devon to attend a conference held by the VIIth Corps Maneuvers Directors Group who had almost completed the first draft of their Field Order, but needed to discuss gunfire, targets, objectives and safety precautions. Here D-Day for the "Tiger" beach assault was confirmed as 27th April, and both Army and Navy agreed that the Navy's operation order should be completed and distributed by 18th April.

Sir David Petrie.

Such a bold commitment by Moon to publish his operation order in only two weeks time meant three frantic days and nights of work for his staff just to produce the skeleton of the order. While they were busy, Admiral Moon took Captain Moran with him to London to confer with Rear Admiral Kirk and the British Admiral Bertram Ramsay. On their return the following day, whatever they discussed in London was passed on during a meeting with Admiral Hall aboard the USS "Ancon" where they were joined by Sir David Petrie. He had been personally appointed by Winston Churchill to reorganize the United Kingdom's intelligence services, and was now in charge of the nation's security. It is remarkable that he should leave London and join such high-ranking US Naval officers, and it can only be speculated as to why the security of the nation should be involved with a totally military operation organized by another Allied nation.

Similar but less grand exercises for American, Canadian and British forces had come and gone, none of which had attracted his attention. So there had to be a very good reason for his interest this time. Allied planning consortiums all operated under the same protective cloak of secrecy relating to personnel and locations, so Sir David could find no fault there. Only a handful of very senior commanders and even fewer of their staff officers knew the details of the projected assault on Normandy. Code named "Bigots"; these individuals had been screened and given security clearance at the very highest level, so any concerns in this respect were negligible. Any security concerns of a more minor nature would not warrant the personal intervention of Sir David, so his involvement had to be for some unique situation or circumstance of a much higher level. This was something so important that the British war effort could be compromised, or some political maneuverings between the Allied nations. Whatever it was, it involved Exercise "Tiger" and the American forces taking part.

Exercise "Splint".

The following day, 11th April 1944, Commander Lowe, Medical Officer on Admiral Moon's staff went to Fowey in Cornwall as an observer of Exercise "Splint". This was a three-day medical demonstration of handling casualties organized by Captain G. B. Dowling (MC) U.S. Navy, a staff officer of Admiral Kirk and involved LSTs 281 and 580 receiving "casualties" from small landing craft, DUKWs, and other ships. There appear to be no conclusions or comments drawn from the proceedings that did not deal with any great number of "casualties", merely transferring a few litter cases from small craft onto an LST. Only LST 281 was due to participate in Exercise "Tiger", landing airborne and anti-aircraft units in the first wave of the assault.

In the wake of Sir David Petrie's Plymouth visit, some very high level meetings were now taking place. On 12th April, Captain Glover of the staff of the Commander in Chief, United States Fleet, had luncheon with Admiral Moon, and the next day Lieutenant Commander Brauer was dispatched to London for a conference with staffs of Task Force 122 and Commander Naval Forces in Europe. There was something very important in the air. Again on 15th April Admiral Moon went aboard the USS "Ancon" to confer with Rear Admiral Hall, and two days later met again with British Admiral Leatham in Plymouth. This was unusually frequent liaison of the closest order and at the highest level for a military exercise, dealing with issues that clearly couldn't be handled by staff officers. [6]

With details now agreed between Army and Navy, army planners were able to make real progress, and by 15th April 1944, VII Corps issued their

Field Order Number 1, defining their objective of Exercise "Tiger" and confirming that live ammunition was to be used by the assaulting units under strict guidelines laid down by VII Corps headquarters. [7]

So D-Day for "Tiger" was the 27th April, with H-Hour at 0730 hours. In all other respects it was a duplicate of what would be executed on the real D-Day including codenaming the Slapton beaches just as "Utah" would be on 6th June - "Tare" and "Uncle" beaches sub-divided by color code, Red and Green. A scaled down version of the aerial and naval beach bombardment was also included. From H minus 60 minutes until H minus 45 minutes, fighter-bombers would attack inland targets as directed by the 101st Airborne Division who would have already made their simulated landing at about H minus four hours, west of the Slapton Sands Range area. During the same time frame, medium bombers were to attack three designated targets along the beach. Air cover was to be maintained so that all these aircraft, if called upon by ground units could attack other targets. In the interests of safety, other simulated missions would be flown with the target areas marked by smoke pots. From H minus 50 minutes until H hour itself, the Royal Navy was to fire upon beach obstacles and if weather conditions were favorable, smoke was to be added to the bombardment by mortars fired from landing craft.

The 101st Airborne Division would be fed into the exercise by road some four hours before the beach assault with the mission of seizing the high ground west of the beach together with all river crossings. Once the 4th Infantry Division reached them, they were to swing south and north to protect the flanks of the advance. 4th Infantry Division units were to consolidate their beachhead by dark on D Day before advancing on to Okehampton, with their reconnaissance units pushing ahead to scout the area for the 359th Regimental Combat Team of the 90th Infantry Division who would land on D+1 and D+2 then advance northwards on the right flank of the 4th. The 359th would hold the ground seized allowing the 4th Infantry Division to advance to Okehampton on D+1 with river crossings already seized and held by the 82nd Airborne Division who would be fed into the exercise by road before dawn on D+1. 1st Engineer Special Brigade was to support the assault landings and operate all shore installations for supply, debarkation and evacuation to ensure rapid movement across the beaches. The 101st Airborne units were then to be reinforced late on D+1 by tanks and artillery of the 87th Armored Field Artillery Battalion and Company "C" 746th Tank Battalion. The 11th Anti-Aircraft Artillery Group was to establish themselves ashore to protect the beach area and airstrips in the combat zone.

7 See Appendix 7 –VII Corps Field Order # 1

Taking the US Navy quite by surprise the 4th Infantry Division issued their own LST Landing Table on the 14th April, well ahead of the Navy plans. This detailed vessels that would land on all three tides, listing the vessel and Army serial numbers and on which beach they would land. The only differences between this table and the US Navy's version published four days later were that the U.S. Navy switched two LSTs, 283 and 400, and their loads, and were shown as due to land on different beaches. The army LST Landing Table listed their serial number 442 as landing on the second tide on Green Beach, but according to the navy LST loading plan, no such vessel was assigned to that serial number. However they did assign an additional LST, number 492, but listed it under army serial 447 which number does not even appear on the army landing table. Slipshod record keeping cannot account for an LST and its load to simply disappear. The only explanation is that the U.S. Navy documents were later re-written, deliberately omitting those details and deleting army personnel from participating in the exercise to assist in the mathematics of official casualty and survivor numbers. [8]

Accompanying their Field Order #1 the U.S. Army issued their "LST Boat Assignment Table" detailing which unit was to load onto which craft, using their serial numbers for vessels. These have been matched with U.S. Navy LST numbers and significantly army serial number 496 is missing from the army list, which equates to the doomed U.S. Navy LST 507. The navy have loading lists for LST 507 suggesting this army document has been re-written, deliberately omitting one of the LSTs that was sunk together with it's load of troops. [14] The fate of LST 507 is linked with LST 508 that may or may not have taken part in convoy T-4 and involves the 3rd Battalion of the 8th Infantry Regiment of the 4th Infantry Division whose fate does not become apparent until D-Day, 6th June 1944. [19]

413 men of the 3rd Battalion, 8th Infantry Regiment are shown in Annex 3 to the 4th Division's Field Order as landing on Red Beach from LCVPs in waves 8 and 9 at H+75 and H+85, the last waves of assaulting infantry to hit the beach before artillery and other specialized units were due to land. This is confirmed in their "Boat Assignment Tables", but probably due to a lack of LCVPs they were to land from LCMs launched from HMS "Empire Gauntlet". [11 & 12]

Movement of 679 men from their billets at Honiton to the marshaling area at Torquay is confirmed by the army's "Road Movement Sheet" of 23rd April 1944.[1] But the "Ship Sheet" issued the following day has the number of troops increased to 879, raising doubts as to the true total, and

8 See Appendix 8 – Army LST Landing Table
14 See Appendix 14 – Army Boat Assignment Table
19 See Appendix 19 – LST 508 Loading sheet
11 & 12 See Appendices 11 and 12 – Landing diagram & Boat Assignment Table

whether or not one or both documents have been altered.[2] This total figure question is further confounded when compared with another army document, the "APA Boat Assignment Tables" where again 879 men are shown as due to be loaded on Empire Gauntlet, now raising doubts as to which one or two of these three documents have been falsified. [13]

On both 17th and 18th of April, several high ranking officers of the US 4th Infantry Division visited the U.S. Assault Training Center at Woolacombe, North Devon. They included Major General Barton and Brigadier General Roosevelt, as well as the division's infantry regimental commanders, all seeking to be updated with the latest in amphibious assault techniques.

On 18th April the Exercise "Tiger" U.S. Navy Operation Order 2-44 was published, just as Admiral Moon had promised, and clearly stated its objective ...

> " this force will firmly establish 7th Corps in position north of Start Point in order (1) to ensure the capture of Okehampton with minimum delay, and (2) to assist in securing a lodgement area as a base for further operations leading to capture of the Devonshire southern coast ports."

Throughout the entire operation order were warnings that ... *"Attack by enemy aircraft, submarines, and E-Boats may be expected en route to and in exercise area."* These may have been routine, cautionary paragraphs common to all operation orders, but their frequency of repetition hints at a built-in touch of realism that had been inserted at the highest level under great secrecy.

The Intelligence Plan, paragraph 10 states that ... *"Surface attack can be expected from a flotilla of 9 to 13 enemy E-boats operating from the French coast."* This among other cautionary and warning information can only be assumed to be an intelligence appreciation of what may happen although the E-boat threat is later elaborated upon ...

> *"A flotilla of 16 E-boats, of which approximately 13 are known to be operational, is based at CHERBOURG, from which attacks on Allied convoys along the South Coast of England have been made. These boats have operated in the START BAY area, and attacks by them on concentrated Allied shipping are expected nightly at any time after dark until approximately 2 hours before sunrise. Attacks from these craft*

13 See Appendix 13 – APA Boat Assignment Table

in the current exercise is a possibility that can not be over emphasized."

The Intelligence plan goes on with greater detail ... *"The newest and largest E-boats are operating in this area. They have a displacement of 95 tons, are 106 feet long, with a beam of 16 feet 6 inches, and draw 5 feet 6 inches. They are fitted with 3 Diesel engines, and are known to make 38 knots, although the newest boats are said to make as high as 46. Speed can be reduced below 12 knots by using one engine."*

Even tactics were known by the exercise planners ...

> *"E-boats start out in a flotilla of 9 and break up into groups of 3 or 4 boats which spread themselves over a 10 mile area and cruise at about 5 knots searching for shipping. Attack is made after the first escort vessel of the convoy has passed the last group of the E-boats. E-boats choose their targets individually, and fire their torpedoes at full speed (38 to 46 knots) at as short a range as 600 yards if possible. They fire their torpedoes singly, and the torpedoes have a range of 6,500 yards. After firing their torpedoes, they make a 180 degree turn out of the range of defending guns and retire in order to reload their torpedo tubes; this reloading normally does not take more than 5 minutes. Direct cooperation between E-boats and aircraft has recently been attempted in the form of aircraft dropping flares to facilitate attacks by the E-boats."*

The day after publication of the Operation Order, Moon's intelligence officers began briefing small craft officers, and at this point several glaring errors were discovered in the Operation Order ... *"which had to be corrected by amendment"*. This meant Moon's staff spent the whole of the next five days making final revisions to the plan, publishing the corrections or altering copies by pen that had not yet been distributed. On the same date 4th Infantry Division published a minor document detailing which of their units were to supply commanding officers for troops aboard LSTs and gives a clue as to which unit was really aboard which vessel, facts that have been altered post exercise. [18]

To keep army units aware of the exercise progress, Supreme Headquarters, Allied Expeditionary Force (SHAEF) issued their own memorandum on 19th April, giving brief details of Exercise "Tiger" which had been condensed and paraphrased from the US Navy Operation Order. [9]

18 See Appendix 18 – Troops CO on ship

The following day VIIth Corps published their troop list as an annex to their Field Order detailing every participating unit in the exercise. [10]

VIIth Corps began their naval command briefing at 9.00 am on 21st April at the Royal Marine Barracks, Plymouth, attended by Admiral Moon, Major General Collins, and Major General Barton. The following day, unit commanders of VIIth Corps units were briefed at South Brent, Devon, by Major General Barton, commanding general of US 4th Infantry Division, with Moon's army liaison officer, Lieutenant Colonel Greear representing his commander.

On Sunday 23rd April, Annex F to the naval operation order, which covered the movement of ships and craft from the loading hards to the beaches, was finally completed after correcting the identified errors. But for some vessel commanders and units it must have been too late and they probably didn't receive the amendments.

To maintain momentum of the exercise and of necessity to ensure troop units arrived on time for embarkation the army had already distributed their "Ship sheets" and "Road Movement Orders" for units that were to load on the APAs. [14 to 17]

On 24th April the final briefing conference for both army and navy was held at the Royal Marine Barracks theatre, Plymouth, starting at 9.45 am, it lasted all morning and most of the afternoon. Moon, Hall, Collins and Barton all attended, and Captain Moran conducted the explanation and discussion. All planning had been completed, now it was time to put it to the test.

9 See Appendix 9 – SHAEF memorandum
10 See Appendix 10 – Troop list
14 to 17 See Appendices 14, 15, 16 & 17 – Ship Sheets & Road Movement Order

Five
___

U.S. Navy Operation
Order 2-44

SECRET Operation Order 2-44 produced by Admiral Moon's staff and published on 18th April 1944 ran to 364 pages, was divided into two volumes, included fifteen annexes each with several appendices, and had a distribution list of over 300 copies. This vast document did not require any alteration to facilitate the documentary cover-up as troop numbers and units were not included, they were detailed in ancillary papers.

The many hand-penned alterations to the original printed version show the minor errors and omissions discovered when the small craft commanders were briefed and the subsequent hurried re-appraisal of the entire contents. One significant alteration to the exercise was that ships and craft that had delivered their cargo to Slapton Sands were originally to make their way to a rendezvous point and await escort to a designated port. However it appears that due to a lack of suitable escort vessels, offloaded craft were to make their own unescorted way back to port.

The Operation order opens with the "Assault Phase Task Organization" which details participating vessels and most of their commanders. On page 3 alterations change the Red Beach Assault Group commander's ship from LCH 86 to LCH 95. On the following page LCT 851 is deleted from the Red LCT Unit and 642 written in. In the list of Close Escort Group vessels the destroyer H.M.S. Skate is crossed out and Krakowiak inserted. Of the four corvettes within that same group H.M.S. Celandine is crossed out with no substitute. Anti-submarine trawlers are also changed; H.M.S.

Rowan is deleted and replaced by H.M.S. Neave, which in turn i
by H.M.S. Skonner.

The second part of the Operation Order entitled "Information" details
standing orders, protocols and agreements that would affect the exercise,
together with a description of the physical limits of the exercise area, the
map grid that would be used, and responsibilities of the various groups of
vessels listed in the previous section.

Less than twenty pages held the outline of exercise "Tiger" with the
detail contained within the fifteen annexes, some of which were again
divided into several appendices. One late addition to the Operation Order,
for it isn't listed in the index, is the "Alternate Operation Plan", to be
implemented if ... " *Information received indicating jeopardy of success
if assault launched in accordance with original Operation Order No. 2-
44.*" This simply shifted the assault slightly northwards to Blackpool
Sands, a beach that was quite incapable of accommodating so many vessels
and therefore simply an afterthought and a paper exercise to complete the
Operation Order.

Listed in detail are the vessels to carry the troops, vehicles and
equipment, which were divided into separately code-numbered convoys
to assemble in Plymouth, Torbay, Salcombe, Brixham, Dartmouth,
Teignmouth and Exmouth. There were troopships, headquarters ships,
landing craft of all sizes, tonnages and types, coasters, trawlers and barges.
Of necessity, some vessels and situations were constructive, or notional,
such as prisoner of war ships. Airborne troops that on D-Day would have
been dropped from the air before the sea borne landings were made, were
trucked into the area before H-Hour, others were to be landed from the
sea. Annex "Fox" to the operation order lists and details the various
convoys of the exercise, including the ill-fated convoy T-4. [20]

Prior to the beach assault, ships of the "Support Craft Group" were to
... " *destroy or neutralize enemy defenses which oppose the landing*",
while the "Close Escort Group" would ... " *provide anti-submarine, anti-
aircraft and anti-E-boat protection from port to transport area.*"

The assault timetable called for the assault phase convoys to arrive in
Start Bay, having completed a clockwise excursion around Lyme Bay, and
be off Slapton Sands in time for the assault at 7.30 am on 27th April 1944.
The following day, according to the 18th April version of the US Navy's
Operation Order, Convoy T-4 with support units aboard was to arrive at
7.30 am on the 28th of April, and commence offloading operations of
follow-up combat troops and support units, the whole exercise to
terminate on the 29th April. [21]

20 See Appendix 20 – Annex "Fox" list of vessels
21 See Appendix 21 - Convoy T4 – Sailing directions

Six

Loading

WHILE both army and navy have undertaken a documentary cover-up, it has been uncoordinated. With the same objective of falsifying their casualties and covering mistakes, both worked from the same formula of sunken ships, a large number of bodies, and men missing from unit rosters. Both have created false documents independently and there has been little or no liaison after an initial agreement of their common goal to minimize the number of casualties.

Each has adjusted troop numbers on some of their documents relating to vessel loadings, the details of which simply do not stand comparison with more reliable sources. This has created a crazy patchwork of anomalies as not every document has been altered to the same unit, vessel, serial number or total numbers suggesting a haphazard, rushed and incomplete job as many relevant documents were forgotten, lost or couldn't be located in time.

This brings into question the veracity of documents publicly available that relate to Exercise "Tiger" LSTs, their loads of troops and vehicles. Some alterations are quite crude and obvious, others are clumsy and confusing transpositions of Army Serial numbers and LST numbers, and some are simply incorrect additions of troop numbers.

Complete units were never loaded on the same vessel. This was a valuable lesson learned by the army from earlier amphibious landing operations, and was applied during these build-up exercises and for the actual invasion. In case of mis-navigation or sinking, either of which would compromise the success of the whole mission, by dispersing a unit among several vessels should ensure at least some of them would reach their designated landing zone, enabling the assigned mission to be carried out in part if not completely.

Allocation of vessels to the army's needs was particularly difficult as shipping of all classes was at a premium and none more so than LSTs. Each one in the United Kingdom was already assigned to Operation "Overlord" leaving none in reserve and every craft that had already been allocated to Task Force "U" for Normandy was to be employed on exercise "Tiger". The principal troop carrying ships were three APA (Attack Transport) ships, the USS Dickman, USS Bayfield, USS Barnett, and the converted passenger vessel HMS Empire Gauntlet. These were all capable of carrying large numbers of combat infantry, and the small landing craft that would take them to the enemy shore. In addition, and for this rehearsal, thirty LSTs were required to carry troops, tanks and vehicles to land on all three tides of the exercise period, with a host of smaller craft to accommodate the surplus, as well as specialized craft necessary to establish and maintain a beachhead.

The army had already supplied the navy with details of which units they required to be landed, where and in which order, and the application of the navy principle was thereafter straightforward by balancing requirements against vessel capacity.

The U.S. Army's "Boat Assignment Table" for LSTs that was drafted by the army prior to the publication of the Exercise "Tiger" Operation Order on 18th April 1944 contains several mysteries when compared with navy documents published afterwards.

After much calculation, on the 21st April 1944, the "LST Loading Plan" was published by the US Navy, listing all LSTs under their port of embarkation, with times of loading, and to which berths or "hards" they were assigned to receive their cargo of men and vehicles in those ports. Both this list and the "LST Assignment table" show the US Navy's LST numbers against the US Army's serial numbers, and between the two documents there are some differences, which suggest that vessels were either substituted, replaced, or simply didn't sail according to the Operation Order of the 18th of April 1944, or the documents were altered. [22]

The army's serial numbers starting with 426 running sequentially to 502, and match the U.S. Navy LST numbers until serial number 434 where the army had allocated 167 troops. It is matched with LST 501, but in the next documentary step to the navy's "LST Assignment Table", produced as an annex to the navy's operation order of 18th April, serial number 434 still matches with LST 501 but now with 429 troops. In the navy's "LST Loading plan" dated 21st April they have matched army serial

LSTs loading at Brixham for D-Day.

number 434 to LST 231, and LST 501 is now matched against serial number 427. Matching serial 434 with LST 231 further confuses the situation. It may be a typographical error between 231 and 281. Serial number 427 of 54 troops on the army's "Boat Assignment Table" is matched with LST 281 but that LST is missing from the navy's "LST Loading Plan". LST 231 does appear in the navy's "LST Loading Plan" yet is missing from the previous navy "LST Loading Table". All this suggests the documents have been tampered with for the anomalies are so diverse they cannot be simple typographical errors or swapping vessels, more a paper shifting of troop numbers.

LST 499 loaded at Brixham, her log showing that loading of troops and vehicles started at 16:40 pm on 24th April, taking on 19 vehicles and 343 army personnel, a completely different mixture of units and numbers to the "LST Assignment Table".

The army had already matched their serial number 442 with LST 492, which agrees with the "LST Loading Table", yet serial 442 of 468 troops has completely disappeared from the "LST Loading Plan".

LST 283 is shown on the "LST Assignment Table" as being army serial number 445, but on the "LST Loading Plan" it is serial number 432. This is further complicated as serial 445 was originally due to load at Plymouth

Loading an Attack Transport ship for Exercise Tiger.

and unload on "Uncle Red" beach on the second tide. Now, in the latest document it is shown as due to load at Dartmouth under army serial number 432, a designation originally held by LST 400 which now loads at Plymouth and is due to unload on "Tare Green" beach, again on the second tide. This may be a case of simply swapping craft and beaches, but the units aboard are very different. A truck company, glider infantry and a tank service company on LST 283, and on LST 400, glider infantry, anti-aircraft gunners, medics and engineers.

It is interesting to note that for LST 283, the typed number of personnel of the 3807th QM Truck Company has been clumsily altered to suit the total number aboard. This may of course have been a typographical error, but then the total would need to be altered as well, and it isn't. Another probable typing error occurs on the total number of personnel aboard LST 511. Only by one, but in light of the above example, it could be expected that a component figure would also have been altered, but it hasn't.

Calculations of loads for the four APAs were also inaccurate. According to the US Navy's "Boat Assignment Table", the USS Barnett was to receive a total of 936 personnel but in the Operation Order that figure was 1,313, and the US Army "Ship Sheet" dated the 24th April 1944 lists 1,403. Some unit and personnel figures agree between two of the documents, but the overload shown on the army list all come from specialized units of the 1st Engineer Special Brigade.

According to army documents there were 81 more personnel on the USS "Dickman" than originally allocated, all from airborne anti-aircraft units.

The Operation Order, the US Navy's Boat Assignment Tables and Ship Sheet agree the "Empire Gauntlet" was loaded with 1316 personnel.

Appendix three to Annex "Fox" of the navy's Operation Order dated 18th April is a plan of the T-4 convoy showing four LSTs of the Brixham section astern of the Plymouth section, and the last ship is LST 508. This is significant as documents written after the E-Boat attack suggest that

LST 507 at Dartmouth.

LST 508 did not sail in the convoy. Navy records show this was due to 508 being damaged en route from Fowey to Brixham on 23rd April when she encountered dense fog, remarking that visibility was down to fifty yards. A British merchant vessel was seen traveling in the opposite direction, and at 5.18 pm both collided. A glancing blow port to port created a hole in the hull, the anchor was lost and one of the bow doors was sprung rendering the bow doors inoperable. 508 continued to Torbay where she anchored at 10.00 pm the same night. The ship's log details that she returned to Falmouth the following day and went into dry-dock for repair.

If this was the case then her cargo of 345 army personnel, 65 vehicles and 42 trailers had either to be loaded onto other vessels already berthed in Brixham, LSTs 289, 499, or 507, or sent by road to Plymouth to board T-4 convoy LSTs there, but most of them were already loaded and standing out from the loading hards. Alternatively the units could be fed into the exercise by road but this would compromise the realism of making an amphibious landing. Every LST engaged in T-4 was fully loaded with personnel and vehicles, but LST 507 was carrying fewer vehicles than most and therefore did have room to take part if not all, of 508's load. It was already in Brixham, and was due to land on the same beach and on the same tide as LST 508, so seems the most logical solution.

A chart complied from various documents of 1944 shows the discrepancies, omissions and additions described above. [23]

Seven

Landings

THE U.S. Navy had four phases for Exercise "Tiger". Pre-Assault, Assault, Follow up, and Build up. The transition from the Navy's "Pre-Assault phase" to their ""Assault phase" occurred when the ships arrived in the transport area on Thursday 27th April 1944. Defined by the navy as ...

> "the movement of a combat loaded assault force into the area to make the initial landings and seize the area."

This would be followed by the "Follow-up phase", in this case Convoy T-4, being ...

> "the movement of pre-loaded vessels into the assault area to augment the assault forces with personnel, equipment and supplies."

There was to be a "Build-up phase" but for Tiger it was only to be a paper exercise at Plymouth.

At 4.27 am the USS "Bayfield" began lowering her boats. By 5.05 am all boats were waterborne, and at 6.26 am troops climbed down cargo nets from the Bayfield's deck into their craft. Once loaded they sheared away to circle at the rendezvous point waiting for the entire wave before deploying in line abreast at the departure line for the assault run-in to the beach. Major General Collins and his staff also left the Bayfield at 5.55 am for the beach to observe the landings scheduled for 7.30 am.

The US Navy's "Landing Schedule" showed 2nd Battalion, 8th Infantry

Troops landing from an LCI.

Regiment landing on Red Beach from LCVPs and LCTs at H Hour from the "Barnett". At the same time the 1st Battalion would land on Green Beach having debarked from the "Joseph T Dickman". Seventy five minutes later 3rd Battalion, 8th Infantry would land from LCMs on Red Beach from "Empire Gauntlet" alongside 3rd Battalion 22nd Infantry Regiment from "Bayfield" for Green Beach. LCI(L)s would then land 2nd Battalion, 22nd Infantry on Red Beach, and 1st Battalion, 22nd Infantry on Green Beach at H + 205 minutes. One officer of Headquarters Company, 3rd Battalion, and 8th Infantry Regiment is convinced he landed on schedule, but his Sergeant is equally convinced the entire unit was still in camp during the exercise. This is a conflict of recollection so different as to raise suspicions that for some reason one is not telling the truth in order to maintain a lie about their losses during Exercise "Tiger"

But at 6.20 am the Green Assault Group commander had reported to Admiral Moon that some of his LCTs carrying important new army weapons were behind schedule in arriving and that he recommended delaying H-Hour from 0730 to 0830. As General Collins had already left the ship, Moon was unable to judge the tactical importance of these LCTs, so acting without advice, ordered H-Hour to be delayed by one hour. Inevitably some ships and vessels failed to receive the signal. Many small craft had already passed through the rendezvous point and were making their way at 6 to 9 knots to the departure line, uncontactable and preparing for their run-in to the shore. Their craft bucked through the seas heading for the shore under the naval bombardment of beach defenses that were pounding pre-designated targets just behind the shoreline. [24]

At the original H-Hour the first troops ashore on Red beach were the 2nd Battalion, 8th Infantry Regiment from APA 5 "Barnett", and on Green beach the 1st Battalion landed from APA 13 "Joseph T. Dickman". Just three minutes ahead of them were sixteen tanks from 70th Tank Battalion landed from four LCTs, and seven minutes behind them in the second wave were more LCVPs and LCT(A)s bringing more infantry.

An LCVP heads for shore.

As wave numbers 1 and 2 of the 8th Infantry Regiment landed on Green Beach at the original time, they came under fire from Royal Navy ships still bombarding the beach defenses for the revised H-Hour. Alongside them were craft carrying personnel from Companies A and C of the 237th Engineer Combat Battalion who also suffered casualties from this naval fire, and worse was to come. [25 & 26]

Among them were men of Company G, 8th Infantry Regiment whose commander Captain James Haley told his radioman Ralph Wires to radio the ships to stop the shelling, which they did. After this initial aberration the landing proceeded – according to official records ... "as planned with fair precision".

Troops of the 4th Infantry Division weren't issued with any ammunition, convincing them they were on another exercise, despite the FUSA letter of 21st March 1944 to VIIth Corps stating that live ammunition would be fired. After being shelled by the Royal Navy, troops of the first waves were shocked to be fired on by the "enemy" ashore. This was the U.S. 1st Infantry Division lined up on the high ground overlooking the beach and firing live ammunition into the troops struggling in the surf to climb the beach. It was planned to add realism to the beach assault but had gone horribly wrong. It only lasted a few minutes but the effects were devastating.

There are no official figures of infantry dead and wounded for the army have never acknowledged that such an incident took place despite a number of witnesses. Henry Aaron was General Gerhardt's regular driver and that morning ... *"drove the general to inspect the exercise that day. I let him out then parked the jeep near the top of village hill. I had a real view of the rehearsal looking out to sea."* Henry then moved the jeep away to a group of three soldiers nearby then live rounds began hitting the ground at his feet so he ... " left the three soldiers. Five minutes after going a shell killed all three. "

Major Edwin Wolf of the 6th Engineer Special Brigade and late of the U.S. Assault Training Center in north Devon had a special interest in this exercise. He had shrewdly ordered two of his captains to travel with the follow up convoy T-4, as observers to watch how the 1st Engineer Special Brigade troops handled the follow up operation. Something he and his unit would soon be asked to undertake during Exercise "Fabius I" for to know in advance any problems or mistakes should help his own operation run more smoothly. So, as an observer onshore he watched intently as the first waves of infantry came ashore, knowing they were to be met by "enemy fire" provided by units of the 1st Infantry Division ranged along the high ground behind Slapton Ley to provide another touch of realism to the rehearsal. Just as the first landing craft dropped their ramps on the pebbly shore, Wolf saw the debarking infantry fall down and instantly realized that the defenders to either side of his observation point were using live ammunition and murdering their comrades in the surf. He shouted and yelled for the firing to stop, but his voice was drowned by the deafening sound of machine gun and rifle fire. He ran to the firing lines, searching for an officer responsible for the shooting to get it stopped, and eventually locating one, the order to cease-fire was given.

An ironic observation made by personnel of U.S. Army's Southern Base Section in their report of the exercise reads ...

"The actual landings were favored by good weather, and the exercise proceeded according to plan. Assault troops went ashore after a pre-H Hour naval bombardment of the simulated enemy defenses, reduced the pillboxes, cut through wire entanglements, and made their way inland to join the elements of the 101st Abn Div, which had arrived previously. As in previous exercises, the greatest deficiency noted was the failure of many combat soldiers to take adequate cover. "

This incident didn't stop the assault timetable on the other beaches, and unloading of troops and supplies continued throughout the day. At 3.26 pm with the beachhead declared secure, Bayfield moved in closer to observe the situation, anchoring about 8 miles from the beach. Major General Collins had already returned to the Bayfield and called a conference of group commanders for 8.00 pm. The Bayfield remained overnight at anchor off Slapton Sands with Admiral Moon's staff directing the unloading of supplies. At 6 am on April 28th Moon sent his Chief of Staff, Captain Tompkins to the surviving LSTs of convoy T-4 enquire into the attack. Navy and Army officers arrived and departed the Bayfield throughout the day for conferences with staff officers until 3.03 pm when Bayfield moved to shallower water.

At 4.30 pm Admiral Moon advised the force off Slapton Sands ...

"E-Boat attack may occur tonight. All isolated vessels will close to within three thousand yard circle from Bayfield prior to 2100 hours. After 2130 all movement of craft must cease and unloading will be postponed until 290600, Green Very star indicates an unidentified vessel is approaching anchorage. Red Very star indicates it is hostile craft. All ships will maintain alert watches and man half battery, and will report radar contacts of suspicious nature."

At 8.02 am Admiral Moon, clearly rattled by the attack on convoy T-4, informed Major General Collins that unloading would be completed except for one coaster at noon on the 29th April and that he proposed sailing naval forces to avoid E-Boat hazards of another night in the area.

Dawn broke on 29th April over the Bayfield at anchor in Start Bay and although several suspicious targets were picked up during the night, no attack occurred. At 8.00 am all ships lowered their colors to half-mast after receiving news of the death of the secretary of the Navy, the Hon Frank Knox. Just after 9.00 am Captain M T Richardson, USN commander of Green Assault Group and officers of his staff arrived aboard the Bayfield for conference with Admiral Moon, and at 12.20 pm Moon signaled that naval participation in Exercise Tiger had been completed. Bayfield began preparations for getting under way at 1.00 pm, then proceeded through swept channels back to Plymouth Sound where she anchored just after 5.00 pm. Moon immediately departed for a conference with Admiral Leatham, RN, Rear Admiral Kirk, Rear Admiral Wilkes, and Rear Admiral Struble regarding the attack on the LSTs. of convoy T-4.

The problem of what to do with bodies from the beach remained. There were those killed by naval gunfire and those killed by the beach "defenders". The decision was made that they would be buried locally and retrieved later for re-burial in a military cemetery. Selection of a suitable site was based upon logic and common sense. It had to be large enough o accommodate all the bodies, close enough to a main road for ease of transportation and access, yet sufficiently distant from the coast and lines of advance so as not to be seen by exercise personnel moving across the beach or pushing inland.

A field behind Wadstray House, near the village of Blackawton was selected, next to the main road that formed the northern boundary of the exercise area. Burial pits were dug and bodies began to arrive by truck. At

Aid Station at Slapton Sands

the same time a young girl, Dorothy Seekings was on the scene. Her father was a local baker who supplied the Americans with bread and she had often accompanied him on his rounds so was well known to the troops. She had hitched a lift in an army truck that stopped on the main road at Wadstray House and when she went around the rear of the truck she saw it was piled high with bodies. She watched as they were carried into the field where she saw mounds of dirt, and piles of bodies.

The story of bodies buried in Devonshire fields has been attacked many times, some have promoted the suggestion that what was seen was a rehearsal for graves registration troops, but there is no mention of it in the navy's operation order. There was, however, a rehearsal for handling simulated casualties written into the navy's Operation Order as Appendix Two. This was for army troops to be tagged as casualties by umpires once they were ashore, to test the medical unit's ability to cope with the anticipated number of wounded during the actual invasion of Normandy.[27]

These "casualties" would be tagged by army umpires to endure the medical procedures of evacuation to provide practice to all units within that chain. Many "casualties" became so bored with their inactivity they simply tore off their casualty tags and walked back to the beach to search for their unit.

27 See Appendix 27 – Plan for simulated casualties

Eight

E-Boat attack – German view

THE CALM, ink-black sea was sliced by the bows of nine German E-Boats roaring at high speed across the Channel towards the English coast, leaving phosphorescent wakes shimmering under a quarter moon. They had left Cherbourg at 10.00 pm on 27th April on a calm sea with a light breeze and a forecast of light coastal mist towards morning, and were heading for Start Bay to intercept and attack a convoy sighted earlier by one of their reconnaissance aircraft.

The attack group comprised of six vessels of the 5th Flotilla, S100 and S 143 of the first squadron, S140 and S142 of the second squadron, and S136 and S138 from the third squadron. With them that night were S150, S130 and S145 from Number 9 Flotilla. Their agreed and usual tactics were that 5th Flotilla boats would take a parallel course to

Typical German "E – Boat"

the east and act as decoys for escort vessels of the convoy allowing 9th Flotilla boats to commence the attack.

US Navy intelligence already knew that enemy reconnaissance aircraft operated in the Start Bay area ...

> *"principally FW 190, and make as many as four to six sorties*
> *a day in good weather. The planes usually come over singly,*
> *very low over the water, and fast."*

A British intelligence signal had also been received exactly predicting the E-Boat departure, but it wasn't to be deciphered until late on April 28th.

The nine E-boats advanced at 36 knots in two parallel lines north of the Channel Islands with radio silence to attack the convoy now known to be in the approximate area ten miles west of Portland Bill, with an estimated time of attack of half past midnight.

Entering Lyme Bay at 11.17 pm and dispersing for attack, they saw a searchlight on shore signaling in Morse code to Allied shipping warning them of the presence of E-Boats, a routine the E-Boats already understood.

All boats then received the radio message that the convoy they were seeking had now been fixed by radiolocation in quadrant 2398 on their charts.

Just one minute after midnight on 28th April 1944 Captain Jurgenmeyer of Number 3 Squadron on S136 spotted a pair of "two-stack" destroyers ahead of his vessel and his partner boat S138. Both slowed to 7 knots and at 2,000 metres S138 fired a double shot of torpedoes at the destroyer furthest from them, S136 did the same just a few seconds later resulting in a

> " ... *Significant detonation with flames. Strong shock waves in*
> *our boat (S136). S138 observes hit on rearmost destroyer at*
> *second smokestack. At same time, both torpedoes from S136*
> *detonate. The second destroyer fires poorly aimed light*
> *weapons ...* "

S100 had heard S138's sighting of the two destroyers, then heard the detonation of their torpedoes and saw two high water spouts, but got no response from either S136 or S138 to confirm torpedo hits, and assumed two high flying aircraft were responsible for the explosions. Boats of 9th Flotilla had also seen the flashes and assumed they were S138's hits on the destroyer.

S136 and S138 had not responded to Squadron One's enquiry as they were withdrawing from their attack at high speed towards the southeast for a few moments. They stopped and then slowly returned to their attack position to assess the effect. They saw the hit destroyer stopped in the water and the second destroyer attempting to go alongside. S136 launched two more torpedoes aimed at the rescuer but missed as it turned towards them zigzagging and firing in their general direction.

Again S136 and S138 withdrew at high speed and after ten minutes, having lost the pursuing destroyer, decided to return yet again and watch the destroyer sink or finish it off with their 4 cm guns, and pick up any survivors.

Somewhat belatedly S142 and S140 turned northeast intending to assist in attacking the second destroyer and asked S138 for its position, but no reply was received.

At 12.58 am S138 sent a radio message to S136 *"... Destroyer sinks."* Both ran over the torpedoing point and saw nothing. Searching for ten minutes they saw no debris, no survivors, no boats, and with ammunition expended returned to Cherbourg after receiving information that two destroyers were closing in on them from the east.

The attack was witnessed by boats of 9th Flotilla commanded by 1st Lieutenant Beer whose vessel made a possible contact to their southwest. This was probably the second Allied destroyer searching for S136 and S138, and as Lieutenant Beer closed on the position found S140 attacking it with its 4 cm gun.

Only a minute later S140 spotted three steamers and gave S142 permission to attack. Slowing to around ten knots, S142 launched a double shot of torpedoes from 1,800 metres at a depth of 3 metres, but both missed, so launched two single shots at a depth of 2 metres. Again both missed.

At 1.13 am S140 fired two torpedoes at one of the three ships, both of which missed their target. S140 stopped to discuss with S142 their failure to hit the ships and could only conclude that their targets had either varied their speed or the torpedoes had gone underneath the vessels having a shallow draught, such as tank landing boats. Just then two torpedoes were seen to detonate on the shore

A minute later S100 and S143 hearing that S140 had located the convoy some seven miles away, raced to intercept it. S100 asked S140 for his position to clarify their approach and was advised the convoy was on a southerly course. Almost immediately 1st Squadron saw S140 attacking both ships with their 4cm gun using red tracer, and closing from 600 to 300 metres as there was no answering fire. S140 then withdrew signaling "pulling back", to allow other E-Boats the opportunity to attack having shown them the convoy's location.

Boats of 9th Flotilla had closed in on the convoy by now. S145 was the first to see the vessels but wasn't in a position to attack being too far astern, so attacked smaller vessels, although it is unknown what they were, while S150 and S130 initiated their torpedo attack.

S145 fired a torpedo but it developed into a "surface runner" having problems with its depth control and hit an LST that was later reported to be LST 289.

S140 standing off the attack area saw two flashing buoys which were probably "dan buoys" laid by the British "Smokey Joes" of 4th Minesweeping Flotilla that night, marking the swept channel used by the convoy.

Precisely at 2.00 am S150 fired two torpedoes at what was believed to be a tanker. After a two and a half minute run the torpedoes hit and the ship immediately erupted in flames and was raked with gunfire from the other E-Boats. There was no return fire so S150 went south after the rest of the convoy, looking for another target.

Having taken nearly fifteen minutes to maneuver into a good firing position S100 had in their sights a 2,000 to 3,000 ton steamer and were about to fire when it was torpedoed by another boat. Quickly taking the next steamer as their target at a distance of 1,500 metres, S100 fired two torpedoes, both of which missed and seemed to have undershot.

While maneuvering for this target, the crew had seen a large tanker to the north, burning brightly with huge black smoke billows that covered the southern part of Lyme Bay.

At 2.16 am S143 fired two torpedoes at a 1,500-ton steamer, both hit after 76 seconds engulfing the vessel in flames, which sank within minutes. Both S140 and S143 headed southeast towards another visible target, reloading as they went and ignoring what they describe as "uncoordinated fire" from the surviving convoy vessels. But their attack was baulked as their new target kept disappearing in smoke and the close proximity of S130 and S150 both angling to attack.

But S130 was having problems reloading torpedoes so S150 fired two torpedoes and after only 56 seconds gets two hits on a steamer, which immediately goes up in flames. There is no doubt in Lieutenant Beer's mind that both vessels in flames did sink, but with their position now known by Allied destroyers and strong defensive fire directed at the 1st Squadron, Lieutenant Beer ordered his boats to turn for home at 2.40 am. By now the E-boats had seen three ships hit and on fire.

S145 was attacking two smaller craft of 200 tons and despite evasive action collided with the stern of one whilst under heavy but uncoordinated return fire. It is most likely this was an LCI, of approximately 200 tons, loaded with approximately sixty infantrymen of the 8th Infantry

Regiment. Frank Schoren of Headquarters Company was aboard one LCI and recalls several of these vessels were sailing behind the LST convoy when the LSTs were torpedoed. Dale Rodman who survived the attack on the LSTs remembers seeing many dead soldiers wearing full combat equipment floating in the sea, and confirms that infantrymen aboard LCIs were required to wear full equipment at all times.

By 2.30 am, 1st Squadron is ordered to return to Cherbourg with the warning that Allied destroyers are waiting to intercept them. Half an hour traveling south at 36 knots brings S100 and S143 up behind two destroyers firing south at an unknown target. This was HMS "Offa" and "Orwell", part of the outer screen. With two torpedoes left on each boat they decide to take advantage of their position and after a megaphone discussion, decide who will take which target, but before their attack can be implemented one destroyer turns, spots S143 and fires causing slight damage. S100 tries to press his attack on the other destroyer but alerted to their presence it starts to bear down on S100 who decides to call off his attack and speeds west.

9th Flotilla heading for Cherbourg was alerted to a patrolling destroyer group by S140 and passing it to the east came under heavy attack. This was presumed to be an escort vessel for four landing ships seen heading eastwards.

What Lieutenant Beer witnessed then was unbelievable ...

> "*Destroyer fires heavily on a landing boat, so it was clear to me that the destroyer did not know of its presence in this area. I believe these landing boats are dispersed units from an exercise group.*"

This information is passed to 1st Squadron who speed to the location given but cannot find anything, and low on fuel do not make a full search of the area.

By 5.35 am all nine E-Boats have returned safely to Cherbourg.

The following day, 29th April 1944, a British newspaper published a news item taken from a German news agency that reported ...

> "*Last night German speedboats attacked destroyers and a British convoy off the south coast of Britain, west of the Isle of Wight. In spite of extremely strong enemy defense the German boats sank three ships totaling 6,400 tons and torpedoed another of 200 tons the loss of which may be presumed. In hard*

LCI 94 at Dartmouth.

defensive clashes one enemy destroyer was so heavily hit that its loss can be assumed."

There are no admitted losses of any Allied warships during this E-Boat attack, but Clifford Graves of Company D, 261st Medical battalion witnessed the sinking of an Allied warship and assumed it was a corvette. The only sinking of a destroyer in home waters around the same time is H.M.S. "Athabaskan", a Canadian ship sunk by E-Boats on 29th April 1944 which curiously had been on the outer defensive screen for Exercise "Tiger". The *"200 ton vessel"* is most likely to be an LCI loaded with 4th Infantry Division combat troops.

There was another American convoy in Lyme Bay that night, sailing from Falmouth, Cornwall to Portland. LSTs 51, 133, 157, 184, 285, 286 and 502 were all towing RHF pontoons together with LCTs 458 and 530, and their escort vessels. At 02:30 am when General Quarters was sounded following receipt of a radioed E-boat alert the escort fired star shells. Laurence B James aboard LST 502 recalls …

"it was pitch black on deck, and the lookouts could hardly see beyond the bow of the ship. Everyone was tense. The existence and positions of the other LSTs and escorts was assured only by reference to radar. Unexpectedly the sky was emblazoned by

star shells. It was suddenly bright as day and a panorama of ships appeared in the vicinity. This was too much for some gunners and a few rounds were fired. Nobody was hurt but one of our LCVP steel davits suffered a 40mm puncture."

H.M.C.S. *"Athabaskan".*

Nine

E-Boat attack – American view

ON THURSDAY morning, the 27th of April 1944, five heavily laden, lumbering LSTs, cynically nick-named by their crews as "Large Slow Targets", moved slowly away from their various anchorages in Plymouth waters heading south east, out into the English Channel. They were all to rendezvous outside Plymouth Sound at 9.50 am and form up in line astern to take a complicated route to Slapton Sands as Convoy T-4 of Exercise "Tiger". All were loaded with US Army units of the assault follow-up force heading for the assembly area off the beaches where the mock assault had already begun at 7.30 am that morning and they were due to arrive in the ship assembly area at 7.30 am the next day, when their cargoes were to be fed into the exercise.

These five ships, LSTs 515, 496, 511, 531 and 58 towing two pontoon causeways were to sail in that order on a prescribed route through mine swept channels, past Slapton Sands to commence an overnight clockwise voyage around Lyme Bay. Passing Brixham at 7.00 pm that evening, three more LSTs that had loaded troops and vehicles in Brixham, would fall in astern to complete the convoy.

The Plymouth section's brief stay in Plymouth had not been without incident in waters teeming with vessels of all types and sizes. Warships and merchantmen, landing craft and motor launches, all moving between quays, anchorages and buoys. LST 511 had been hit in the stern by a drifting British freighter, and later hit another British ship herself, but reported no damage from either collision. LST 58 while making for

Turnchapel Hard to load sustained damage to her port side when she collided with LST 491. Commander B. J. Skahill of LST 515, designated as T-4 convoy commander, had already loaded his ship at Turnchapel Hard the day before, and then wisely anchored in Cawsand Bay, well away from the bustle of the inner harbor. LSTs 511 and 58 copied his example and joined him later that day.

By mid-morning of 27th April all was going to plan, proceeding in formation at 5 knots, the Plymouth section of T-4 sailed eastwards around the south Devon coast to meet their escort vessels, the corvette HMS "Azalea", and the destroyer HMS "Scimitar" who would detach from guarding the ship assembly area off Slapton Sands to rendezvous with them at 11.00 am.

Before escorting convoy T-4, HMS "Scimitar" and HMS "Azalea" took the role of "reference vessels" together with Motor Launch (ML) 214. They were to take station at points where the initial assault convoys were to make navigational turns to maintain their allocated courses to ensure they made progress along channels swept of mines. As one of the early convoys (T-1B) was heading from Salcombe to Lyme Bay, the first and probably most significant incident of the exercise occurred. HMS "Scimitar" was involved in a collision and returned to Plymouth for repairs.

The signal from Scimitar to Plymouth Command advising of her damaged state should have been addressed to the commander of Force U and repeated to C in C, Plymouth. Plymouth command did not repeat the signal to Com Force U. On arrival at Plymouth, Scimitar received a signal from C in C Plymouth to go to Number 6 buoy to refuel, but questioned the order and advised C in C Plymouth that she was supposed to rendezvous with the Plymouth section of convoy T4 outside the port at 0950 hours the next morning (27th April). But no decision was made as ... *"no one seemed to know"*. Scimitar was brought alongside for the damage to be assessed and temporary repairs to be effected if these could be done quickly. In the event the dockyard were unable to make repairs until the morning of 28th April, and although seaworthy in the prevailing fine, calm weather, the decision was taken by Plymouth Command to keep her in harbor.

This decision was made without reference to the responsible staff officer, Plymouth, who was under the impression that the American Force commander and the captain of HMS Tanatside, Commander B J St Croix, RN, being Senior Officer Escorts, were aware of the damage and had ordered Scimitar to Plymouth. Shortly after 7.30 pm on the 27th April, a

Royal Navy staff officer realizing something was amiss, sent for Scimitar's captain, and then fully appreciating the situation, put Scimitar on four hours notice to put to sea. A signal timed at 11.06 pm was sent by C in C, Plymouth to the captain of HMS Tanatside, which, by the time it had been decoded, was delivered to Commander St Croix at about 12.45 am on 28th April. He took immediate action and detailed HMS Saladin, already in Start Bay, to act as relief escort for convoy T4. Saladin left her patrol at 1.37 am on 28th April. Too late.

Precisely on time T-4 sighted "Azalea" at 50' 13" N, 4' 12" W, and she took up her station ahead of the convoy, but there was no sign of Scimitar. She had already passed the convoy on her way back to Plymouth for minor repairs, and her absence over the next few hours would have a catastrophic effect upon events that were about to unfold.

The Plymouth section changed course three times after Azalea joined them. LST 511 recorded these at 11.00 am to 096' true, at 12.47 pm to 101' true, and at 2.43 pm to 033' true, lining up for the Brixham section to join them.

LST 289 at Dartmouth.

The Brixham section of convoy T-4 comprised of four LSTs, 499, 289, 507 and 508. All four are assigned on the US Navy Operation Order dated 18th April 1944, and on the LST loading sheets complete with details of their loads, but curiously LST 508 is not mentioned in any of the US Navy after action reports, except in that of LST 496 dated 30th April 1944, which states that …

> "At 1930B, on reaching point E, convoy was joined by the Brixham section, Green LST Unit No. 3 consisting of LSTs 499, 289, 507, 508". Quickly added to that paragraph was … "It is believed that LST 508 did not join convoy as scheduled".

Most of the other LST after action reports state that LST 508 was part of the convoy, and the US Army reports are positive that she was there. While the inexperienced skippers may understandably not keep time-perfect deck logs, they should know how many ships were in their convoy. It does appear that all navy reports were hurriedly written and based upon details taken directly from the Operation Order and only later amended, either through the authors being told that LST 508 did not sail that day. Or more suspiciously, they were tampered with after submission. One example of poor log keeping or later alterations comes from LST 58 which confusingly records that at "Point E" the Brixham section joined the convoy at 7.30 pm, then again at 8.05 pm records three LSTs joining the convoy at a quite different location.

Commander Skahill, the convoy commander in LST 515, logs the Brixham section joining at 7.00 pm, exactly on schedule. Perhaps another example of copying details straight from the Operation Order, because the last page of his report is devoted to amendments of times and courses, not only to his own report, but also correcting details of the other LST captain's reports so they all conform to his version of events.

Once the Brixham section had fallen into line, the convoy speed was increased to 6 knots, took a course of 023' true, and continued uneventfully for over two hours. LST 515 unconcernedly noting the appearance of small craft off her starboard bow at 9.45 pm. They weren't positively identified but nevertheless considered "friendly" even though they could not be participants of the exercise, being too far from the rehearsal area, so were ignored. Perhaps they were British minesweepers clearing the channel ahead of the convoy, or Free French MTBs from Dartmouth shadowing the convoy and waiting for nightfall.

Sweeping a channel ahead of convoy T-4 was Tom Saxby, an Able Seaman serving aboard HMS Selkirk, a fleet minesweeper of the 4th Minesweeping Flotilla, which had arrived at Portland on 7th March 1944. It consisted of nine sweepers and two dan-layers, HM ships Kellett, Albury, Elgin, Lydd, Pangbourne, Ross, Saltash, Selkirk and Sutton. They were the last purpose-built coal-burners, which remained in the Royal Navy and were known affectionately as "Smokey Joes". For the next few weeks the flotilla practiced day and night maneuvers in Lyme Bay and was twice attacked by enemy bombers. According to Tom's diary the flotilla left Portland after sundown on 27th April 1944 and proceeded to sweep a buoyed channel across Lyme Bay towards Slapton Sands. The minesweepers formed up in echelon and at seven and a half knots with their accompanying "Dan-laying" trawlers keeping pace, began sweeping a buoyed channel around Lyme Bay towards Slapton Sands. Once the minesweepers had cleared a channel, their accompanying dan-laying trawlers would mark the edges of the swept channel by dropping dan-buoys. Night sweeping was always a tense time and the dimly lit torches attached to their Oropesa floats astern created an eerie atmosphere.

At 10.10 pm LST 515 changed course to 90' true, LST 531 followed, changing course twelve minutes later, logging the turn at 50' 34" W, 3' 14.5" W.

For an hour and a half the convoy proceeded at 5 knots, each LST finding difficulty in maintaining station, often drifting far out of line. Then LST 499 saw two white flares illuminate some considerable distance off her starboard bow. LST 58 saw them as well, and so too did three US patrol craft numbers 564, 565 and 567, who were escorting another convoy of eight LSTs from Swansea to Portland. No action was taken and no enquiries made, the captains complacently assuming all was in order as it may have been part of the exercise scenario, and the Royal Navy, out of sight, was protecting them.

LST 515 records that at midnight on 27th/28th of April, she and the convoy continued on a course of 90' true proceeding at 5 knots until 12.19 am when course was changed to 145' true. At the same time, LST 58 that hadn't yet made the turn saw two white flares off her starboard bow, estimated as being seven miles away, but had no radar contact. LSTs 499 and 289 saw them as well, all off their starboard bows, then 499 saw another fifteen to twenty flares immediately afterwards. Again, no action was taken; the ships were not alerted to "General quarters", and no orders given by the convoy commander.

All LSTs in Convoy T-4 had been ordered to maintain a continuous radio watch on the "Group Transport" net at 490 Kc, but only the convoy commander aboard LST 515 had been ordered to keep a continuous radio watch on the "Plymouth Port Wave" at 2300 Kc. This was a radio channel specifically for the passing of information of enemy attack. If LST 515 had monitored HMS "Onslow's" report of E-Boat activity to Plymouth Command on that wavelength, it was not disseminated to the other LSTs in the convoy via the Group Transport Net, and neither was the 12:30 am Plymouth Command broadcast of E-Boat activity on the "Plymouth Port Wave" passed on to the convoy.

It has been suggested that convoy T-4 were monitoring a different radio frequency due to a typographical error in their orders that deprived them of receiving those vital warnings of E-Boat activity. Whether that incorrect frequency given was for the Group Transport Net monitored by the convoy, or LST 515's transmissions were mis-tuned remains unknown, but complicating this issue was that radio silence had been ordered from sortie to the assault area. Radiomen were warned that bogus traffic would be sent throughout the exercise, there was a procedure in place to authenticate genuine transmissions, but this does not appear to have been implemented.

By now LST 499 had counted fifteen flares off their starboard bow and despite becoming nervous of their significance and frequency, especially with no radio contact from their British escort, she obediently changed course to 145' true at 12.50 am. As the Brixham section of LSTs turned to follow, they were spotted by E-Boats. S142 fired two torpedoes at them, which appeared to miss, so fired another pair, which also failed to hit their target but LST 289 had felt two slight jars as S142's torpedoes scraped under their hull.

LSTs 496 and 511 were dawdling at only 4 knots trying to maintain station, and the convoy leader, LST 515 reduced his speed to 5 knots to try and maintain formation. At this time LST 511 believed the convoy had two escorts, HMS "Azalea" and HMS "Saladin". Their entry for 1.00 am in their action report dated 30th April 1944 is incorrect as "Saladin" was still guarding the assembly area off Slapton Sands and would not leave there for another half an hour.

At 1.14 am both 499 and 511 saw a pair of white flares about two miles distant off their port side and 499 felt an explosive vibration from an undetermined direction or distance. At 1.23 am, 499 felt a second explosive vibration. Both were torpedoes fired from E-Boats S140 and S142 that had missed the Brixham section, scraped under the hull of LST 289, and had now exploded on the shore.

At 1.30 am both LST 531 and 507 heard gunfire and saw tracer astern, so sounded General Quarters, as did LST 515 at the head of the convoy. 289 saw this fire directed at 507 some 600 yards astern and watched her veer to port and increase speed to try and evade the attack by E-Boats S140 and S142. LST 58 saw the action and sounded General Quarters just as some red (German) tracer passed over the ship.

By now LSTs 515, 289, 496, 499 and 511 were all at General Quarters and still maintaining a southerly course. HMS "Azalea" was about 2,000 yards ahead of the convoy that now stretched for almost three miles; still believing it consisted of nine LSTs. Despite the gunfire, she calmly altered course to 206' true at Point H as planned at 3 ½ knots, ignoring the tracer, either because she hadn't seen it, which is most unlikely, or it was expected as part of some added realism to the exercise, and orders were to take no action.

By 1.40 am LST 58 at General Quarters heard gunfire astern and saw flares in what she believed to be the vicinity of LST 507. But within minutes the attack was over. LST 507 moved back into formation astern of 289 and the whole convoy closed up, following their escort turning to 206' true at Point H, following the wake of the ship in front.

One baffling account of the E-Boat attack is made by Frank Schroer of Headquarters Company, 8th Infantry Division who was with the regimental Colonel and sixty other men aboard an LCI. He states his ship was right behind the convoy as the first torpedo struck the LSTs ...

> *"the sky lit up and we headed for shore. " But just offshore his ship ... "hit a sand bar and dumped some of us off, the water was about seven feet deep. I dropped everything and had to swim to shore at night. We lost three men. The LCI backed off and made another run down the shore, this time they went right in with no trouble."*

Despite the 8th Regiment losing three men in this episode, there is no record at all of their death or being missing in action on this date in any official document or record.

No sooner had LST 531 secured from General Quarters at 1.50 am than 289 heard an explosion and saw the LST 507 astern, blow up. This was the result of the co-coordinated torpedo attack of E-Boats S150 and S130, followed up by other E-Boats raking the ship with 40mm tracer gunfire. LST 511 noted the attack occurred at 50' 28" 15 N, 02' 49" 00 W, and sounded General Quarters. LST 58 saw 507 on fire then both "Azalea" and 289 heard an explosion, 289 seeing the LST directly in front of her hit and immediately catch fire.

LST 58 recorded that at 2.02 am she saw a burning ship and changed course to 203' true, just as LST 499 sheared to port and moved up on her port beam about 300 yards away, then 58 heard an explosion from astern and saw flames from the last ship in the convoy, which was confirmed by radar to be LST 507. 499 had heard and felt the same explosion astern and saw LST 507 in flames. But suddenly she had her own problems. Spotting a torpedo wake heading for the bow, full left rudder was applied and with relief watched the torpedo miss by only 20 feet. Her maneuvering had placed her on the port side of LST 58 and briefly remained there to try and mask any further attack from the same direction.

At the head of the convoy, LST 515 saw a ship on fire and sounded General Quarters. Believing it to be the last ship in the convoy that was hit, they watched as the column of LSTs fired to starboard although 515 could see no target. A few moments later seeing a large explosion followed by fire, 511 estimated from the position that 531 had been hit in addition to 507.

LST 507 had been torpedoed at 2.04 am on the starboard side by E-Boat S100. All electric power failed, the engines stopped and the ship was immediately engulfed in flames. LST 515 saw it burning, but because it seemed so far away, no information was received, and "Azalea" maintained station ahead of the convoy, 515 believed the burning ship was not part of their convoy.

Tom Saxby aboard the minesweeper HMS "Selkirk" well ahead of the convoy was ...

> " steering the ship at the time the U.S. landing ships were hit, which I noted at the time was 02.20 hours. The US fleet had been due to gradually overhaul us during the night. The explosions happened some miles astern of us, towards Portland. The voice pipe from the bridge was at my ear, and I could listen quite clearly to what was being said up there. Radio messages soon came through that three ships had been hit. There were, the signals said, a lot of men in the water."

No action was taken and HMS "Selkirk" returned to Portland at about 5.00 a.m. Aboard LST 507, US Navy crewman "John" had his ...

> "battle station on the #2 20mm forward gun. We left the gun on account of the fire. We tried to get the portable pumps going but they wouldn't start. We couldn't get any water from the hydrants – no water because the power was out. That's when the boat coxswain called me to help lower the boat. When we got it down we had quite a load in the boat, when we couldn't get the cable unhooked and the shells were exploding most of the guys jumped over the side. That's when the soldier came over with the carbine. I can still feel the drop of the boat. The soldier looked an old man to me maybe because he was unshaven; I was only 17 at the time. As we took off we started to pick up survivors, I know we had more than we should have because the water was starting to reach the gunwales. I know we passed up a few because we couldn't steer the boat around with all the weight on board."

Part of the 33rd Chemical Decontamination Company was aboard the same ship and "Ed" ...

> " *Was on fire guard duty from 10:00 pm to 12:00 pm. Came off duty, was talking to First Sergeant Spitler on the top deck, told him that the officers who brought up that exercise had no common sense. Why all our belongings and service records were taken on the trip is beyond me – all were lost. As time went by we were under machine gun fire by a German E Boat. Spitler just laughed and said that it was just practice prior to our landing on the beach at daylight. We spread our blankets under a truck on the top deck. I couldn't sleep thinking that we were sitting ducks for German E Boats. The LST wasn't moving – we were in the middle of nowhere – no land in sight. The torpedo hit us on the port side, the ship listed to the starboard side. I turned my head to ask Sergeant Spitler if he was okay – saw him as he rolled off the ship – no cries, no words from him, he must have been sleeping. When the ship righted itself I went to look but couldn't see Spitler, he was gone, either straight down or under the ship. Thought that I was the only one left on the ship, went many times back and forth, wondering whether to jump off the ship. Was very scared – then I wasn't scared – then I became afraid again. Kept thinking that I've got to be cool and try and control my feelings. Had been ducking items that were flying around. The ship was burning, gas cans exploding, ammunition going off – was a heck of a feeling. Heard voices coming from the tank deck, they said they were trying to get the doors open to get some DUKWs out. Got into a Higgins boat and when daylight came went aboard an LST. We were taken to Weymouth, to a hotel that had double decker beds. Others with me were Gentile, Kurz, two or three others, they may have been Cole and Koen – these were saved with me.* "

Vince Rolleri of the same unit ...

> "*Could not get Rosowski to get out of his bunk, and that was the last time I saw him. I and others were standing by the only LCVP that went into the water, someone with a carbine shot the cable, which held us to the LST; otherwise we would not have gotten away.* "

Arthur Victor had been ...

*"**awakened** by loud banging noises that sounded like hammers being pounded on the top deck. I had been asleep in an upper berth, in one of the compartments with seven other corpsmen. All told there were (a number) of us assigned to the 507 along with two surgeons. I could hear the other guys scrambling around "what the hell's going on?" I wanted to know. "We're under attack!" someone shouted back from the darkness. I jumped from my bunk onto the cold deck and wasted no time getting dressed but in the excitement and rush forgot my life belt – an almost fatal error. I dashed from the compartment with other guys pushing and shoving up the ladder to topside. But when I went thru the hatch and stepped on deck I was surprised to see how calm and quiet was. No shooting, no shelling. In fact it was breath-taking, heart pounding panorama of beautiful sky, lit up by a bright moon and a myriad of blinking stars. The air was brisk and chilled and felt good. It was night for love, not war. I went to my battle station which was at the stern, the other corpsmen I was on duty with were already there – Dailey PhM2/c (in charge), Lewis HA2/c and Rutherford HA2/c. They were quietly staring out to sea. We were on maneuvers and the ship was **packed with about 500 soldiers (infantrymen and combat engineers)** who were veterans of the Salerno and Sicily campaigns. In addition there were amphibious ducks, jeeps, trucks and small weapons of all shapes and sizes, loaded from one end of the ship to the other, top deck and tank deck. We were a floating arsenal. I crouched at my post whispering to my buddies about the incident and was told that the pounding I thought I heard was actually tracers aimed at the gun turrets. We guessed they were fired from a submarine or German E boat, but because it had become silent we hoped that whoever it was withdrew and returned to base."*

Leslie Morse of the 557th QM Railhead Company ...

"was bedded down a little aft of the lifeboat davits on the starboard side. I was asleep when the thing started but the fellow beside me had just come up from a poker game in the

*crew's quarters, poked me with foot and spoke. When I opened
my eyes the air was full of tracers. I put on my helmet and stood
up. Everything was black. There were quite a few jumping over
the side; I think maybe some onto the ones ahead. The fire was
getting closer and they started on the lifeboat but someone was
in a hurry and lifted the counter balance and the boat started
down but the pin was still in place and blocked it. I stood there
and waited as they were trying to drive the pin out with a
sledgehammer. It was getting rather warm and I decided they
would never make it so I went down the ladder into the water.
Then I looked up and the boat was coming down, so between
getting from under the boat and getting clear of the burning oil
I lost contact with everyone."*

W. W. Redieske a navy crewman of LST 507 remembers ...

*"When GQ alarm sounded a friend and I immediately went
topside and were standing forward when the torpedo hit. I was
knocked off my feet and fortunately the only injury sustained
was a slightly scraped knee. As the canvas covered army
vehicles topside started to burn I found temporary refuge
behind an air vent. Behind the vent I saw a lifeboat being
lowered and when I reached the side the boat was below deck
level. By this time the vehicles were burning heavily and
ammunition was exploding. As I jumped down into the lifeboat
my fall was broken by others already there. The bow was
touching the water but the rear cable was jammed and was
holding the stern probably 8 to 10 feet out of the water. A
soldier fired several shots from his rifle and severed the cable.
The steering mechanism was damaged when the stern hit the
water and the lifeboat was left without steering capabilities The
cries from those in the water were numerous at first and we
picked up the men who could reach the boat. As the night wore
on the survivors rescued became fewer and fewer and the cries
for help became less and less. Shortly after daybreak we were
rescued from the lifeboat by the 515. I remember seeing covered
bodies of men who did not survive their wounds, lying on the
deck."*

All LSTs with radar had their operators intently watching their screens trying to make sense of the confusing past few minutes. 515's radar showed two enemy craft cross the convoy column from starboard, one ahead and one astern of LST 531 which is quite remarkable as the LSTs were fitted with type "SG" radar that their operators classed as ... *"not too precise."* Their experience was that it could show large vessels such as other ships in the convoy, but not smaller craft such as E-Boats.

LST 511 sounded General Quarters and increased speed to all ahead two thirds; just a moment before 289 was hit by a torpedo in the stern. Captain Theodore R. Wilkinson, commanding officer of the 462nd Amphibian Truck Company aboard 511 with 144 of his men, reached the deck and saw three LSTs in flames.

"Azalea" saw LSTs firing tracer, and receiving fire to her port sounded Action Stations just as the LSTs steadied themselves by regrouping and resuming convoy speed. HMS "Saladin" steaming as fast as she could from the southwest saw the same exchange of tracer ahead, then a sheet of flame as an LST was hit, so altered course to 60' towards the action.

Just as LST 531 had opened fire at unseen targets in the darkness, E-Boat S143 fired two torpedoes at it and watched them hit as did LST 58 who also heard the E-Boats they were so close. LST 531 hit by both torpedoes on the starboard side instantly burst into flames, all electric power failed and the engines stopped. "Azalea" had just made radar contact with the attackers when 515 opened fire to starboard on the same radar contact and increased to flank speed taking evasive action at the same time. 496 saw 515 open fire and could see blue tracer return fire from low in the water. German E-Boats were using red tracer.

At 2.19 am LST 289 was under attack and saw one torpedo wake pass astern and another across the port bow. 511 saw an unidentified object some 600 yards off the starboard beam and believing it to be an enemy craft about to launch an attack, pushed her engines to all ahead full. 499 saw 531 being fired on and returned fire having seen it burst into flames and list almost immediately to starboard. LST 515 was still firing on their radar contact at 2,500 yards but observed no hits despite changing course and increasing speed to 11 knots.

By 2.21 am LST 496 could see two burning ships, and to escape the confusion and danger changed course 90' to port, increased to flank speed and opened fire on a radar target behind her as she started to zigzag away from the action

LST 511 opened fire on their radar target as did 496, but 496's guns strafed 511's decks wounding some personnel, so both ceased fire just as an E-Boat crossed 511's bows. During this confusing gun battle,

Lieutenant Yacevich commanding LST 511 told Captain Wilkinson commanding the 462nd Amphibian Truck Company aboard his ship, that two vessels had been picked up by radar prior to the attack, but he had been told they were other ships in the convoy. He also told Wilkinson that he estimated they were 15 miles off the French coast, and they had been struck twice by torpedoes that failed to explode. Just as General Quarters was sounded, Wilkinson records in his report, he and Yacevich agreed three ships were on fire.

In his after action report dated 30th April, Yacevich was able to detail this attack from witnesses aboard his ship, S2c W.P. Waiter, SC1C R. Edralin, S1c W.L. Benson and S2c C. Dorfman who ...

> *"First heard the motors, which were initially reported to be an airplane, as it sounded much like one. The sound, though loud, had a muffled quality. The boat approached at about 40 knots on a course heading from port to starboard, passing directly in front of the ship by no more than 15 yards. At this point none of our guns were able to depress sufficiently to fire on it. The boat then made two sharp turns, first ninety degrees to starboard, then back to its original course to port. The boat then disappeared from view. No description of the craft can be given due to the darkness and it's coloring. Only the wake and its gunfire were seen. It commenced firing when slightly off our port bow and continued until lost from sight to starboard. It was noticed that the tracers from its gunfire were green in color. From the size of the bullet holes noted on our ship, its guns must have been approximately 30 caliber."*

It should again be noted that the attacking E-Boats were armed with 40mm guns that had recently replaced 20mm versions, and were using red tracer ammunition.

At 2.24 am LST 531 rolled over and started to sink. LST 58 was under attack from E-Boats and was desperately firing in the general direction of their unseen attackers. At the very moment the gunners first saw the E-Boat, a torpedo was also seen approaching the port bow about 1,500 yards away and was narrowly avoided by rapid use of the helm. LST 515 was still firing at targets they could now see but no hits were seen.

HMS "Saladin" was dashing from one incident to another, and on seeing this latest intense exchange of tracer, altered course to intercept just as 496 heard "Azalea" radio Portsmouth that the convoy was under E-

Boat attack 16 miles from Portland Bill on a bearing of 250'. Belatedly Azalea's captain must have realized this attack was genuine, and not the mock attack he had been briefed to expect.

By 2.30 am LST 289 was again under attack. Her port guns opened fire on a *"fast white boat"* while all the other guns were firing at a torpedo wake coming in fast from the port side. But the torpedo hit the fantail causing considerable damage and jamming the steering, forced her to circle towards two blazing LSTs before she could regain some steerage and head away from them. The fires on 289 were eventually brought under control, and after assessing the damage her captain decided to make for port. With her steering still inoperative, he ingeniously lowered small landing craft, secured them to the ship sides and used them to propel and steer the LST towards Dartmouth.

Another convoy of seven LSTs and two LCTs en route from Falmouth to Portland steering on north easterly course, heard the E-Boat alert broadcast and immediately went to General Quarters, but despite their escorts firing several star shells no E-Boats were seen and no contact was made.

LST 58 had seen 289 firing her guns and had seen the torpedo hit, then heard another explosion astern and briefly saw a searchlight off her port quarter. Unnerved by it all, the decision was taken to leave the area, taking a zigzag course.

HMS "Saladin" was being frustrated by not making contact with any enemy craft but soon made another radar contact some 4,000 yards away and illuminated the area with star shells which were seen by LST 515, but "Saladin" again found nothing.

LST 499 had already radioed a distress message, and at 2.32 am LST 515 advised Portland for the second time of the attack which was heard by 496 who was now at flank speed making for West Bay, just west of Portland having repaired her port engine that had given out under the strain of prolonged flank speed.

The convoy had scattered in all directions by now, and LST 515 was some 10,000 yards from the attack area but could still clearly see two LSTs burning fiercely.

At 2.37 am LST 58 was still zigzagging away from the attack when her lookouts saw and heard a torpedo pass her bow. Saving the ship and its cargo was of paramount importance, and LST 58 was hampered by the two pontoons she was towing, so wisely cast them adrift.

By now LST 507 was a lost cause. It was on fire from end to end; men trapped below decks were burned to death. Blazing vehicles slid across the decks as the ship heeled over and the lucky few to escape the flames jumped over the rails into the freezing cold sea.

On LST 496, First Lieutenant Thomas A Welstead, second in command of the 704th Maintenance Company saw from the deck that the sky was ablaze with machine gun and 40mm fire. As the attack abated the ship's commander, Lieutenant (junior grade) Grode conferred with Welstead and they decided to head for shore.

LST 515 had been maneuvering around the attack area all this time, logging flare sightings and burning ships. "Saladin" had been frantically hunting for the enemy, chasing radar contacts at every opportunity, but by 2.56 am her only radar blips were of the scattering convoy.

Just after 3.00 am, LST 499 had the same radar picture of ships heading towards Portland and followed at a distance of four miles, trying to catch up and zigzag at the same time.

LST 58 was heading for Portland and for the next half hour saw E-Boats and more and more flares as "Saladin" vainly tried to hunt them down.

Azalea's radar confirmed the convoy scattering towards the northeast, her lookouts could see the burning ships, and at 4.00 am requested assistance from her flotilla commander aboard HMS "Tanatside".

"Saladin" approached these burning wrecks illuminating them with star shells and could see about fifteen feet of the bows of one LST still above water with fifty men clinging to it and after careful maneuvering managed to pull alongside and take them off.

By 4.15 am LST 515 had changed course to 226' true, and against orders was returning to the attack area to search for survivors. Having confirmed that LSTs 58, 511, 496 and 499 had safely reached West Bay, a dispatch was prepared stating two LSTs had been torpedoed. 511 saw that two LSTs were still burning, and as 515 approached them, survivors of 507 in the water saw the 515 lower boats to pick them up. Saladin also saw 515 picking up survivors just as HMS "Onslow" returned after fruitlessly chasing the E-Boats.

Captain Wilkinson of 462nd Amphibian Truck Company aboard LST 511 could still see two burning LSTs, and was surprised that no rafts, vests or boats had been put overboard to help any men in the water, and that no rescue attempt had been made.

At 5.20 am Azalea was heading west searching for the convoy LSTs, finding 289 at 280', 12 miles from Portland Bill, struggling for Dartmouth. She also found Saladin still standing by the burning LSTs. One mile north and half an hour later Saladin found the bows of another LST protruding above water with two survivors on it. These were taken off and the bows sunk by gunfire and depth charges. Once this had been done at about 6.00 am, Saladin saw Azalea to her north escorting LST 289 and reported to Azalea that she considered three LSTs had been sunk and radioed this to Admiral Moon aboard the USS Bayfield, as headquarters ship for Exercise "Tiger", adding that she was searching for survivors. On receipt of this, Moon immediately dispatched his Chief of Staff, Captain Tompkins to enquire into the incident.

By now British warships involved in the exercise were starting to arrive in the attack area. HMS "Obedient" and "Brissenden" joined the search for survivors with orders to take them to Portland.

Lieutenant Welstead on LST 496 remembers ...

"As dawn broke, the horrible sight of hundreds of bodies floating head down appeared. It is a mental picture never to be forgotten."

Surviving LSTs had all anchored in West Bay and were sending their casualties ashore in small boats to a waiting line of military ambulances that would take the dead and wounded to a military hospital near Salisbury.

HMS "Onslow" had picked up a few survivors, including Ensign D. G. Harlander, and several bodies that she landed at Portland. LST 515's boats had returned and she made for Portland with 118 walking survivors, 14 stretcher cases of wounded and 45 bodies. American and Royal Navy ships were still searching for, and collecting bodies from the now calm waters of Lyme Bay.

LST 289 was in dire trouble. Her one good propeller came off at 9.30 am and she was obliged to ask for a tow from a French tug, eventually arriving in Dartmouth at 2.30 pm.

By the evening of 28th April 1944, the surviving LSTs of convoy T-4, having offloaded their casualties, sailed for Slapton Sands to continue with the exercise and discharge their loads of men and vehicles.

Paul H. Atkins, a navy crewman aboard LST 511 remembers General Quarters being sounded at 02:07 am on 28th April and seeing the last ship in the convoy, LST 507, on fire from stem to stern with ammunition constantly exploding. LSTs 496 and 531 started firing ...

"LST 496 on our bow directly in front of us fired and hit our number 4 gun. The gun captain was badly hurt, put on a

stretcher and carried below; another of the gun crew was hit in the arm. Then our guns began to fire, LST 531 was torpedoed off our fantail and set on fire, a torpedo was seen passing under our bow, and then we were fired on by E-boats. Our ship commenced to leave the area, leaving two ships burning on the horizon. "

Arthur Victor on LST 507 ...

" after a few minutes of silently waiting and staring out to sea looking for any movement and seeing or hearing nothing, I walked to the railing on the port side and stood beside the raft. I leaned on the rail, caught in the beauty of the night, when I was joined by Rutherford who leaned on the rail on the other side of the raft. Feeling nostalgic we started talking about love and stuff when suddenly there was a tremendous explosion. I was lifted off my feet and hurled back against the bulkhead. My head smashed sideways against the steel plate so hard that I almost passed out but fortunately my helmet absorbed the shock and I was merely dazed. Somehow I hauled myself up and staggered back to the raft. Rutherford was at my side, his face was ashen. Mine probably was too from the shock. I asked if he was OK – he said he was then he said my mouth was bleeding but I could only feel the ringing in my ears as I ran my sleeve across my mouth. We looked down the area where the blast came from and saw giant flames and black smoke billowing from a gaping hole just about midship. A torpedo had torn thru the starboard side and exploded into the tank deck and engine room – a fatal blow, and although we knew our ship would go down we were more afraid of another attack, which we might not survive. It never came. But it was instant pandemonium. Someone yelled "Men overboard!" I turned from the spectacle of fire and saw some guys already in the water, swimming around. All we could do was toss them life preservers. Some never made it and we saw them struggle and go under .At this point Ensign Brown ordered all the ammunition tossed overboard. The deck was getting very hot and we could have blown ourselves up. As I saw the cartridges hit the water and sink from view I knew our situation was desperate. Mr. Brown then ordered us to release the raft. We

removed the holding pins and gave it a shove, over it went, but to our dismay it landed upside down with survival gear underneath. Then Mr. Brown asked for a volunteer to go over the side and keep it in tow when a corpsman by the name of Star said he would go and leaped overboard. Rutherford and I wanted to go too but Mr. Brown said one was enough so we stayed at our post and watched Star scamper onto the raft. I must admit it's where I wanted to be. After watching Star take over the raft I turned toward Mr. Brown for further orders and saw Bailey standing there alone, looking lost and confused. I went over and asked him if he was OK. He said he could swim but was afraid to jump. His life belt was inflated and his helmet was off, so I led him to the railing and told him to jump when Mr. Brown gave the order. I said if he didn't jump I'd throw him over. He told me he was OK and could do it. He looked all right so I returned to where I was. That's the last I ever saw of him."

An extraordinary witness to the attack was Peter Nevill. A pilot of a modified Beaufighter TFX with a Special Service Unit detached from 604 Auxiliary Air Force night fighter squadron based at Bolt Head airstrip, which was on top of a 400 ft cliff between Bolt Tail and Hope Cove. His unit's role was to intercept enemy bombers and long-range fighters on nocturnal raids. They were also instructed to take any opportunity to hit back at enemy shipping.

On his 20th birthday – 27th April 1944, Nevill was given unusual instructions. He and his navigator were told to keep well clear of Lyme Bay, in particular the Slapton Sands area. Early in the patrol as he flew west on the first leg, he and his Aussie navigator saw a convoy of tank landing ships sailing slowly towards Lyme Bay.

Towards the end of Nevill's second leg of the patrol, they passed their airstrip and continued east to turn back to Start Point. They were flying a few miles out from the coast by now and he and his navigator could look into Lyme Bay. A ship was on fire over towards Portland Bill. Every so often it was rocked by a loud explosion, followed by a bright orange fireball that lit up the darkness and the surrounding water. Tracer fire was flying in all directions and seemed to be striking at anything afloat on the water.

Nevill knew the army held exercises in battle conditions, even going so far as to fire live ammunition ...

Bristol Beaufighter.

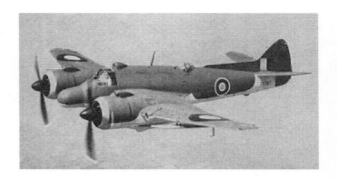

> " *But what I saw before me that night seemed to be a naval exercise that had gone completely over the top. Ships that had been in the convoy we had flown over some hours earlier were scattered all over the bay and seemed to be firing indiscriminately in all directions. It was quite obvious a large ship was ablaze.* "

Nevill urgently reported the sighting to their control and was told to keep clear. He repeatedly expressed concern that there was something seriously wrong but was again told to stay away.

> *"It was terrible, I knew there were people dying down there who needed my help, so against orders we decided to stay around a little while longer".*

He had described the scenes he had witnessed to his base but was told *"This is only an exercise"*. He knew differently –

> *"I knew that the men down below needed help and I decided off my own bat that we were going to try and help them. I knew that a single aircraft couldn't do much, but I couldn't ignore what was happening in front of my eyes."*

His navigator spotted three fast moving vessels on the sea and after they had established that they were German E boats. Nevill proceeded to launch an attack as they sped away from Lyme Bay. During this attack his navigator lost sight of the other two boats and they had to return to base to refuel where they were privately congratulated by their commanding officer but warned to say nothing of the incident for the rest of their lives.

Ten

E-Boat attack – British view

AT 11.00 a.m. on 27th April, "Azalea" joined convoy T4 as escort, watched "Scimitar" returning to Plymouth, and proceeded alone at the convoy speed of 5 knots as T-4's one and only escort. When Lieutenant Commander G. C. Giddes later submitted his secret report dated 28th April it contained his belief that he had nine LSTs in the convoy, not eight

H.M.S. "Azalea".

as shown in all subsequent documentation from other sources. When interviewed on the 29th April by Admiral Moon, Lieutenant Commander Thayer and Commodore Moreno, Giddes admitted he thought it strange that he should be the sole convoy escort, but made no protest at the time.

As "Azalea" escorted convoy T-4 through the night, reports of E-Boat activity were first received on the "Port Wave" from HMS "Onslow" at 12.11 a.m. on the 28th April as she encountered a solitary E-boat heading north just off Portland Bill and which retired southwards a few minutes later. Onslow's report was monitored by HMS "Saladin" and re-broadcast by Plymouth shore base on the area radio net at 12.39 a.m. C in C Portsmouth also reported two groups of E-Boats south west of Portland Bill on the Port Wave. At about 12.20 a.m. three groups of E-Boats were plotted by "Onslow" between 10 and 20 miles WSW Portland Bill steering northwest. These groups were also plotted by Portland who broadcast their presence and was heard by "Saladin". Then the first unidentified radar plot from shore stations was received at Plymouth at 12.22 a.m. and classified as hostile three minutes later. As more information came in, it was broadcast at intervals on both the Area net and Plymouth Port Wave. C in C, Plymouth had sent a signal to HMS "Tanatside" concerning HMS Scimitar's absence at 11.06 p.m. Its delivery to the captain was delayed by decoding until about 12.45 a.m. who then took decisive and immediate action by detailing HMS "Saladin", already in Start (Lyme) Bay, to act as relief escort for convoy T4. An extract from the "Secret" report of Lieutenant Commander P. E. King RNVR, commanding HMS "Saladin" dated 29th April 1944 confirms the timing ...

> " At 1.30 am on 28th April HMS Saladin received radio message from HMS Onslow reporting E-Boats. As the captain reached the bridge another radio message was being received from the flotilla command ship HMS Tanatside ordering Saladin to join the T4 convoy escort HMS Azalea."

Unaware that help was on its way, at 1.35 a.m. "Azalea" altered course 2,000 yards ahead of the convoy of LSTs that now stretched for over three miles, traveling at three and a half knots. "Saladin" had been patrolling an area between the Dart buoy and the Mewstone in Lyme Bay and at 1.37 a.m. on receipt of Tanatside's complete orders set a course ENE at a speed of 23 knots, estimating she was some thirty miles from the convoy. Despite the urgency her speed was limited due to the unreliability of one of the three boilers, but the course selected anticipated meeting the convoy at about 2.45 a.m. approximately 17 miles from Portland Bill. During their dash across Lyme Bay, one of the crew saw two E-Boats traveling in the same direction until one cut across the bows and the other across the stern but they were so fast he had no chance to fire his gun.

According to "Azalea" she heard an explosion at 2.00 a.m. and ten minutes later saw tracer being fired to port by an LST. Azalea sounded "action stations" and closed with the convoy. Five minutes later an LST at the rear of the convoy was torpedoed and set on fire. Only a minute later saw another LST was torpedoed and on fire. Azalea zigzagged down the starboard side of the convoy and was fired at by an LST. She made a brief radar contact close to and in line with three LSTs but sighted no E-Boat. "Azalea" had received shore station reports of E-Boats but the attack started whilst studying them.

At 2.25 a.m. LST 496 in the convoy heard Azalea radio Portsmouth that they were under E-Boat attack, giving their position as 16 miles, bearing 250 degrees from Portland Bill. A minute later the same LST heard Azalea calling for assistance. Shortly afterwards star shells were seen in various directions, mainly ahead and at 2.15 am an exchange of tracer was seen followed by a sheet of flame. "Saladin" saw this LST on fire and altered course towards it, believing this was the convoy under attack.

Azalea's first report of the attack timed at 2.20 a.m. did not reach Saladin until some three hours later. At 2.25 am another tracer exchange was seen to the south of the convoy's estimated position and Saladin swung south on an interception course. Five minutes later she made a small radar contact at a distance of four thousand yards and the area was illuminated with star shell but nothing was seen, the contact faded and no asdic was reported to support the radar blip. Tracer was seen back in the direction of the convoy and a second ship seen to be on fire, so Saladin again returned to her original course towards the convoy sending a signal to Azalea of her course to avoid any mis-identification. But there was no radar contact with the convoy which should have been possible if the convoy was within the swept channel, and it wasn't until 2.56 am that the first radar contact was made with one of the stricken ships which was some two and a half miles eastward of the swept channel.

Radar was now showing the whole convoy had scattered. Saladin determined that Azalea was to her southeast so continued northeastward to search for the convoy. Reports were now coming in thick and fast from Lyme Bay shore stations of E-Boat activity but due to the time delay of these reports Saladin stood little chance of intercepting any E-Boat except by sheer chance. By 3.10 am the convoy was scattering in a northeasterly direction and Azalea took up position to their south, zigzagging to give some form of screening and protection. Five minutes later Azalea saw star shells sent up by Saladin at about 3.15 am to identify the bows of an LST still above water.

By 3.15 am as Saladin approached the attack area one LST which appeared to be intact was blazing fiercely from end to end until it was seen to turn over and sink. An unidentified object when illuminated by star shell, proved to be the bows of another LST protruding about 15 feet out of the water with about 50 survivors clinging to it. As Saladin went alongside and took off the survivors, many more survivors were seen in the water, but as small craft were already rescuing these in a flat calm sea, Saladin opted to move away. Nearby was a smaller conflagration that appeared to be a section of an LST and was presumed to be part of the bow section from which survivors had been rescued. After a brief assessment of the situation, Saladin's initial radio report stated that three LSTs had been sunk.

Almost an hour later at 4.00 a.m. Azalea contacted HMS Tanatside requesting assistance for the burning LSTs. C in C Plymouth later stated that Azalea's signal log showed that she received all signals originated by British authorities, and in his opinion had maintained an excellent W/T watch

Saladin picked up reports that E-Boats were returning to their base by 4.40 am and then was granted permission to pick up survivors. Twenty minutes later she saw LST 515 return from the northeast and lower boats to pick up survivors. Saladin's captain considered these small craft were better placed for this task while he searched for outlying groups of survivors.

With such a momentous and tragic incident taking place in British home waters, each Royal Navy captain felt a moral obligation as well as a duty to quickly inform their superiors of what had happened. This was unfortunate for the US Navy because they couldn't reach these officers before they wrote their reports to ensure details and timings corresponded with their own version of the incident that they were engineering. Lieutenant Commander G. C. Giddes commanding the corvette, HMS "Azalea" had already written his report of the attack the very day it happened, but this contained several aspects the US Navy urgently needed to adjust to ensure all reports told the same story. The report was already within the upward chain of communication having reached Admiral Leatham's office, and in between too many people had already seen it to simply locate and destroy it, so another method of discrediting its contents had to be found. The U.S. Navy decided upon a personal interview between Admiral Moon and Commander Giddes was their best option, where carefully framed questions would elicit responses that would bring his view of the attack back into line.

In reply to a seemingly innocuous question from Admiral Moon, Giddes stated he had not seen any blue tracers. The color must have been significant for Admiral Moon to pose the question. The E-Boats had used red tracer, so who was using blue tracer? That question is answered by HMS "Onslow" when at about 12.10 a.m. she plotted three groups of E-Boats between 10 and 20 miles WSW of Portland Bill steering northwest and they were also plotted by Portland shore station. The German 5th and 9th Flotillas undoubtedly represented two of these three groups as this was their agreed tactical approach to the T-4 convoy, and had not yet dispersed for their attack. The E-Boats did not have the benefit of radar, so must have been unaware that a third group of vessels were also approaching the convoy from the same direction. If Onslow also identified this third group as "E-Boats" it must have somehow given that impression to experienced radar operators by their speed, which suggests this group of vessels was either another unknown squadron of E-Boats, or Allied MTBs.

Lieutenant Commander King commanding HMS "Saladin" had written his secret report, dated it the 29th April 1944, and submitted it to Plymouth Command, also depriving the US Navy of the opportunity of changing or influencing the contents. But Saladin had been a latecomer to the action and the report contained nothing contentious as far as the U.S. Navy were concerned, except for the number of sunken LSTs that King had seen.

One group of small Allied vessels that approached the attack area from the Portland direction and can therefore be discounted, as the third group seen by Onslow, were British rescue launches. John Cullen was second coxswain on Royal Navy Rescue Motor Launch number 532 based at Portland Dockyard. He remembers ...

"In the very early hours of the 28th April 1944, we were tied up at the Torpedo Boat pens in Portland Harbour. 532 was part of a flotilla of six Rescue Motor Launches all of similar age and each crewed by the same number of personnel. As senior officer, Commander Scott received a signal to take all six boats into Lyme Bay, where an American convoy was in danger of attack by German E-Boats. Very quickly, all six ML's went into line ahead through Portland Harbour, into Weymouth Bay, up to and around Portland Bill into Lyme Bay. This took approximately twenty minutes. The intention was to try to engage the E-Boats and protect the convoy of Tank Landing Ships that was proceeding at very slow speed towards the Devon Coast. It was ideal E-Boat weather, calm sea and very low cloud, which would protect them from attack by aircraft. Being April it was fairly cold but I was comfortable wearing plenty of woollens under a boiler suit insulated with kapok. Commander Scott issued orders for the Battle ensign to be raised. (a flag approximately ten to twelve times larger than an ordinary ensign). Also the port and starboard lights on the yardarm to be turned on in order that friendly ships would recognize us. When we rounded Portland Bill we could not see the convoy but we picked it up on radar as being eighteen to twenty miles away. We also spotted some shapes moving fast towards the convoy from the shore side. All during this time we were being conned by H.M.S Attack, a shore based establishment situated on top of Portland Bill with a

panoramic view of the English Channel that extended for approximately thirty miles in all directions.

"The Bridge was very busy, with the Skipper continually calling for radio reports from Nobby Hall our radio operator and also from our radar operator. The First Lieutenant appeared to be permanently engaged with the Aldis Lamp signaling H.M.S Attack and the other Five M L's of the flotilla. We were approximately fifteen miles from the convoy, when I first saw gun flashes reflected by the low cloud then some flares, followed later by some large explosions. We were blind to what was going on as our Radio Operator (Nobby Hall) reported that he could not raise any signals from the American ships. It was HMS Attack that informed us that two American LST's had been sunk and another was in difficulty because her stem had been blown away. This information reached us approximately 45 minutes after I had first sighted the gun flashes. As a result of receiving this information the Skipper issued orders to prepare for survivors. Scrambling nets were rolled out, covers were removed from the two searchlights, the dinghy was slung outboard and Jamie Hyman, our Medical Artificer proceeded to layout a dozen Heath Robinson stretchers on the quarter Deck. By this time we were within five miles of the convoy. The gunfire and tracer appeared to be increasing. The Skipper was using his binoculars continuously and I realized that he had to make a decision to take his ships within range of the LST gunfire. The Americans were hopping mad and appeared to be firing at shadows. Our Radar operator also reported that some of the LST's had turned and were heading back in our direction."

The situation was resolved by the Rear Admiral at HMS Attack issuing orders for us to return to Portland as it was judged that we may have been mistaken for E-Boats and would have come under fire from the American ships. To this day I am convinced that this was the right decision for. I feel that we would have come under friendly lire that would have turned us from being saviors into victims. Still, it was a bitter disappointment, for we all felt that given the opportunity, each boat could have saved perhaps fifty men resulting in something like three hundred being saved. The E-Boats had departed before we followed orders and turned back to Portland."

Eleven

Survivors

HUNDREDS of sailors and soldiers were now in the near freezing water. Many had drowned almost as soon as they jumped from the stricken ships, some simply drifted away to slide quietly beneath the gentle waves. Others were desperately clinging to anything that floated, but the intense cold was penetrating their very souls as the darkness increased their feelings of isolation and helplessness.

Leslie Morse of the 557th Railhead Company ...

> *"tried to float but it was too cold. Had to keep moving to keep a little warmth."*

Arthur Victor on LST 507 had heard Ensign Brown shout, *"Abandon ship"* and saw ...

> *"...guys started over the side in droves. Many landed on top of one another with a thud. Many soldiers, who for some reason were dressed for battle, pitched forward in the water with legs up and faces down. They were top heavy and struggled unsuccessfully to overcome it, even tho I could see they were wearing lifebelts. It was unbelievable. Those who survived the jump swam towards the raft."*

> *"I looked to where Dailey had been standing – he was gone. Rutherford wasted no time. Said he'd see me later and took off. I threw down my helmet and started over when I heard someone frantically calling my name. I turned and saw another corpsman*

standing there shaking with fear. I took his hand and led him to the railing and told him we would jump together, but for God's sake don't grab onto me, to rely on his lifebelt for support. I had to keep reassuring him that we would be OK. Then we slowly climbed over the railing together and before he had time to hesitate I grabbed his hand and jumped, pulling him down."

"*We hit the water together, our grasp broken as we sank deep into the freezing English Channel. It seemed an eternity before we reached the surface. I stayed where I was, holding on and treading water, getting my breath. After a few minutes I tried heading for the raft which surprisingly was still in sight, lit up by the burning 507. The 507 was sinking slowly at the stern and I knew there wasn't much time left, and without a lifebelt I wasn't sure I could make it to the raft if I delayed any longer. So I turned and started to move away, another corpsman screamed at me to come back. I stopped, turned and told him to let go and work his way to me (which was no more than a few feet) but he said he was too scared and couldn't do it. Reluctantly I turned, wished him luck and swam away. I never looked back even tho he kept shrieking at me to return. I was sure he was going to die. I was sick at heart. ."*

"*I made it to the raft and strangely enough there was only a handful of men clinging to the side. I thought by now it would be overcrowded. I guess a lot of guys floundered and died before they even got started. When I got their Star was kneeling alone on the top. I found an open space on the side and took hold. It wasn't long before we were swarmed by men who quickly filled the other open spaces along the sides. Those who didn't make it to an open space had to hold onto those who did. It was made clear that only one guy was allowed on top. It wasn't challenged – yet. But the extreme cold and hysteria were already taking their toll. Guys without lifebelts and waterlogged clothing were in a constant struggle to stay afloat, holding on to guys with belts or Mae West's. Even those with preservers were struggling because of the freezing water and the desperate situation we were in. Men were dying all around in those first few minutes of trying to settle into our perilous predicament. It puzzled me how young healthy men could give up and die so easily. It still does."*

"*As many died, there were still as many to take their place, so we were loading up pretty fast. We spotted another raft about two hundred feet away, but further out to sea, with just a cluster of men clinging to it. I volunteered to swim there to help relieve the load on ours. Some of the others said they would go with me, so I removed my jacket which had become heavy with water and would be a burden to swim in and let it drift away, but during this intervening time, the other raft became full so I stayed put. However without my jacket I was left bare from the waist up which put me at the mercy of the freezing cold water that splashed over us. It was like being naked in a pool of ice water. We were now about 100 yards out when I felt a sharp heat strike the back of my neck, then someone started screaming that the water was on fire. I turned quickly and stared at mile high flames and billowing black smoke making a wide circle, when by some miracle the fire suddenly died out not more than 20 feet away. "*

"There were about 75 of us now, jammed around and about the raft holding onto each other as before. Guys came and guys went. It was hard to keep count. Across from me were six other corpsmen clinging to the side including Rutherford who had one of them hanging on piggyback. One of the doctors was to the left of me at one end holding up a soldier who kept moaning that his leg was broken. The other doctor was opposite with the corpsmen. Dailey wasn't there. Neither was Lewis. We were so packed in that the raft was arm length under water from the sheer weight of us so we had to extend our arms to keep our heads above water. It was agonizing."

"Guys were dying off all around us. Those without life preservers just let go, struggled a bit, then disappeared. Dead weight made it impossible to do much of anything to help them. One of the first to go was a corpsman who was only 19 years old, married and the father of a 4-month-old son. He wasn't wearing a lifebelt and had been holding on next to Rutherford. Suddenly and without warning he was struggling in the water, screaming for help. Star couldn't reach him and Rutherford (who was still holding up the other corpsman) threw him his leg to grab onto. He managed to get hold of the foot but slid off and sank beneath the surface. We waited for him to pop up, but he never did. In a twinkling he was gone. We were dumbfounded and devastated and prayed for him. That's all we could do. But no sooner was he gone when the boy on Rutherford's back let go and started sliding down. Rutherford reached back to try and hold him up but he was too heavy and wet and kept going straight down. Star tried to

help but it was too late. He never said a word and never tried to stop himself. Just quietly disappeared beneath the surface and never came up. It happened to be his 19th birthday. "

"The 507 could be seen, still afloat, still aflame, listing at the stern. There were men still running about her decks. Off to our left was the LST 531 and we started kicking in her direction hoping to be picked up. Then we heard two thunderous explosions and great columns of fire and smoke rising from her belly. Ammunition started firing from her bow guns and shot straight up into the sky, which looked like a 4th of July celebration. Bodies hurled from her deck like rag dummies, parts of bodies too. A few guys managed to jump and swim for their lives as the 531 split and went down in a matter of minutes. In the blink of an eye it blew up and disappeared taking most of its crew and soldiers with it. When the 531 went down guys started shrieking despairingly that it was the end of the world. They cried we would be gunned down in the water. Desperate men were praying aloud, begging, pleading to be saved. They started packing in closer and tighter to the raft pushing it further under. Then a few soldiers banded together and worked their way closer. They threatened to get on the raft and take it over. They said that because we were sailors we were fish-like and better in the water than they were. "

"I had become almost unbearably cold by now. I had also been swallowing oily tasting salt water that made me nauseous and I started puking. I pissed my pants to feel the warmth. I remember how good it felt pouring over my thighs, but I kept puking my guts. I was numb as we continued drifting and losing men. They seemed to just give up and slip under without much of a struggle, or died in their preservers where they were. The 507 was still in sight but fading from view. Fog was beginning to surround us. We could still hear cries for help. We called out and flashed our lights to give our position but only a few managed to make it to us. We finally drifted beyond sight of the still burning 507, shrouded in fog and mist. We could hear the drone of an engine, hoping it wasn't the Germans looking for survivors to pick off. But someone said it sounded like one of our small boats, so we took the chance and yelled and shouted and kept signaling with a flashlight that we were able to pull free from the underside of the raft, but the boat never came. Later we learned it was only picking up lone swimmers. We continued drifting in a thick fog and heavy swells.

Guys became seasick and threw up, taking in water as they gulped, making them sicker and weaker and hopeless. Guys were dying off in a steady stream. They died and drifted away or died and went under. By losing so many men the raft had been slowly rising to the surface so we could lean on it. The soldier with a broken leg was allowed on top where he sprawled out. He was a big man and covered almost the entire top of the raft. With him on and us leaning, the raft went under again so we were back to extended arms and heads held high. At some point in time we were joined by Lewis, a bear of a boy who came swimming out of the darkness. I couldn't believe it. After he rested he said "Bye" and took off. It was even more amazing that he survived. After about five hours we were down to about 20 of us and the raft had risen to the surface. We were able to lean again. It felt wonderful."

Leslie Morse finally ...

"made contact with another fellow and shortly we saw a boat and yelled. We were the last two they picked up except for a sailor swimming with no preserver and in his underwear. Someone said he was a long distance swimmer as a civilian. A fellow in the boat I knew was dry and gave me his field jacket; I put it around my head and shoulders. I have no idea how long I sat back to the side of the boat. After a time I got on my hands and knees and finally stood up. Then I held the rail in my hands and started to walk in place. I felt that if I didn't exercise then I never would. When we pulled alongside the LST after daylight I started up the net but a few feet from the top started to black out. A couple of sailors jumped over the rail and grabbed me. On deck I was stripped and someone handed me a cup of hot coffee and I went below into a bunk and sleep."

There is no doubt that many individual acts of courage, sacrifice and quick-thinking saved lives after the torpedo attack. Staff Sergeant Edward G. Polovitch of the 33rd Chemical Company scrambled into the forward, port side LCVP but it was held by the lowering cable to the side of the sinking LST. He called to Staff Sergeant Francis P. Gentile of his unit to shoot the cable with his carbine, but someone else in the LCVP shot the cable and freed the craft.

An identical situation on another LST was experienced by T/5 Ernest D

Rodman, also of the 33rd Chemical Company. The aft cable was jammed, preventing the LCVP from dropping into the water until an infantryman shot away the cable.

Charles W. Kusman, a Staff Sergeant of the 478th Amphibian Truck Company had survived the sinking of LST 507.

> *"After I was picked up by the British destroyer, they opened fire on the capsized LST, which had to be the 531, and sank it. As you know the casualties list says the 478th lost 28 men. My Company commander says there was 80. "*

As daylight was starting to break Arthur Victor heard ...

> *"someone yelling he could see a ship. We thought he had gone mad, and then suddenly we saw the outline of a ship loom before us as though it had risen out of the water. We didn't know if it was enemy or friendly, and didn't much care. We started hollering and drifted close enough to see a small boat being lowered from an LST. It hit water and headed in our direction. We would be saved! The LCVP pulled up to the raft with the bow door down and we scrambled onto the raft in turn but when I started crawling onto the bow the boat drifted back and I fell in between. The end of the bow door kept ramming my legs against the raft but I felt nothing. Finally someone grabbed me by the belt and hauled me into the boat and gave me his jacket. It felt like fur against my skin. We were told to lay down and were covered with tarpaulin. I couldn't stand anyway. We were taken back to our rescue ship, the LST 515. Some were hoisted on stretchers, others went up the ladder. When we landed on board we were led to the crew's quarters, stripped, given a shot of brandy and put to bed. The guys from the other raft were already there and greeted us like it was party time, including the one I left at the fender. He wouldn't speak to me. "*

Those who survived those freezing, dark hours were rescued by many ships, including HMS "Onslow" who detailed survivors and bodies recovered in a report dated 29th April 1944. [28]

28 See Appendix 28 – H.M.S. Onslow's report

Twelve

Bodies and Wreckage

PROBABLY the first vessel to arrive on the scene of the E-Boat attack that was not involved with Exercise "Tiger" was MTB 704. Returning to Portland from patrol off the French coast where they had been hunting for German shipping, she received an urgent message to divert to Lyme Bay. Archie Jelly aboard the Motor Torpedo Boat remembers arriving there ...

"as daylight was coming in. There were bodies floating about everyone everywhere. We counted seventy. Some had their eyes open, one had a split open in his head by a boats propellers.

H.M.S. "Obedient".

Our officers started to crook them in, to get their identity, then a message came through to leave them there, so that the Americans could pick them up. We put them back in the water again. It made our crew very down-hearted, we thought if that's an exercise for D-Day – God help us."

HMS "Obedient" on the outer protective screen of the exercise had heard the attack and watched it on the distant horizon. She had offered to assist but had been ordered to maintain her station until just before dawn when she was given orders to proceed to the vicinity of the action and assist where possible. As she approached, the crew could see an LST on the horizon, still on fire. Drawing nearer they were confronted with two LSTs, both with their bows in the air and sterns submerged. Black smoke billowed from the wrecks and flames rose from the middle of the bows. It was then a crewman, Tom Cull became ...

"aware of all the dead men in the water, stretching for what seemed miles. We were all puzzled by the fact that virtually all the dead men were floating in a similar manner, i.e. head down and feet out of the water. My shipmates and I concluded that they were top heavy due to either too much equipment or incorrectly fitted life belts."

"Obedient" immediately began searching for survivors on the flat calm sea. Their motorboat was lowered into the water and searched in earnest, especially as some of the crew thought they heard cries for help. Only one survivor was plucked from the sea by "Obedient", but he died shortly afterwards in the ships wardroom despite the efforts of the ships' doctor.

Just as soon as Admiral Moon heard of the attack he assumed command of the Royal Navy screen vessels and ordered HMS "Dianthus" and "Primrose", together with the USS "Tide", to the scene to protect the surviving LSTs and to search for survivors. He also requested an air search from C in C, Plymouth.

HMS "Sutton" was also searching for survivors having just left Portland. Crewman Leslie Johnson remembers the 28th April was a beautiful day with a near cloudless sky ...

"and the sea was like a mirror with hardly a ripple to be seen."
The ship took on their fill of coal and cast off but to Leslie's surprise they did not head back to their anchorage. Instead the

message was piped around the ship for special and duty men to go to their stations and the forenoon watch to stand by for leaving harbor. As naval custom dictated, the forenoon watch lined the upper deck as they left Portland. The sun was rising into a now cloudless sky, lookouts were posted and ratings started to hose down the decks, as coal dust was everywhere. But no orders for minesweeping had been given and the crew was puzzled. They were not kept in suspense for very long when the captain mustered the crew and informed them that they were heading for Start Point, and the area where the night before, German E-Boats had sunk some LSTs, and HMS Sutton was to pick up any survivors. The crew was dismissed and went about their duties as the ships engines increased to full speed ahead heading westwards on a flat calm sea."

Alongside "Sutton", HMS "Selkirk" and the dan-laying trawlers were also heading westward from Portland and Tom Saxby watched aghast as "Selkirk" sailed through groups of bodies of soldiers, some still wearing steel helmets, all floating vertically in the water supported by their life jackets. They were told to leave them as other boats were picking them up, but if any were seen on their return they should gather them in, no matter how long it took. The flotilla then separated to search different areas and Derrick Willcocks on the bridge of "Selkirk" as lookout was told to stand in the forepeak and was the first to see what seemed to him to be bundles of clothing floating on the surface of the calm sea.

Lookouts on HMS "Sutton" had also spotted bundles floating on the surface, so the ship decreased speed and the order came to man the sea boat. Leslie Johnson with a Petty Officer and five seamen to man the oars boarded the whaler as it was lowered on its davits to deck level, taking a dozen rope strops with them. As the ship closed with the bundles the engines were stopped and the sea boat lowered to the water. As soon as they neared the first bundle Leslie could tell at a glance it was the body of an American serviceman by the green battledress, badges and insignia, floating face downwards, wearing a cork life belt and a backpack. He managed to get a rope strop over the legs of the body and work it up over the life belt and pack until it was under the armpits. The strop was then lifted over one of the rowlocks, securing the body to the side of the sea boat.

They repeated the procedure until all five rowlocks had a body secured to them by rope strops, then returned to the stern of the "Sutton" and attached a strop and body to the port davit and one to the starboard davit. As the two bodies were hoisted inboard, Leslie will …

> *"never forget that sight as the two bodies were being hoisted inboard by the strops. They hung there with sea water dripping from their bodies, foam around their mouths, and gazing down with sightless eyes at our sea boat's crew."*

But there were still more bodies to bring back to the "Sutton", so with more strops the sea boat cast off and started rowing to the nearest group. The near flat calm sea helped in the recovery of bodies by Sutton's crew who had noticed that there were no signs of them having any mutilation or shot wounds, or signs of blood on the uniforms which made their task a little easier to bear.

As the morning wore on, HMS Obedient's boats were still vainly searching for survivors when a small American landing craft from an LST came alongside and requested three or four men to help them retrieve the bodies. Tom Cull watched as the landing craft lowered the front ramp and dragged bodies up the ramp.

He was on Obedient's quarterdeck and helped lift the bodies aboard. Then an order was issued to prepare the bodies for burial at sea, but before it could be done the American landing craft returned alongside and the bodies were lowered onto its deck. Tom was told the bodies were to be shipped back to America.

Ray Siddons on HMS "Selkirk" was given a rope to haul the bodies in from the sea boat. He was terrified but hauled the first body in that fell apart in front of him. His next order was to help lay the bodies on the quarterdeck and to read their identity disc. That's how he knew they were American …

> *"I remember one was a coloured boy and another was only a boy not much younger than myself. Some had no clothes on, and some in shorts. One had his eyeballs hanging on his cheeks, and the smell was terrible.".*

Six bodies lay on the quarterdeck with feet towards the stern as the Coxswain emptied their pockets, carefully listing every item before placing it in an envelope. Derrick Willcocks helped in hauling the bodies on board and noticed one body had blood coming from the mouth, another had his boots on the wrong feet, but all wore nearly new uniforms and lifebelts.

Returning to Portland HMS "Selkirk" respectfully lowered their White Ensign to half-mast.

Leslie Johnson was still collecting bodies. As he secured one, he watched sadly as written postcards slipped from a pocket and floated slowly down in the sea. On one body he found a length of rope was fastened to his waist and attached to another body nearby. They wondered if they had been brothers, or very good friends who had not wanted to be separated as they jumped over the side of their ship. As the sea boat crew cleared one area of bodies, the "Sutton" would pass them a line and tow them to another group. They had been so preoccupied with their grisly task that only now did they notice two or three more "Smokey Joes" nearby also recovering bodies until no more were seen and the sea boat was recalled. Boarding the ship Leslie saw the bodies had been placed on both sides of the upper deck, and some on the quarterdeck, with tarpaulins covering them and a seaman standing silently by each group of bodies.

At about 8.00 pm HMS "Selkirk" arrived back at Portland with their sad cargo, and Derrick Willcocks was horrified by what he saw ...

> "The sight of our own quarterdeck was bad enough, but it was terrible to see the bodies on the dan layer. They were piled on top of each other on the upper deck perhaps forty or fifty altogether and the pile was perhaps six feet high."

John Cullen on rescue launch 532 had arrived at Portland ...

> "at approximately 4.30am. A meeting of all the officers took place and apparently orders were issued to instigate a search of various areas of the channel at first light for evidence of the attack, each boat being allocated its own search area. We had breakfast at 5.00am and shortly afterwards proceeded to our search area. It was just breaking daylight when we arrived, and it was soon evident that we were at the site of the attack as there was debris spread over a very large area. In the centre of this was a Rhino, a prefabricated pontoon approximately 250ft long by 100 ft wide. It was constructed of a series of rectangular steel tanks each approximately 20ft x 8ft x 8 ft and bolted together with four sets of railway lines running fore and aft."

But this Rhino did not come from LST 58. At 2:39 am that morning John E. Wachter, commanding officer of LST 58 had given the order to cast off the pontoon causeway they were towing. They were desperate to flee the attack and felt that their maneuverability would be increased sufficiently to warrant it. In his report dated 3rd May 1944 he recalls there was ...

> "some difficulty (jamming) experienced with the winch holding the cable and there was delay carrying out this order. At 0300 the tow was cast off."

The skipper of RML 532 ...

> "decided that we would tow the Rhino back to Portland, as apart from any thing else it was a navigational hazard. So it was that the First Lieutenant and I launched the dinghy. We made our way to the Rhino and managed to attach a towline to the stem bollards. Slowly 532 took the strain and then started to rev up but nothing moved. We had not realized that the Rhino was firmly secured to the sunken LST. At that moment there were a lot or shouts and gestures from the Quarter Deck. We looked over the side and realized the reason, the wash from the twin propellers had brought into view a considerable amount of flotsam and more importantly quite a number of bodies."

The next time John Cullen was to see a "Rhino" would be after D-Day and under very different circumstances with a most sinister purpose.

Cullen's crew ...

> "let go the towline and rowed back to 532. The Skipper was concerned that if he took the boat among debris there was a chance of something fouling the propellers. He therefore instructed me to go into the water and bring each body to the ship's side where it would be winched inboard. Being late April the water temperature in the channel was in the low forties. I very quickly realised that I would have to work vigorously for the first few minutes in order to become acclimatised. To say that the water was cold would be an understatement. I spent between one and a half to two hours in the water until I had recovered all the sighted bodies from the area. Some were in a

dreadful state. Some were trapped beneath Carly Rafts with arms and legs entwined in the netting. I had to swim under and cut them free."

"When the Skipper was satisfied that all of the bodies had been recovered he came down to the side of the ship and helped me onboard. I was absolutely shattered and very close to exhaustion. I quickly donned three or four woolen blankets. I could not stop shivering. After all this time I still remember the atmosphere so very well. There was absolute silence, the engines were stopped, there was no barking of orders, the crew spoke in hushed tones and even the seabirds were quiet. It was as if the world was paying reverence to the brave dead men lying on the deck."

"We got under way and headed back to Portland. The Skipper issued me with a couple of tots of neat rum. I then went below and changed in to No.1 uniform ready to pipe each poor soul ashore. We arrived back at Portland at approximately 11.00am. The dockyard appeared deserted except for a line of American lorries at the end of the quay, waiting to accept the bodies. One of the first people to come onboard was the Rear Admiral from HMS Attack. He stood and reverently watched each body being gently lowered to the quay as I piped each one ashore and handed over to the American military."

There was a contingency plan for actual casualties of the exercise. And there were strict instructions regarding the disposal of the dead, whether navy or army ...

"Retain remains of dead occurring afloat on board for burial ashore. Burials at sea will be held to the extreme minimum and will be done only when it is impracticable to retain on board for delivery ashore." [29]

Thirteen

Portland and Brookwood convoy

A T FIRST light on 28th April 1944 the British crew of an anti-aircraft gun on the ridge overlooking Chesil Beach waited for their NCO to arrive on his routine morning inspection. The sentry met him, pointed to the sea below the cliffs at Weston, handed him his binoculars ...

"What do you make of that lot?"

Tecwyn Morgan took the binoculars and saw two LSTs anchored side by side a short distance from the foot of the cliffs off Blacknor Point. One had its bow doors open and the loading ramp lowered. Both ships were obscured from amidships to stern by smoke but he could see that one ship, anchored some forty yards behind the other appeared undamaged. But from the interior of the closest he saw black smoke billowing out, reaching up several hundred feet into the sky, and every so often a mass of orange flames erupted through the bows as small boats moved around the starboard side of the ship.

Watching this puzzling scene was interrupted by a convoy of more than two dozen U.S. military ambulances approaching them along the shoreline road. When they reached the gun site, all turned round and waited. Small boats from the LSTs landed on the beach in front of the gun site and stretcher parties carried their loads up the beach, past the gun crew to the road and the waiting ambulances.

Also watching was a Royal Navy Petty Officer who waited until the dinghies had returned to their LST before telling Morgan and his gun crew what he understood had happened. He left, but returned in less than an hour to address the gun crew, telling them ...

> *"What you have seen this morning must be blotted from your mind; you haven't seen it – you can't talk about it because you know nothing of it – it's something that's never happened."*

It is curious that only two LSTs were seen, because according to LST 499's ship's log her radar saw the surviving convoy ships heading for Portland and she had followed four miles behind, anchoring at 05:15 am in West Bay alongside LSTs 58, 496 and 511. LST 58's action report states they arrived in West Bay at 04:32 am and also anchored alongside three other LSTs.

Paul Atkins, a navy crewman on LST 511 remembers when ...

> *"we finally sighted land. We sighted three other LSTs that had escaped also. LST 515 went back to pick up survivors. Held General Quarters all night. Morning nothing but gun flashes on horizon at 0600. It seemed as the sun would never rise. Two of our small boats lowered in water began to put wounded ashore. My boat and another. Nine men from the crew wounded and six army men."*

At 4 pm that same afternoon, 28th April 1944, the gravel car park in front of Greenhill House, Bodicote, Oxfordshire, was cluttered with US army vehicles. Some six-wheel trucks were parked in ranks, others reversing to their allotted space among them, and all the while jeeps weaving between each other at speed, dashing across the marshalling area adding to the gray dust cloud settling on the parked trucks. Unseen officers were shouting orders confirming to men of the 605th Graves Registration Company that something big and urgent was happening. One jeep, driven by the company commander, Captain William C. Barefield, stopped beside Squad Sergeant Rodney Russell and told him that he had been ordered to take two platoons to Portland on the south coast of England to deal with an incident. He was going on ahead with First Lieutenant Ernest W. Carlson, and told Sergeant Russell that he was to load up the 4th platoon, without their 2nd and 3rd Sections, and follow within the next hour.

Enlisted men of the unit had already been told to pack, including Wayne G Starnizer, who recalls the order but remembers not being told where they were going or why.

The 2nd Platoon with their platoon commander, Lieutenant Francis M. Koch, but without their 3rd Section had left just a quarter of an hour earlier under the same orders, but were sent to another of their unit's bases at Shedfield in Hampshire where they arrived at 9.30 pm that night. With only time to refuel their convoy they left for Portland, now being joined by one officer and twenty five men from the 3231st QM Service Company who were being trained as Graves Registration troops.

As they drove through the blackness of the southern English countryside, so Lieutenant Louis B. Weiss and 10 men of his 1st Platoon were also making their way directly to Portland from Bodicote.

The 605th operated under direct orders of the American Southern Base Section and had three detachments from Bodicote to cover Plymouth, Dorchester and Southampton. All had been busy laying out cemeteries at three locations along the south coast of England for expected use in case of attack on the concentration areas where troops would soon start massing for embarkation for D Day. They had been made responsible for handling all graves registration services for American deceased within Southern Base Section. So far, usually from accidental or natural causes, yet soon, bodies returned to the southern British shores from European battlefields.

Apart from these three stand-by plots, American burials were being made at Brookwood in Surrey and at Cambridge where negotiations had recently secured the enlargement of the cemetery allowing the number of burials at Brookwood to be reduced. Once the estimate of casualties of Exercise Tiger became known, Colonel Hutchins, the Quartermaster of Southern Base Section, was prepared to bury them in the stand-by plot which had been reserved near Portsmouth but Major Whitney intervened and ordered the bodies to be taken to Brookwood.

A Graves Registration Company comprised of four platoons, plus a headquarters platoon, which totaled about 140 men. Each platoon had three squads. Each squad had a Sergeant, Medic, truck driver, two record clerks and five other men. Headquarters platoon consisted of the commissioned officers, the First Sergeant, Headquarters administrative clerks, cooks, kitchen help and some truck drivers. Graves Registration people did very little burying of bodies. Most of their work involved processing bodies, keeping records and filling out forms, and transporting bodies to a cemetery. To "process" a body, first a Medic examined the body and filled out a Death Certificate. Then someone had to search the body to remove all personal effects. These were listed on special forms, then placed in a Personal Effects bag, sealed and sent to the Headquarters. From there, they went through the proper channels to be sent to the family of the deceased.

It was half past midnight when Sergeant Russell arrived at the field hospital at Portland where Captain Barefield told him there had been a bombing raid and that about 300 bodies had been brought in. He

emphasized that the job had to be done before daybreak. Whether or not the Captain's explanation of a bombing raid was an attempt to disguise the true cause of the casualties, or had been simply repeating what he had been told was soon shattered. As his platoon began processing the bodies

50th Field Hospital at Weymouth (during Normandy invasion)

they found them wet, some with life vests on, so they knew the disaster happened on water. As more bodies were brought in by ambulance crews, they told them that some LST's had been sunk.

Their gruesome task was carried out in hospital tents hastily erected between hospital buildings, and they had to work in eerie, blackout conditions with only gas lanterns inside the tents and flashlights outside. According to Standard Operating Procedure, their mission was to identify each body, list the personal effects and secure this information to the body for transportation to the cemetery.

Wayne Starnizer was the first to lift the flap of the first tent, and by the light of flickering gas lanterns, he saw bodies had been placed in two neat, orderly rows with their heads to the center of the tent, and their clothes were quite obviously wet. Blackout conditions were essential as just after starting their task German planes flew over, so all lights were extinguished to wait for the all clear before getting back to work.

All night there was a seemingly endless procession of military ambulances delivering more bodies for processing. As more rescue ships docked with their sad cargo throughout the night and into the early morning hours, bodies were stretchered into the waiting ambulances for transport to the long line of tents. The sheer number of dead almost overwhelmed the emotions of some Graves Registration men as well as the condition of some bodies. Some were missing arms and legs, some were horribly disfigured, but no one saw anything that resembled bullet wounds.

Geoffrey Cassidy had been posted to the Royal Navy base, HMS Grasshopper, at Weymouth to learn how to load tanks and trucks onto landing craft with the US Navy. On Friday 28th April his landing craft was berthed in Weymouth harbor for the night. He was duty watch and had been told …

> *"I would be called on to do guard duty that night. So after tea I got my orders. I had to draw a rifle and bayonet and go on guard on the quay. My duty was to keep all sightseers away from the harbour. Craft of the US Navy and Royal Navy started to unload dead US soldiers and sailors. They were placed side by side on Weymouth quay. I was told there were 1,000 dead from three US tank landing craft. By 9 pm that night US ambulances were taking the dead away 6 bodies to a van. By 4 am the following morning all had been taken away."*

Wilson Smith was a Military Police motorcyclist at Weymouth and all during the day of the 27th April he had been escorting convoys from a parking lot to ships docked at the harbor and helping to waterproof vehicles. He and seven others had gone home and gone to bed, but about 1:00 am he and his roommates were woken and told to report to the harbor.

LSTs unloading casualties at Weymouth (during Normandy invasion).

"No one told us what was going

on. We got down there, and it was dark, and there was mass
confusion. Everyone was shouting – no one knew what was
going on. Army officials were there, medics, ambulances, and
bodies were already being brought in. We asked what was going
on and they said these ships had been in the English Channel
and the Germans had got them."

Through the night and into the next day, Jones and the other MPs
escorted ambulances filled with bodies to the 50th Field Hospital where
the 605th Graves Registration Company were carrying out their
identification work.

Wayne Starnizer, working in the mortuary tents had a brief
conversation with a group of survivors who were all suffering from cold
and hypothermia later that morning and one told him he was in the
cold water for some time and that some of the German E-Boats returned
after their attack and made a pass at them, firing at survivors in the
water.

Another survivor stood shivering on the Portland quayside. Patsy J.
Giacchi was in one of the QM Railhead companies on LST 507 and had
been picked up by a Royal Navy vessel. He saw an LST arrive and watched
as the two huge bow doors opened and saw piles of dead soldiers and
sailors. But the doors were closed almost immediately as there were too
many British dockworkers and other civilians around to witness the scale
of the event. Around midnight of 28th April, a QM Major from SHAEF
headquarters had awoken Lieutenant William R. Albright, platoon
commander of the 146th QM TRUCK COMPANY, at his bivouac area
south of Dorchester. Albright was told the 146th were to perform a secret
mission and that not only was he to be the convoy commander, but also
held responsible for preserving the secrecy of the mission as far as his men
were concerned.

After a rapid shakedown of their forty-eight operational vehicles,
ensuring that each were equipped with tarpaulins and rear curtains, the
convoy moved off at around 2.00 am following the Major to Portland.

As they drove with blackout lights, the Major told Lieutenant Albright
the brief circumstances of the E-Boat attack, and emphasized that secrecy
was paramount to ensure the scale of the disaster never became public
knowledge. He added that the American and British staffs at SHAEF were
at each other's throats over the incident, and secrecy was important to
avoid bickering at staff levels, as co-operation over the next few months
was vital.

Sergeant Russell's platoon had been processing bodies continuously through the night, and finally their task at Portland was completed. Now the bodies were to be transported to Brookwood cemetery by a long convoy of trucks that had arrived while they had been working, and it was his job to oversee the loading of the trucks. He recalls loading twelve bodies on each truck. Each was on a stretcher placed across the body of the truck, six on the floor and six on the drop-down seats. The tarpaulin covers were tied down so that no one could see inside but a First Lieutenant was able to find a hole where he could see a foot and admonished Sergeant Russell for not doing his job properly.

Frederick Cox of 146th QM Truck Company was one of the truck drivers and recalls there were forty-five of his unit's trucks in the convoy. One truck ran empty in case of breakdown, which came from the 147th.

Rudy Weber also of the 146th remembers a strange smell in the air when he arrived, and when asked about it was told to look into some very large, long tents. When he looked inside he saw row upon row of dead, wrapped in blankets on stretchers.

Freddy Cox recalls how his unit's trucks were loaded at Portland ...

"The first layer of blanket enshrouded bodies, lying on canvas stretchers, was placed crosswise, in the bed of the truck. The troop seats were then let down, so the handles of the second layer of stretchers could rest on the troop seats and were thereby suspended above the first layer. The bodies filled three-fourths of the truck body; the space framed by the first four bows.

The rear curtain was suspended from the fourth bow to hide the cargo. Some of the trucks had GI blankets pinned to the bows (possibly because the rear curtains weren't with the trucks). The seat between the bodies and the tailgate of the trucks carried a medical or graves registration personnel to prevent anyone from lifting the curtain or blanket. We were present at the loading of the bodies and assisted somewhat at the actual placing of the stretchers on the truck."

His estimate of the convoy length was forty-five trucks, each laden with thirteen bodies, giving a total of 585 bodies. This approximates with the 605th Graves Registration unofficial body count by Wayne Starnizer where he and Lieutenant Carlson ... *"led a convoy of trucks loaded with 527 bodies going to Brookwood Military Cemetery."* Lieutenant Albright's estimate is also 527 bodies. Rudy Weber, also a 146th truck driver, agrees with Cox's estimate of bodies ...

> " *We loaded 13 dead on each GMC 6x6, two tiers high, also a rope down the center of the truck over the bodies to prevent them bouncing off the stretcher. A blanket was used as a curtain at the second last bow. A soldier from Graves Registration in Class A uniform with rifle sat at the back of each truck as Honor guard."*

His sergeant, Louis J Brienza is convinced that in addition to the 146th, their sister unit the 147th QM truck Company were also there with some of their trucks. This view is reinforced by Weber's recollection of a seventy-truck convoy, and Albright remembering ...

> *"there were more bodies to be transported that our company trucks could accommodate. We recommended that the Major call in a platoon from a sister company, the 147th QM Truck Company, to accommodate the overflow – another 12 trucks."*

When the loading was completed, Albright ...

> *"checked all the trucks to see that tarpaulin covers and curtains were securely lashed in place. Convoy orders were issued to fully fuel all vehicles, and to be prepared to operate non-stop to our destination, to not communicate with civilians or any military personnel, other than our personnel serving on the assignment."*

Then all personnel involved in the processing of the bodies, together with the convoy drivers were assembled alongside the trucks and given a long talk by a First Lieutenant from General Eisenhower's office. He told them it was vital the enemy should not learn how badly the Allies had been hit then informed the assembly that they would be traveling in a guarded convoy to Brookwood and any man who ever talked about their cargo would be court martialled. Should anyone ask, their reply should be – we don't talk about it.

Once loaded, the convoy left Portland for Brookwood cemetery to the west of London. A Military Police motorcycle escort led the convoy from Weymouth over the road route, which took them to the cemetery in London. As convoy commander, Albright …

> *"traveled at the rear of the convoy in my jeep with the kitchen truck and Maintenance tow truck just ahead of me. Also in the convoy was an empty truck from the 147th QM Truck Company to be used in the event we had a breakdown and found it necessary to transfer cargo. Fortunately we had no maintenance problems and the convoy arrived at the cemetery about noon."*

Sergeant Russell rode with the convoy to Brookwood; Wayne Starnizer rode in a jeep with his platoon commander Lieutenant Carlson having counted five hundred and twenty seven bodies loaded on the trucks. Motorcycle MPs leapfrogged the convoy from one road intersection to the next; stopping all other traffic to ensure a continuously moving convoy that would drive for an hour, then take a ten minute break for the drivers to check their cargo.

The convoy was patrolled by military police, as Weber believed was … *"to keep other traffic out."* Sergeant Rodney Russell of the 605th GR Company traveled with the convoy and saw …

> *"an MP at every intersection so no truck would have to stop."*

While driving to Brookwood Cox remembers the convoy passing …

> *"through a village with narrow sidewalks and houses built close to the curbs. The exhaust pipe from the engine came out about knee high just in front of the left rear wheels. Because we were driving down the left side of the street, the roar of the engines as we downshifted resounded against the stone. I wondered if this convoy, traveling through town in the middle of the night, was something they were accustomed to, or were they startled and frightened by this unusual event."*

Garland Coghill remembers having 13 bodies on his truck …

> *" and going through towns and villages, seemed like we were*

there in early morning, and we would see people looking up at
the back of the trucks expecting to see troops or something,
and saw the tarpaulins closed. You could see a kind of puzzled
expression on their faces."

Rudy Weber remembers the large convoy ran with tight spacing and it was difficult driving because the chosen speed forced constant gear changing. He saw the MPs patrolling the convoy to keep other traffic away, and at the end of the trip the MPs told him it was the best convoy they ever saw. Rudy remembers thinking that these dead deserved it.

The convoy arrived at Brookwood cemetery but the truck drivers didn't unload the dead, instead, most of the drivers simply walked around the cemetery.

The convoy progressed across southern England until it arrived at Brookwood cemetery and unloading of the bodies began. MP Wilson Jones and his colleagues slept that night in the now empty trucks and returned to Weymouth the next morning. Wayne Starnizer watched the trucks park in and around the cemetery, helped unload the bodies, then his platoon erected "pup" tents, had a meal and tried to sleep but some men had problems sleeping so close to the unloaded bodies.

Albright states ...

> *"there was an American QM Graves Registration unit on hand*
> *at the cemetery to process our cargo. It was a nice sunlit day,*
> *and the litters were unloaded from each truck and placed in*
> *rows on the ground to be processed. The bodies were not in*
> *any state of decomposition, as they were being processed within*
> *24 hours of their drowning. The unloading proceeded slowly,*
> *truck by truck. After unloading, the driver would park*
> *alongside the road, maintaining his original convoy position,*
> *and would visit the kitchen truck on foot before returning to his*
> *vehicle and taking a brief nap."*

As the drivers wandered around the cemetery, Cox came across ...

> *"the morgue of the cemetery, we looked in the windows and*
> *saw the bodies lying on the tables, dressed in green fatigue*
> *uniforms. While looking at the bodies I was impressed by the*

fact that there were no signs of injuries. But for the pallor of their faces and hands, they could have been asleep. We were told that most had died either from drowning or hypothermia. On their left shoulders they wore a medium blue rectangular patch embossed with a golden anchor. I had heard this patch signified "Combined Operations".

Smith, the motorcyclist ...

"didn't have anywhere to sleep that night, so we slept in the trucks and the next morning headed back to Weymouth."

Sergeant Russell, 1st Platoon, 605th GR Company ...

"stayed at Brookwood for about five days. We assisted personnel at Brookwood to dress and bury all of those victims in Class A uniforms." It was a period of intense pressure mentioned in the unit history. There ... "was a great many bodies to handle and the personnel had to work very long hours for four days. They had very little sleep during this period and the strain was great."

Back at Portland, John Cullen aboard Rescue Launch 532 went back to normal ship's routine after the truck convoy departed the quayside at Portland ...

"Lunch was cooked and served and at approximately 2.00pm the Skipper came up forward and issued instructions to the full crew that no one was to speak about what had happened in the early hours of that morning. He explained that German Command would dearly like to know of how many casualties that they had caused, but even more important, the incident and resulting losses of life would have had a huge effect on the morale of Allied Invasion Forces if it became widely known."

From testimony of the 146th Truck Company drivers in that convoy, all trucks carried bodies of U.S. Army personnel, identified by their olive green clothing. None of the drivers can recall bodies dressed in U.S. Navy uniform confirming that naval casualties were dealt with separately from the army. Captain McDevitt, who headed a detail of army personnel to

Brookwood to identify the bodies, tells of a similar detail of the U.S. Navy being sent to Salisbury Plain to identify their dead, further evidences this. This was probably at Odstock Hospital on the outskirts of Salisbury.

Fourteen

Brookwood burials

SOME bodies carried to Brookwood had not been identified by the 605th Graves Registration Company when they processed them at Portland. The U.S. Army Service of Supply report dated 30th April 1944 stated some bodies recovered did not have identification tags, which may be explained by HMS Onslow's actions of recovering identification tags from bodies they found, then returning the bodies to sea.

To resolve this issue a group of officers and senior NCOs from army units that had suffered casualties, was hurriedly assembled and dispatched from the exercise area to Brookwood cemetery.

It was headed by Captain James C. McDevitt, commanding officer of the 3207th QM Service Company, which had only just returned from the exercise amid rumors of tragedy. On 29th April he was summoned to 1st Engineer Shore Brigade headquarters and ordered by the commanding officer, Colonel Eugene M. Caffey to take the detail to Brookwood.

The group left south Devon ...

> *"...by train the following day, arriving during the evening to be escorted to billets for an overnight stay. Early on Monday morning they were taken to the cemetery, briefed by the Graves Registration personnel, and then shown the unidentified bodies in a separate area. Captain McDevitt remembers ... "Each body was wrapped in a GI blanket. Many heads were wrapped in something similar to an elastic bandage, in order to keep the features intact for better identification. We went to each individual, the wraps were pulled away, and if someone could identify the person they would raise their hand or call out, and*

the information would be taken from them, and they would move on to the next individual. This continued until noon when we had to break for lunch. The graves registration people were able to pull off their rubber gloves and aprons and go to lunch, but I didn't see any of our people participating."

Missing among Captain McDevitt's detail were representatives from units that had lost men. These included 557th Railhead Company (74); 478th Amphibious Truck Company (28); 1605th Map Section (3); 3206th Service Company (195); 607th Graves Registration Company (16); 3891st Truck Company (3); 35th Signal Construction Company (28) totaling 349 casualties. So it has to be assumed, and at this stage is very unlikely that these units knew precisely who had been killed and who was missing, and were content that their casualties had all been identified at Portland. The 556th Railhead Company clearly weren't so sure if they had suffered any casualties at all and sent representatives

1st Lt Marvin E. Shaw	0-1551241	625 Ord Amm Co
S/Sgt Raymond Lather	32396701	625 Ord Amm Co
1st Lt Carroll W. Wright	0-1035625	33rd Cml Decon Co
S/Sgt Joseph J. Lasky	130-7931	33rd Cml Decon Co
Capt James E. McDevitt	0-408325	3207th QM Svc Co
S/Sgt Alexander J. Platt	32633872	3207th QM Svc Co
Sgt James L. Telesco	39095742	556th QM Rhd Co
Cpl Jerome (NMI) Estarman	12153040	556th QM Rhd Co
1st Lt Gene P. Wood	0-1297463	462nd Amph Trk Co
1st Sgt EltonE. Langley	14016069	462nd Amph Trk Co
1st Lt Roger R. Grist	0-1100506	Co "D" 531st ESR
Sgt Lawrence J. Stenstead	37268643	Co "D" 531st ESR
1st Lt Paul O. Retchie	0-350090	Hq Co 2nd Bn 531st ESR
S/Sgt Ralph W. Nelson	37254336	Hq Co 2nd Bn 531st ESR
1st Lt david C. Loup	0-430178	Co "E" 531st ESR
Sgt Melvin N. Wright	38048203	Co "E" 531st ESR
1st Lt Kermit J. Thompson	0-1108366	Co "F" 531st ESR
T/5 Albert H. Bloencaux	35377877	Co "F" 531st ESR
1st Lt Marchant G. Cottingham	0-327057	Co "A" 531st ESR
1st Elmer F. Garrett	0-428283	Co "C" 531st ESR
Sgt Harold D. Bennett	37158032	Co "C" 531st ESR
1st Lt Harry H. Mitchell	0-432371	Co "B" 531st ESR
1st Lt Frank W. Miller	0-350948	Hq Co 1st Bn 531st ESR
Sgt Darrell B. Doby	14015768	Hq Co 1st Bn 531st ESR
Sgt Dillard J. Morrell	14024233	Co "A" 531st ESR
T/Sgt Carl (NMI) Faiterson	14020203	Co "B" 531st ESR

along with Captain McDevitt's detail, not knowing at that time that they had suffered no losses whatever.

The 605th Graves Registration Company was the only GR unit involved in the processing of these bodies both at Portland and Brookwood cemetery. Lieutenant Weiss's platoon had ridden with the convoy and was met at Brookwood by Lieutenant Kenneth J. Hellwig and his 3rd Platoon to identify and bury the dead, which took several days of concentrated work. Some of the GR personnel returned to their base by 4th May, others remained at the cemetery until 7th May.

Wayne Starnizer of the 605th does not ...

"remember if the bodies were buried in the cemetery in boxes or mattress covers – each did have a single grave."

Although an official history of GR matters in the UK states ...

"All remains buried in Brookwood and Cambridge cemeteries were embalmed and placed in wooden caskets purchased locally which became known as U.K. caskets."

Graves Registration team at work.

U.S. Navy bodies had been taken directly from the beaches at Portland to the 158th General Hospital at Odstock near Salisbury for identification as confirmed by Captain McDevitt who was aware of a detail similar to his being dispatched there. They were later convoyed to Brookwood cemetery arriving after army casualties, which is confirmed by the majority of navy bodies being buried on dates after the army bodies were interred.

The Quartermaster Graves Registration Service in Great Britain made weekly reports of U.S. service personnel they had buried at the three permanent cemeteries under their control, Brookwood, Cambridge and Lisnabreeny in Northern Ireland. The principle adopted by the Graves Registration Service used London as a dividing point of England whereby casualties to the south of the capital were buried at Brookwood, and those to the north, principally aircrew from the airfields scattered

Exercise "Tiger" casualties at Brookwood cemetery.

across East Anglia, were buried at Cambridge. Lisnabreeny had long been in use since American soldiers first arrived in Northern Ireland in 1942. So it was quite a normal procedure for "Tiger" casualties to be buried at Brookwood.

A single weekly burial report included all three cemetery interments based upon information supplied by Graves Registration units involved with the actual burials at the individual cemeteries.

In excess of 500 "Tiger" army casualties had been transported from Portland to Brookwood, yet only 268 army and navy burials are detailed on these weekly reports, suggesting that at some point in the documentary trail at least 232 army burials have been deliberately omitted, or the original weekly reports have been replaced by newer, edited versions that conveniently halve the total casualty numbers.

It had obviously been the practice when completing weekly reports to sequentially number the burials, and it appears this practice was started with "Tiger" casualties. But some reports wildly deviate from the ordered numbering creating duplicate numbers, suggesting the author of re-written reports had no access to the original numbering sequence and simply took a guess as to the number that should be entered.

The question of where these missing bodies are cannot be answered, as no records exist of the initial identifications at Portland that would have provided a comparison before and after transportation to Brookwood.

Examination of the weekly burial reports does reveal discrepancies. Some may be due to inaccurate record keeping, others must be deliberate, and some may be due to mis-identification. Further confusion arises as many casualties were listed in their unit's Morning Reports as "Missing", but they were listed as being buried at Brookwood. Some were re-buried at the Cambridge cemetery, some were repatriated, and others that were buried at Brookwood have no known re-burial site. [30]

Floyd E. Blake, a Technician 4th grade of the 557th Railhead Company was killed on 28th April 1944, and according to weekly burial reports was buried at Brookwood on 1st May 1944. On that report his service number is shown as 35410567, a number that was not issued, his correct service number being 33271593. The U.S. Army Military History Institute states his body was repatriated, but it may be another soldier bearing the false service number.

Donald S. Bryant from Massachusetts, a Private First Class in the 531st Engineer Shore Regiment is listed by the U.S. Army Military History Archives as being killed in action on the 28th April 1944. There is no record of him being buried at Brookwood, but there is a record of his burial at the Long Island National Cemetery in New York where his date of death is recorded as 6th June 1944. Perhaps he is one example of the falsification of dates of death to minimize the number of "Tiger" casualties.

Harold G. Foster, a Private First Class with the 818th Port Battalion according to the U.S. Army Military History Institute was killed in action on 28th April 1944 and his body repatriated. There is no record of his burial at Brookwood. The American Battle Monuments Commission declare that Harold G. Foster, service number 12098159 was a Private First Class with the 818th Truck Company killed on 12th August 1944 and is buried in Normandy.

Private Robert Grissom of the 35th Signal Construction Company is commemorated as Missing in action at the American Battle Monuments Commission cemetery in Cambridge, when in fact he is buried at Long Cemetery, Van Buren, Tennessee.

Private Robert P. Motley from Virginia is recorded in his unit's Morning Report as being killed in action on 28th April 1944, and he is buried in Normandy with the service number 33042133. This number, according to the U.S. National Archives and Records Administration, was issued to another soldier, Jeffress S, Dortch Jr.

Oris A. Stokes, Private 31110688 of the 33rd Chemical Decon-tamination Company was reported in Morning Reports as being killed in action on 28th April 1944, and recorded as being buried at Brook-

30 See Appendix 30 – Brookwood burial summary

wood cemetery on 1st May 1944. The American Battle Monuments Commission has no record of his further burial, which suggests his body was repatriated. Coincidentally, the body of Private Horace A. Stokes, service number 14124810 who had been aboard LST 507 was also repatriated.

Richard E. Swanson, a Technician Sergeant, service number 19016503 of the 1605th Engineer Depot Map Company is recorded as being buried at Brookwood on 1st May 1944, and his body repatriated to a civilian cemetery where his date of death is shown as 6th June 1944.

The body of Second Lieutenant Lester Wright of the 35th Signal Construction Battalion had been found in the sea by HMS Onslow, his identity disc removed and his body returned to the sea. According to the Weekly Burial Reports at Brookwood, he was buried there on 2nd May 1944.

There is a striking similarity between the service numbers 37416153 issued to Private Melvin A. Roberson of the 3206th Service Company, and 37416157 issued to Private James E. Roberson of the same unit. Melvin Roberson was buried at Brookwood and was most probably repatriated; James Roberson is listed as Missing in action and commemorated at Cambridge cemetery. Perhaps they were brothers; they certainly enlisted at the same place on the same date.

Private First Class Fay E. Thomas, service number 37504430 of the 3206th Service Company is listed as being buried at Brookwood on 1st May 1944, but this service number was not issued. The U.S. Army Military History Institute states Pfc Fay E. Thomas, service number 35083542 was killed in action on 28th April 1944 and his body later repatriated. But this service number was issued to a Fay Lambert and there is no record of him being a casualty.

One very personal instance of tragedy surrounds William Schriber. He had lied about his age and joined the U.S. Navy at fifteen years of age but later admitted this to his superior officers and asked to go home. His sixteenth birthday was April 27th 1944 so it was decided that his naval service would begin on that day. He was killed aboard LST 507 and his official date of death is 28th April 1944. Because of the time difference between England and the United States his family believe he was killed on his birthday and the U.S. Navy record his length of service as less than one day. But the tragedy continues as his casket was returned to his family before the war's end. His mother was desperate to see her son for the last time and pleaded with the two armed sailors escorting the casket to open it but no matter how much she begged, they refused and by their actions

William Schriber's mother believed to the day she died that her son's body was not there.

The only logical explanation for such disparities between the number of army bodies carried by the 146th Truck Company and the number of recorded interments is that documents have been altered or re-written. This is compounded by that fact that 116 navy bodies have been included in the Brookwood burial reports and their total number should be added to the army casualty figure, which is in excess of 500. Taking the official total figure of casualties as being 749 killed and missing, this leaves 133 army and navy casualties classified as "Missing in action". But there are exactly 300 army casualties and 84 navy casualties listed from various sources as "Missing in action". Even using the official casualty figure of 749, deducting the 268 recorded as buried at Brookwood leaves 481 that by official reckoning should be "Missing in action", but as above only 384 "Missing" can be traced leaving a shortfall of nearly 100 bodies that official figures cannot account for.

Fifteen

First reports

LATE in the afternoon of 28th April 1944, Teletype machines began clattering with top-secret messages of the attack on convoy T-4. There was initial confusion and contradiction in original reports suggesting honest, truthful reporting and only later, as the enormity of the disaster became known to the U.S. Navy were "correcting" messages concocted to minimize the loss of life and shipping.

```
          TOP  SECRET  —  PRIORITY


                    FROM: ANCXF
                    TO: SCAEF
REF NO:       281629B                    28 April 1944


Regret to report that enemy E boats attacked a force of
8 LST Western Task Force South of Lyme Bay during night
Thursday 27th / Friday 28th. LST were loaded and taking
part in Exercise TIGER. No details are yet available
but it is reported that 3 LST were sunk and one LST was
torpedoed but has arrived in harbour. I greatly regret
that present reports indicate 300 to 400 casualties but
until  a  complete  count  of  survivors  can  be  made  any
figures should be treated with reserve.
```

This was followed up the next morning by the following.

```
                    TOP SECRET — PRIORITY
FROM: ANCXF
TO:    SCAEF
REF NO:        291147B        APRIL 1944

My 281629

For "3 LST sunk" read "2 LST sunk"
```

Casualty numbers were at this early stage understandably confusing for the ANCXF (Allied Naval Commander Expeditionary Force) War Diary recorded on 28th April 1944 there were 638 killed and 89 wounded.

Admiral Moon was obliged to make an early, detailed report, and based upon information given to him by his staff that afternoon advised the Commander in Chief, U.S. Navy.

```
                    SECRET — TOP PRIORITY
FROM:          CTF 125
TO FOR ACTION:       COMINCH, CTF 122, CTF 127
REF NO:              291408B / CR-1032 : 29 April 1944

Convoy of 7 US LST's in command of Commander B J SCAHILL,
USN, in force "U" Training Exercises TIGER attacked by
hostile E-Boats April 280220B, 252 Degrees, Portland Bill
15 miles.

Regret to report LST's 507, 531 loaded with estimated 744
Army and 282 Navy personnel sunk by torpedoes. Total known
ambulatory survivors 257, litter cases 33.

LST 289 received following torpedo damage wrecked steering
gear and crew's quarters. Crack appearing amidships. 4 of
crew dead, 9 missing, 18 wounded 1 critically. 4 Army
personnel wounded. LST 289 towed to DARTMOUTH.

LST 511, no damage, some Naval personnel wounded by
gunfire. Number not yet reported.

Have directed convoy Commander to forward required
reports.
```

It is upon this message that the official death toll of 749 is based. A figure that persists to this day and still quoted by all official documents, it is based upon very early, panicky reports with no corroboration. But already this figure was being questioned as casualty numbers began to vary with different message authors drawing upon their own sources of information.

The U.S. Army's report of April 29th is puzzling. The number of bodies on the truck convoy to Brookwood were counted by graves registration personnel and the drivers to be in excess of 500 and taken non-stop directly to the cemetery. Yet the U.S. Army Southern Base Section states that only 248 were taken to Brookwood. This suggests the U.S. Army was either, naively accepting what the U.S. Navy was telling them, they were already falsifying the number of casualties quite independently from the U.S. Navy who were undertaking a parallel exercise, or there had been early liaison between army and navy to instigate a cover-up. Any of these options are possible and one of them was certainly adopted, but the documentary cover-up is challenged and confounded by eyewitnesses. Those that processed and counted the bodies and those that loaded and counted the bodies.

```
              SECRET — PRIORITY
FROM:        SBS, FROM CG CS SECTION, SIGNED THRASHER
TO:          ETOUSA, ATTENTION CHIEF OF STAFF
PASSED TO:   SHAEF FOR INFORMATION
REF NO:           13592 29 April 1944
Latest reports on casualties exercise TIGER indicate 248
dead sent to BROOKWOOD, 253 walking patients being
accommodated at BLANDFORD, and 63 hospitalized in vicinity
of DORCHESTER.

Walking patients being interrogated, segregated and will
be returned to home stations. 20 of those hospitalized
will be released today.
```

Amid all the bad news, there were glimmers of hope that were eagerly seized upon, especially when they seemed to support a minimizing of casualty numbers. LST 289's return to Dartmouth was quickly passed to higher headquarters. But army survivors were sent to Stover camp near Newton Abbot, Devon, and not returned to their home bases. This is probably convenient for interrogation about the incident and indoctrination of the official storyline that was rapidly evolving between the army and navy.

```
            SECRET — PRIORITY
FROM:        HQ SBS, SIGNED THRASHER
TO:          ETOUSA ATTENTION CHIEF OF STAFF
PASSED TO:   SHAEF FOR INFORMATION
REF NO:           CS-13593, 29 APRIL 1944
Supplementing and in addition to D area casualty reports
transmitted by teletype 1392 this Headquarters and by
General THRASHER to Colonel STRATTON, the following
information has been received from K area.

"LST 289 returned to DARTMOUTH at 1700 hours, 28 April 44,
with 4 wounded Army personnel, 18 wounded Navy personnel,
4 Navy dead, 6 Navy missing. 9 Officers and 342 EM from
this LST being evacuated to STOVER B."
```

Details of the incident were working their way right up the chain of command, through Eisenhower's office and on to the Combined Chiefs of Staff.

```
            SECRET — OUT LOG
TO:          AGWAR
REF NO:          S-50910
TIME SENT:   291111B
For COMBINED CHIEFS OF STAFF signed EISENHOWER
SCAF 18
German reaction to first phase of FABIUS was an E-boat
attack. Details not available but first report is that
three LST's were sunk and one damaged, but arrived in
harbor. 300 to 400 casualties probable.
ORIGINATOR CHIEF OF STAFF
```

By the 30th April 1944, Moon's staff was getting to grips with the disaster that was far worse than they first believed, and they were now striving to play down casualty numbers by making no mention of them at all. Moon seems somewhat resigned to the facts and was probably unaware of the true casualty numbers, instead being fed information by his staff hinting at the Royal Navy's shortcomings in the exercise in anticipation of searching enquiries by higher authorities.

```
INCOMING MESSAGE

APRIL 301508B

SECRET
OPERATIONAL PRIORITY

FROM:         CTF 125
TO FOR ACTION:      COMINCH, CTF 122, CTF 127
FOR INFO:     COMNAVEU, CTF 124, CG VII CORPS, ANCXF, CG
FIRST US ARMY, CG 4TH DIVISION
PASSED TO :  SHAEF FOR INFO
REF NO:             1248/301508B          30 April 1944

Amplifying  my  291408B  Convoy  T-4  was  proceeding
independently as a follow up convoy for exercise TIGER to
arrive at SLAPTON BEACH Lat 50 degs 17 North Long 3 degs
38.5 West at 0730B, 28 April. At the time of the attack it
was approximately 33 miles from this destination.

Force U after landing 4th Division of VII Corps in assault
during 27 April at nightfall had under protection in
transport area SLAPTON BEACH 1 APA, 21 LST's, 28 LCI's, 65
LCT's 14 miscellaneous and 92 small landing craft or total
of 221 awaiting unloading and sailing empty at daylight.

Representative CINC PLYMOUTH informs all available escorts
had been assigned to Assault Force Convoys patrols and
screens.

4 special patrols totaling 3 motor torpedo boats, 2 motor
gunboats and 40 class DD's were stationed on a patrol line
from start point to off PORTLAND BILL. A 5th patrol of 3
motor torpedo boats was stationed off CHERBOURG to
intercept any departing E boats.
                                          Page 1
```

Page 2

HMS Scimitar's suffering slight damage although still operational resulted in a mix up in PLYMOUTH Command in regard to her orders and she was not sailed with convoy leaving corvette HMS AZALEA as only escort.

This was unknown to anyone in authority until discovered by PLYMOUTH Command too late to provide an additional escort before attack. SALADIN proceeding to reinforce as result of CINC PLYMOUTH action after discovery arrived in time to pick up survivors but not assist in repelling attack. E boats penetrated screen and operated freely inside LYME BAY until convoy was picked up and attacked. Timely reports of E boat movements fro Radar plot were made by CINC PLYMOUTH. Commander SCAHILL, Convoy Commander, now in Plymouth, contacting scattered LST Commanders and senior survivors in preparation of reports.

Captain Skahill had already been briefed by Moon's staff as to the content and detail expected in reports from commanders of ships in his convoy, which would present a unanimous account of the action. But the army's Southern Base Section were taking an altogether practical view of the losses, looking to fulfilling their responsibilities of replacing men and vehicles lost in the exercise.

```
OUTGOING MESSAGE
TOP SECRET
PRIORITY
THIS IS A REPRODUCTION OF AN ETOUSA OUTGOING MESSAGE
TO:    CG SBS
FROM:  LEE
REF NO:        E-26467
```

The following information is available in this Headquarters on recent incident and loss by First Army thru enemy action during exercise "TIGER".

LST number 507 (Army serial number 496) assumed lost.

Had following loading list:
Personnel from478 Amphibian Truck Company,
557 Quartermaster railhead Company,
33 Chemical Company,
1st Platoon 440 Engineer Company
3891 Quartermaster Truck Company.
Equipment - 2 each truck ¼ ton 4x4
            1 each truck ¾ ton 4x4
            13 each truck 2 ½ ton 6x6
            22 each truck Amphibian 2 ½ ton 6x6 (DUKW)

LST number 531 (Army serial number 495) assumed lost.

Had following loading list:
Personnel from 462 Amphibian Truck Company,
3206 Quartermaster Service Company
Equipment -   1 Truck 1 ton 4x4
            3 each truck ¾ ton 4x4
            13 each truck 2 ½ ton 6x6
            22 each truck Amphibian 2 ½ ton (DUKW)

LST number 289 (Army serial number 501) damaged aft.

Had following loading list:
Personnel from 478 Amphibian Truck Company,
556 Quartermaster Railhead Company,
4th Medical Battalion.
Equipment -   3 each truck ¼ ton 4x4
            1 truck ¾ ton 4x4
            13 each truck 2 ½ ton 6x6
            22 each truck Amphibian 2 ½ ton 6x6 (DUKW)

Request list of major items of equipment actually lost or damages beyond repair and advice as to your action being taken to replace this material.
```
```

An administrative and moral obligation to notify casualties' next of kin was becoming more pressing after nearly two weeks, and a decision had to be made what to do.

INCOMING MESSAGE
CONFIDENTIAL
ROUTINE

FROM: AGWAR, FROM SURLES
TO: ETOUSA FOR EISENHOWER, FOR PRO
PASSED TO :   SHAEF FOR INFORMATION
REF NO: W-34801, 10 May 1944

Relatives of 200 Army personnel are being notified of casualty status, most of them being missing, wounded or dead near ENGLAND 28 April.

Suggest limited announcement there of ship lost and total of personnel dead or missing would remove prospective pressure for information or undue comment.

But Eisenhower's decision was both decisive and predictable, with D-Day only a matter of a few weeks ahead he could not afford to break the security blanket that was about to descend on Britain.

OUTGOING MESSAGE

TOP SECRET
ROUTINE

THIS IS A REPRODUCTION OF AN ETOUSA OUTGOING MESSAGE

TO: AGWAR FOR SURLES
FROM: LEE, SIGNED EISENHOWER
REF NO: E-27684

Supreme Headquarters strongly recommends against release at this time of information concerning ships lost and casualties sustained 28 April 1944 for security reasons.

11th May 1944
Out 14 May 1944

By now the U.S. Navy knew the true extent of those killed and missing and was weaving their web of deception through dis-information as illustrated by the following message.

```
OUTGOING MESSAGE


PRIORITY


THIS IS A REPRODUCTION OF AN ETOUSA OUTGOING MESSAGE



TO:         AGWAR FOR CASUALTY BRANCH
FOR INFO:   FOR GROSS
FROM:       EISENHOWER
REF NO:         E-27603


Tabulation of total casualties reported all LST's in April
28 incident:


KIA, QM 80, TC 18, Signal 5, Engineer 8, CWS 10, Ordnance
2, Cavalry 1, Infantry 2, total 126


MIA, QM 226, TC 50, Signal 16, Engineer 12, Ordnance 10,
total 314.


13 May 1944
```

By the late 1940's questions were already being asked about the true number of casualties and the U.S. Army felt it necessary to produce an official report. It was a compilation of data and reports from army sources made in the wake of the attack upon convoy T-4.

> "*Most of the casualties were from LST 531. There were only 290 survivors of 744 soldiers and 282 sailors. Aboard LST 507 there were 13 dead and 22 wounded. The 1st Brigade suffered most heavily in the action with 413 dead and 16 wounded. The 3206th Quartermaster Service Company was virtually wiped out. Of 251 officers and men, 201 were killed or wounded. The*

557th Quartermaster Railhead Company also had heavy losses,
69 casualties in all. A complete list of casualties is not available,
but Army records, possibly not complete, state that 749 were
killed and more than 300 either insured or suffering from severe
exposures."

Organization	KIA O	KIA EM	WIA O	WIA EM	MIA* O	MIA* EM	Total O	Total EM
Hq 1st Engr Sp Brig	2	0	0	0	0	0	2	0
531st Engr Shore Regt	0	9	0	0	0	10	0	19
3206th QM Sv Co	1	38	1	8	1	155	3	201
3207th QM Sv Co	0	1	0	0	0	1	0	2
607th Graves Reg Co	0	6	0	1	0	9	1	28
462d Amph Trk Co	1	4	0	0	0	37	1	41
478th Amph Trk Co	1	14	0	1	0	13	1	28
306th QM Bn	0	0	1	0	0	0	1	0
556th QM Rhd Co	0	2	0	1	0	1	0	4
557th QM Rhd Co	3	45	0	1	2	23	5	69
625th Ord Co	0	2	0	0	1	9	1	11
33d Chem Decon Co	1	9	0	2	0	8	1	19
1605th Engr Map Depot	0	3	0	0	0	0	0	3
TOTALS	9	133	2	14	5	266	16	413

• Status of all men MIA changed to KIA 8 July 1944.

In a defensive statement the army also issued a table of casualties that was ... "compiled by the 1st Engineer Special Brigade and checked by a representative of Historical Section ETOUSA from unit casualty reports:

Controversy surrounding casualties of Exercise "Tiger" was only just beginning. For decades, analyses and arguments over the true total of dead and missing have been promoted and dismissed, and even today there is no definitive answer. Except that it has to be many more than 749, that figure so tenaciously promoted by official documents and government departments as the truth, when in reality that figure is based upon 1944 reports that are inaccurate through lack of information, omission by poor record keeping, and later manipulation to hide the truth.

Many attempts have been made to discredit this figure of 749 casualties through common sense, eyewitness accounts, document analysis, or simple addition and subtraction of numbers. All have had to work from documents or archive material available, of which many are suspected of having been re-written or falsified.

Sixteen

Threats and bribes

THE WOUNDED and injured had arrived at the U.S. Army 228th Field Hospital at Sherborne, Dorset. Built in only a few weeks it had already treated American servicemen of the 1st Infantry Division, suffering from malaria and hepatitis as they returned from the Mediterranean theatre. But the hospital's location was deliberately chosen, close to the south coast ports, it was ideally situated to deal with anticipated casualties of the amphibious assault on Europe, already designated as D-Day, and only some five weeks ahead.

Building of 228th Field Hospital, Sherborne

Colonel James Kendall the hospital's Commanding Officer summoned his staff of 40 Medical Officers and 80 nurses at 8:00 am and told them ...

"In about half an hour we're going to receive hundreds of cases of immersion shock, hypothermia and blast injuries. You are to treat them as they lie. Ask no questions, take no names, keep no records. Anybody that discusses this matter or is found talking about it, even in the future is subject to court martial."

An order reinforced by the sudden arrival of guards surrounding the hospital compound.

Late that same afternoon, Saturday 29th April 1944, the US Southern Base Section, responsible for men and equipment, had sent a priority secret message to ETOUSA ...

"Latest reports on casualties exercise TIGER indicate 248 dead sent to Brookwood, 253 walking patients being accommodated at BLANDFORD, and 63 hospitalized in vicinity of DOR-CHESTER. Walking patients being interrogated, segregated and will be returned to home stations. 20 of those hospitalized will be released today."

The statistics of fatalities were based upon information supplied by the US Navy, and at complete variance to the evidence of the 146th Truck Company and recollections of 605th Graves Registration Company. Survivor numbers being treated at hospitals could not be challenged, they were facts calculated by the Army. Army survivors would be returned to their units, Navy survivors would be sent to "survivor camps" in Plymouth where they could be separately interrogated and mingled with personnel posing as survivors, tasked with convincing them to comply with the official storyline.

At 4.02 am on Sunday 30th April, details of casualties aboard LST 289 that had finally made Dartmouth were transmitted ...

"LST 289 returned to DARTMOUTH at 1700 hours, 28 April 44, with 4 wounded Army personnel, 18 wounded Navy personnel, 4 Navy dead, 6 Navy missing. 9 officers and 342 EM from this LST being evacuated to STOVER B ."

Later that day casualty details began filtering through to the Army, and

Lieutenant Colonel B H Grundborg, Commanding Sub-Area V of the D-Day marshalling area was able to submit a report attaching a list of known survivors from LST 531. [31]

John who had survived the sinking of LST 507 remembers ...

> *"they took us to some army camp. We stayed there over two weeks, they wouldn't tell us where, or the name of the camp, it was near some port."* During his stay in camp, he and fellow survivors were ... *"made to unload an ammunition ship, USS Nitro. They took us there at night so we couldn't tell where we were."*

Ed Polovski of the 33rd Chemical Decontamination Company was also a survivor of LST 507, but on landing at Portland was taken to a hotel in Weymouth.

Joseph E McCann Jr was aboard LST 515 when it returned to the attack scene to search for survivors, and ordered to lower his LCVP. He recalls drifting through several bodies until he came upon ...

> *"one of the LSTs life rafts. The inner webbing had been burned out. There were three men on it, one had a very serious head wound and I actually started to pull away because it appeared all three men were dead. One of the crew thought he saw movement and upon checking we found they were alive but unconscious. We were to find out later that we picked up thirty-four men.".*

One body he recognized was that of Lieutenant Henry Q Saucier from LST 507, but his orders were to only pick up the living and he had to be left. His body was subsequently recovered by another vessel. McCann also picked up five men of the 4th Infantry Division who had been on LST 507.

LST 515 also picked up Arthur O Victor who was ...

> *"led to the crew's quarters, stripped, given a shot of brandy and put to bed. We slept for a while, got up and watched them haul dead bodies from the water, which were strewn everywhere. It was a wretched sight. When we hit port we were trucked to an army hospital with the surviving soldiers, checked over physically and put to bed, but we stayed there only a few hours.*

Next we went to a Red Cross station and were given army fatigues, shoes and toilet articles. We slept there overnight. The next day we were taken to an army base and counted in. Then the army boys went one way and we went the other. We never had a chance to say goodbye. Then we were taken to another area and housed in a dilapidated barracks under guard, for three days, and ordered under threat of court martial, not to discuss the incident with anyone outside of our immediate group. At the end of three days we were sent by train to a navy base and stayed there five weeks, with one week spent unloading an ammo ship that was anchored well out in the harbor."

Leslie Morse of 557th QM Railhead Company graphically sums up the casualties suffered by his unit when he estimates 175 were on an LST and when survivors returned to base camp, what were left were in three tents. He had been picked up by LST 515 where ...

"*someone handed me a cup of hot coffee and I went below into a bunk and slept.*" He was woken up in Weymouth and ... "*walked up the street with some sailor's underwear on and a pair of galoshes about size 12 over my bare feet with a white navy blanket around me. Isolated for a couple of days. Back to camp and isolated there. Then to Cardiff to rebuild the company withdrawn from the real invasion.*"

William C Reckord was a Pharmacist's mate aboard LST 507 and was picked up by LST 515 and taken to Portland. His memory is a little hazy about detail but he does remember ...

"*Three days in an army camp, we were not allowed to talk to anyone outside our area. At this time we were required to write a letter home and make sure that April 29th 1944 was clearly shown on the V-Mail letter. On 3rd May some of our group were sent to Plymouth Navy Amphibious Base (Vicarage Camp) to help unload an ammunition ship called the "Nitro".*

Albert Nickson had been aboard LST 507, survived the sinking and had been rescued by LST 515. He found ...

"*the morning of the 28th was a beautiful morning and the water was filled with all kinds of small boats looking for survivors. It was a ghastly sight to see all the bodies floating by – held up by their inflated life jackets. It was impossible to even try to count them. All that morning they were bringing bodies aboard. We were landed in Portland about noon of that day and taken to an army hospital for a check up on our injuries. The ones who didn't need any further treatment were then sent into Weymouth to the Red Cross to be fed and bunked. The only clothes we had were the ones given us by the boys on the 515.*

The next day we were given shoes and clothes if we needed them and then they shipped us off to a camp about 20 miles from Weymouth for "security" reasons. It was an army camp being made over into a hospital. The barracks were not in the best of condition and there was plenty of ventilation with broken windows. It was located in a beautiful spot, but the one bad feature of the place was a huge bomber base, which was located nearby. At night you would think some of the planes were going to crawl in bed with you they came so low. The army tried to do all they could for us under the circumstances although the food was not so hot. They arranged church services for us on Sunday and had movies for us in the evening. They posted guards around the barracks and we were not allowed outside a certain area. We were given more army clothes and shoes and a few toilet articles. We were asked not to say anything to anyone, but everyone we met seemed to know more than us.

After roughing it from Saturday to the following Friday we were again loaded on trucks and taken to the railroad station for our seven hour train ride to Vicarage Sub Base in Plymouth. It was a Sea Bee camp and was all Quonset huts. The chow was very good and we did not have much to do until they figured we would probably be better off if they gave us something to do. The first few days were spent making out new health records and it was like going through the old "boot" camp examination all over again. We were given complete checkups and the only ills I had were a bruised thigh and a bump on my forehead, which gave me a headache for a few days. I felt pretty fortunate that that was all bothering me and I was dam lucky to be alive.

> *We still did not have our Navy clothes so we were restricted to within the limits of that camp, although we used to sneak down to the movies almost every day and at night we would go down to a pub that was close by. One night while we were there, Pete and I were put in charge of a working party to go and unload ammunition from an LST that had just come from the States. The job started at midnight until 8 in the morning. Needless to say we got very little work out of the boys".."*

The business of minimizing casualty numbers had already been started by the US Navy, cleverly increasing the number of survivors from ships that had been sunk. Bob Robertson, a US Navy crewman of LCT 663 had a typical experience ...

> *"The message we sent home to our folks after the LST 507 was sunk. We didn't have a full crew when we were aboard; I believe there were 9 of us and our skipper Ens. Herbst. When we returned to Dartmouth someone from our flotilla headquarters came down and said the nine of us still could be listed as crewmembers of the 507 and they advised us to send a telegram home to our folks. I don't remember the wording but it went something like "Disregard any notice of my health, everything is fine". We had to pay for the telegram. My folks got it but couldn't figure it out of course."*

The tenuous link between this LCT crew and LST 507 was that their landing craft had been shipped across the Atlantic to England aboard the 507.

Robertson recalls their involvement in Exercise Tiger ...

> *"We took aboard troops on April 24th (in the evening) and I believe a couple of tanks or half-tracks. We joined a convoy of LCTs and headed (our crew didn't know where). The soldiers aboard thought we were going on the invasion as they had been issued ammunition. We traveled all night (around in circles I suppose) and in the morning we were off a beach (Slapton Sands). We landed the army we had on board. The following days we practiced unloading trucks from LSTs and making bridges of the LCTs (never worked too well). We saw the 2*

LSTs on fire on the horizon and saw ammunition going up. I don't remember what we did on the 28th. We saw no wreckage or bodies. We left the area and went to Dartmouth (our new base)."

Stanley W Gifford had also been on LST 507 with the 557th QM Railhead Company ...

"There were 180 men in our company, only 80 of us got off alive. I was in the water four hours before being rescued by a British destroyer, which took us back to Weymouth. They put cables around me to bring me out of the water. I was stiff from the salt water and couldn't walk. An order came out that our company would receive the Purple Heart but that was cancelled. Only those that went on sick call, so I didn't receive anything."

Vince Rolleri of the 33rd Chemical Decontamination Company was ...

" picked up by an American destroyer at the first light of dawn, and that was when I saw Jarret, sitting on a latrine, naked and with scorched hair – and stunned."

Walter Bohl's brother, Jacob was with the 557th QM Railhead Company ...

"Thru some letters from home I found out my brother Jacob was headed overseas. Knowing how long it took for me to get mail I thought I could get a letter to him faster if I wrote asap. My first letter sent to his APO # 230 was mailed on May 25th 1944, but I also had written him a letter dated Mar 25 44. Both of these letters were stamped "deceased" by 2nd Lt Robert J Bernhard. This was how I found out that my brother was dead. Shortly after I found out where my brother was buried I asked for time off and borrowed the money for train fare from the Red Cross. My visit to Brookwood was some time in late May or early June of 1944. While there I counted rows and graves in each row, that there were approximately 270 graves from the 557th QM Railhead and LST 507 because all the dates were the same on the graves".

Survivor's vulnerability through natural bewilderment and confusion, trauma and shock in the days immediately after the E-boat attack was exploited by those at the highest level in the cover-up, knowing there would be little or no objection to their manipulation.

Dispersal of survivors was a priority to minimize discussion and comparison of experiences that may lead to a realization of what had truly occurred, and to tighten the gag of silence.

A memorandum from VII Corps Headquarters at Sheplegh Court had been widely distributed. This was not a clear order, more of a threat that anyone discussing the events of Exercise Tiger would be dealt with severely. [32]

This memorandum however was interpreted by some as a firm order, and disseminated it as such throughout their organization so effectively that some soldiers would not talk of it for nearly forty years.

Unwritten orders issued by First U.S. Army to groups of officers summoned to their headquarters at Bristol on 3rd May 1944 began to take effect as small groups of enlisted men were transferred out of participating units and away to other units.

At a time when units knew they had lost men, either killed or missing, but were still unsure of their true casualty numbers, it is inconceivable that any commanding officer would readily agree to part with experienced troops he had trained to a peak of efficiency. Even if an assurance of rapid replacements was given, those men would arrive inexperienced, they would require time to integrate into the unit, and they had to be trained. With D Day only a few short weeks ahead, the receiving unit could never hope to re-achieve their state of readiness and expertise.

Despite this logic and common sense, the 478th Amphibian Truck Company transferred two EM to Headquarters, 24th Amphibian Truck Battalion on 29th April, and on 3rd May transferred another two EM to the 215th QM (Salvage) Repair Company, detailed in their Morning Reports.

First Lieutenant Clayton A Blomquist of the 33rd Chemical Decontamination Company was acting Commanding Officer as Captain Ralph A. Suesse had died shortly after being picked up by HMS "Azalea". Blomquist had been ordered to First Army headquarters at Bristol and upon his return on 5th May, assembled the Company and informed them that sixteen men of their Headquarters unit had perished when their LST was torpedoed and sank. Also lost on that ship were all Company records and Blomquist informed the survivors that everyone would now have to be interviewed to reconstruct them. This didn't happen and yet upon

32 See Appendix 32 – VII Corps memorandum

discharge at the end of the war, all personnel records were complete, including relevant information before, during and after Exercise Tiger. Once unit records were re-constructed to conform to the official version of events, Blomquist was reassigned to First Army headquarters on 19th May 1944.

Reports were daily being received of men missing or killed in action, only to be advised the next day that they had in fact survived. Conversely some believed to have survived had to be listed as missing until their body could be found and identified, or eventually conceded as missing. Some of this confusion would be expected after such a disaster, but the uncertainties were being deliberately exploited to cover the true number of losses.

Some of those who assisted in the falsification of documents to mask the number of casualties were rewarded by promotion that would ensure their silence. Stanley R. Stout and Leslie Morse of the 557th QM Railhead Company recall one such NCO being made First Sergeant almost immediately after the exercise, and the original First Sergeant being transferred as soon as he returned from survivor camp.

No one was in a better position to order and oversee the falsification of casualty documents than the head of the Graves Registration Service in the United Kingdom. Major Whitney arrived in the United Kingdom during May 1943 and was immediately appointed head of the Graves Registration Service. By D-Day he was promoted to Lieutenant Colonel, and by VE Day he was a full Colonel.

First Lieutenant Edgar W. Dortch of 3206th QM Service Company helped prepare the final report of 1st Engineer Special Brigade where he is listed as Captain Edgar W. Dortch of 1st Engineer Special Brigade. This was another illustration of the promotion and transfer policy to ensure silence.

LST 515 deck log records they returned to Portland with approximately one hundred and eighteen walking survivors, fourteen litter cases, and forty-five dead. Arthur Victor had been rescued by LST 515, and after ...

> "We slept for a while, got up and watched them haul dead bodies from the water which were strewn everywhere. It was a wretched sight. When we hit port we were trucked to an army hospital with the surviving soldiers, checked over physically and put to bed. But we stayed there only a few hours. Next we went to a Red Cross station and were given army fatigues, shoes and toilet articles. We slept there overnight. The next day we were taken to an army base and counted in. Then the army boys

*went one way and we went the other. We never had a chance to
say goodbye."*

Others were unwittingly bribed more modestly for their silence by the
simple process of awarding a "Purple Heart". Some whose silence was
essential received more prestigious awards. Others who were omitted in
the immediate aftermath of awards and had survived the hell of D-Day
were recommended for the "Purple Heart" or a plea on their behalf for
battle credit some months later. [33]

In July 1945 it was reported in a provincial newspaper that Corporal
Ernest Dale Rodman had been awarded the French Croix de Guerre with
Palm for ...

*" outstanding courage and heroic achievement in the liberation
of France".*

Modestly, he can recall no personal act of bravery that would merit his
receipt of France's highest military honour, believing it to be a bribe for his
silence.

The process of awarding the "Purple Heart" was justified quite simply.
To qualify, a serviceman had to have been wounded in action, and to
ensure an easy administrative passage for this to happen official reports
were created listing the intended recipients as receiving hospital treatment.
Some like Stanley W Gifford of the 557th QM Railhead Company who
had been aboard LST 507 heard the whole unit was to be awarded the
Purple Heart, but that was cancelled and only those on sick call would be
entitled to it.[34]

There are no records in Morning Reports of Corporal 31115452 Robert
A Kurz, or T/5 37064289 Howard C Dozier of 33rd Chemical Decontamination Company being wounded or hospitalized; yet in September
1944 they both received a Purple Heart for wounds received on April 28th
1944.

Morning Reports were secretly destroyed and re-written as hinted at
by one entry on one of the 33rd Chemical Decontamination Company's
documents.

*"This Morning Report rescinds consolidated morning reports
covering 22 April 44 through 2 May 1944."* [35]

33 See Appendix 33 – 1st ESB letter and citations
34 See Appendix 34 – Purple Heart
35 See Appendix 35 – Morning Report – 33rd Chemical Decon Co

These "Morning Reports" lists 8 men as missing in action, 10 killed, one wounded and 12 survivors. This exactly matches the U.S. Navy report by Lt Murdock of LST 507, but the Company history states 34 men from the headquarters platoon were aboard an unknown LST where 18 were killed and 16 rescued, of whom 4 were wounded. The headquarters group was aboard LST 507 whose loading table only shows 32 men aboard.

So the Morning Reports only account for 13 of the 16 survivors referred to in the Company history. Nine from the headquarters section are accounted for except Jarrett. Three from the 4th Platoon are unaccounted for, and are not listed as survivors. Others not accounted for include Roy Kopoff, Albert O Walters and John Jett who are listed with platoons of the 33rd Chemical Decontamination Company that landed on Slapton Sands on 27th April 1944. This still leaves three more men unaccounted for, Donald Shaw, Dino Volano, and Carl Johnson.

They weren't hospitalized, and some of those listed on rosters of the 115th Station Hospital's for 5th and 14th May 1944 simply were never there. They weren't wounded, injured or sick and they were never in a hospital between the stated dates, but still their names were on those rosters. Just two examples are T/5 39691191 Earnest D Rodman of the 33rd Chemical Decontamination Company and Pvt 14013743 Otway Burns of Company A, 531st Engineer Shore Regiment.

Incorrect details within those same rosters cast doubt upon their accuracy and honesty, suggesting they were partially or completely false. Pvt John O Wilkerson of the Ordnance service is shown with the service number 34228076 when his assigned service number was in truth 38220274. The number shown against his name was for an Edward Tarver, who is not shown as a patient. Again, Pfc Michael V Maley of the Infantry has the service number 35119543 against his name on a roster, but this was assigned to a Charles E Mikesell who also was not a patient.

Neither do these rosters match with units Morning Reports either. Shown as being from the CWS, Pfc Michael J Notek 35518622 and Pvt Biagio L Mascia 32204270 were completely unknown to personnel of the 33rd Chemical Decontamination Company, yet Notek is shown on the 33rd's Morning Report of 14th May 1944 as being released from 115th Station Hospital at Tavistock.

The rosters that declare they list Exercise Tiger casualties contain a high proportion of Infantry patients, yet no reports exist showing that the infantry suffered any casualties in the exercise. Official figures state there were about 330 survivors, but in one survivor camp some soldiers estimated there were at least five hundred occupants, most of them infantry, yet not one infantry survivor or fatality can be found in any records.

One hint was inadvertently given by Admiral Moon when he held an exercise debrief, and his comments are taken from the transcript ...

> *"We tried to get in every unit that could possibly be brought in regardless of training at that time."*

He later refers to the number of men aboard vessels of Exercise "Tiger" ...

> *"Carry men and taking certain risks. LST (crew) 185 men. Putting on 400 – 500 (army) men. Choice of doing that, getting the lift or not getting it"* so suggesting that some LSTs were double, or overloaded with army personnel. Something that Arthur O Victor, a crewmember of LST 507 remembers ... *"the ship was packed with about 500 soldiers, infantrymen and combat engineers."*

But the misery for survivors continued. William W Redieske who had abandoned his ship, LST 507 and was rescued by LST 515 remembers being ...

> *"put ashore later that morning. The survivors were taken by a lengthy truck ride to an isolated location where we spent a short period of time. I later learned there was interrogation of some of the men by military officers although I was not questioned."*

When Leslie Morse of the 557th Railhead Company woke aboard his rescue vessel ...

> *" I think we were in Weymouth, I know I walked up the street with some sailor's underwear on and a pair of galoshes about size 12 over my bare feet with a white navy blanket around me. Isolated for a couple of days. Back to camp and isolated there ".*

Seventeen

Reports

A US Navy ship's captain was at liberty to record incidents on either the ship's log, or the vessel's war diary. Any expansion upon incidents recorded in either of these documents would be written as an "Action report". But the E-Boat attack on 27th/28th April 1944 required more detailed reports from vessel's captains or senior survivors as ships and government property was lost in the action.

Some US Navy reports were written almost immediately after the incident before the authors could be supervised or guided as to the content and detail and were the subject of "correction" by more senior officers. Army reports were also penned while memories were still fresh in the minds of survivors and witnesses, but were beyond the reach of the US Navy to ensure conformity with the official version of events. [36 & 37]

So too were some Royal Navy reports. Lieutenant Commander P.E. King of HMS "Saladin" submitted a comprehensive account of what he had seen when approaching the attack area, including his assertion that he had seen three wrecked LSTs and a fourth damaged, not two that the U.S. Navy were insisting had been sunk with a third damaged and making for port. This report had been submitted through the chain of command so quickly after the incident that it was beyond the reach of the U.S. Navy who were carefully making all official reports quote their facts. [38]

Early in the morning of 28th April 1944, Admiral Moon had dispatched his senior staff officers to meet with vessel commanders of convoy T-4 to assess the incident and doubtless to ensure necessary reports all told the same story. But not all ships could be reached in time.

Lieutenant Commander Thayer had boarded LST 496 at 09:40 am on 29th April to meet with Lieutenant Stanley H Koch; whose report dated 30th April 1944 closely follows timings and details of the Operation

Order. So closely had he duplicated the wording that he had to correct himself by inserting a paragraph ... *"It is believed that LST 508 did not join convoy as scheduled"*. Details are given from the deck log of times and courses and observed fire. LSTs that were sunk are immediately identified at the time and HMS Azalea's radio transmissions of the E-Boat attack are heard and noted. On May 9th Koch submitted a covering report with his war diary to the Commander in chief, US Fleet, which details incidents worthy of noting on his deck log but do not appear there suggesting it had been re-written.

LST 499 was boarded at 09:25 am April 29th by Commander Guillot and Lieutenant Allen of Admiral Moon's staff, and undoubtedly ensured the captain's report included all the facts that were required to conform to the cover up.

Meanwhile, Admiral Moon for the record was officially quizzing Captain Geddes of HMS Azalea, and it is difficult to gauge whether Geddes had been put under pressure to give the responses required. The transcript reads as a routine interview, touching on nothing contentious, except an innocuous question by Moon ... *"Did you notice anything distinguishing about the E-Boat tracers? Blue tracers?"* Geddes replied ... *"No, sir"*. Significantly the German E-Boats were using red and yellow, so the reason for introducing the question of blue tracer suggests other vessels in the attack area were using that color. Despite his negative response, Geddes probably knew who was using blue tracer that night because he had been secretly briefed to expect a dummy attack.

Moon also asked ... *"How many survivors did you pick up?"* Geddes reply was ... *"I didn't pick up the survivors."* A U.S. Navy crewman along with approximately one hundred others was rescued by a ship that he positively identified as a British corvette. It had to be "Azalea" because "Primrose" and "Dianthus" were still some hours away and they made no reports of picking up survivors. Perhaps one reason these questions were posed was to show in a recorded document the answers that were required to support and maintain a cover up and minimize casualty numbers.

Blatant forgery was taking place too. LST 499's log for the 28th April detailing the attack is in a different hand writing to the rest of the log and signed by an untraced individual, G. E. Berry.

Admiral Moon's staff officers were ranging far and wide to spread their false version of events, even reaching the army's Service of Supply headquarters, which issued their own report dated 30th April 1944 stating only LSTs 507, and 531 had been sunk. Paragraph 5 of that report states ...

" The foregoing information was complied from information received from the following persons: Commander Simpson – U.S.N. – Staff Officer of Admiral Wilkes; Commander Bell – U.S.N. – Staff Officer of Admiral Wilkes; 1st Lt. E. W. Dortch, 01584194 – 1st Engineers. "

By May 3rd 1944, all reports from convoy T-4 LST commanders had been written, collated and submitted to the Commander in Chief, US Fleet by the convoy commander, Commander B J Skahill. He includes a list of events with comparative timings from all LSTs, drawing attention to the times of specific events varying by up to thirteen minutes from some ships, and correcting his own deck log timings for his sighting of the second burning ship, and the time LSTs initially opened fire. Some deck logs had slipped past Moon's staff without correction, and were now attached to Skahill's report en route to his commander in chief noting that LSTs 496 and 58 had seen a third LST that was torpedoed and on fire.

Ensign Douglas G Harlander was the senior survivor of LST 531 as the vessel commander; Ensign William H Cantrell was missing in action. Harlander submitted his report on the loss of his ship on 2nd May 1944, making reference to the fact he was assisted in preparing the report with assistance from Commander B J Skahill, the convoy commander. It is brief with a minimum of detail except for the number of personnel originally aboard, those rescued and dead and missing, and he specifically includes the number of army personnel on board his ship as 354. All other reports state this should be 392. To reinforce his statement Harlander wrote another report dated 22nd July 1944 listing survivors.

On the same day, Lieutenant J F Murdock of LST 507 submitted his report in the same clipped style; almost a copy of Ensign Harlander's report, but this time devoting a special paragraph to the number of army personnel aboard, quoting it may have been 282 or 294.

Lieutenant Q M Rhodes, the Executive Officer of LST 515 officially submitted to his commanding officer a copy of the deck log for April 28th 1944. Ensign B W Wahlberg wrote the action details up to 04:00am, and from then until 08:00 am Ensign D G Downing wrote details. Rhodes clearly believed it necessary to endorse the log "Certified to be a true copy" above his signature.

The following day LST 515's commanding officer J H Doyle submitted his report, enclosing the action report, praising his crew for their conduct during the attack and Lieutenant G M B Hawley for his medical skills. [40]

40 See Appendix 40 – LST 515 Deck log

On May 2nd 1944, LST 289's commander, Lieutenant Harry A Mettler submitted a more detailed and informal report on the action and his saving of the vessel despite severe damage, attaching a list of army and navy casualties.

By May 6th, Admiral Moon as commander of Task Force 122 was confident enough to report to Commander in Chief, US Fleet, enclosing transcripts of his interviews with the commanders of HMS Azalea and HMS Scimitar, and reporting on preparatory action by the Royal Navy to protect the exercise.

Lieutenant Commander Geddes had sent a report dated 28th April 1944 to his superior officer on HMS "Tanatside", still convinced he had been escorting nine LSTs, not eight as suggested by the U.S. Navy, and he had noted that one LST anchored off Blacknor Point instead of joining the others in West Bay. [41] This may account for the British anti-aircraft crew not seeing all four LSTs in West Bay but the questions is raised as to why it should anchor there and not offload its casualties alongside the others. And the question remains as to where those casualties went. There has been a suggestion that bodies were offloaded and sealed in the many tunnels running under Portland.

LST 511's report by Lieutenant J Yacevich of April 30th 1944 is comprehensive and detailed, but again appears to have been taken straight from the operation order as he lists HMS "Saladin" as being an escort.

Various army reports of April and May 1944 were collated long after Exercise Tiger into one document that formed the basis of the official army history of events leading up to the invasion of northwestern Europe.

Casualty numbers from Exercise Tiger are included... *"Most of the casualties were from LST 531. There were only 290 survivors of 744 soldiers and 282 sailors."* This number exceeds both the army's original Ship Loading Table of 392 soldiers, and the Navy's LST Loading Table that agrees the number at 392. Surprisingly, the same report states there were only 13 killed or missing from LST 507. The document concludes that ... *"A complete list of casualties is not available, but Army records, possibly not complete, state that 749 were killed."*

Only two army reports have survived the ravages of the cover-up, one was from Captain Theodore R. Wilkinson, commanding officer of the 462nd Amphibious Truck Company, giving a brief account of the E-Boat attack from his vantage point aboard LST 511. The other from Captain David D. Moore, commanding officer of the 478th Amphibious Truck Company aboard LST 289 tells only of the action aboard his vessel.

---

41 See Appendix 41 – H.M.S. Azalea report

Eighteen

Fabius

THE TRAGEDIES at Slapton Sands were to continue after Exercise "Tiger" during Exercise "Fabius I". This exercise plan again closely followed the true sequence of Operation "Neptune". The convoy approached behind minesweepers and marshaled about 10 miles offshore. After a preliminary naval bombardment, DD tanks of the 741st and 743rd Tank Battalions were launched 3,000 yards offshore, landing at H Hour they did not leave the water's edge, instead proceeding under their own power to Torcross and withdrew from the assault.

They were followed by the first waves of infantry. The 16th Regimental Combat Team was to land on the left and 116th Regimental Combat Team on the right. Engineers were to follow immediately, blow underwater obstacles, open up beach exits, and clear mines from suspect areas. At H plus 3 hours the 18th Regimental Combat Team was to land and join the other teams in an attack inland. Three Ranger companies were to land at Blackpool Beach, approximately two miles north of Slapton Sands to destroy enemy artillery installations, just as they were planned to land at Point du Hoc in Normandy. Another company was to land on the right flank of the regular assault beach, while other Rangers were to be landed with the infantry and were to make their way to the right to relieve the flanking company.

Exercise "Fabius" at Slapton Sands.

It was during the dark opening hours of this exercise ten LCVPs, each with thirty Rangers aboard ran into an uncharted sandbar almost one mile offshore from Blackpool Sands. Thinking they were ashore, they were discharged. The LCVPs withdrew leaving the fully equipped soldiers to drown. There is no record of any Ranger fatality on these dates and the only casualties from both 2nd and 5th Ranger Battalions are recorded as 6th June 1944 or later.

Later in the day when the excitement of the initial landings had abated and the assault force were moving inland, Barnett Hoffner of "B" Company, 203rd Engineer Combat Battalion and his squad were practice lifting mines when they saw bodies floating in on the tide ...

> *"We started down the water's edge to get the bodies when I heard a voice yell "Sergeant! Get your men out of there!" I looked up and saw three stars on the shoulders and recognized that it was Major General Huebner of the 1st Infantry Division. I got my squad out of there fast. You don't question anything a general says. He was there with three members of his staff. "*

Local witnesses, who had slipped through the perimeter security and entered the exercise area for unknown reasons, recall seeing bodies on the shore at Blackpool Sands. These were undoubtedly the Rangers who drowned and those witnesses have confused this disaster with Exercise Tiger.

Blackpool Sands.

The problem of what to do with the bodies was exacerbated by the pressing needs of that time. The rehearsal had to go ahead according to the timetable. There was no question of canceling or postponing it, for this was the last opportunity to rehearse the entire assault group for "Omaha" beach with D-Day only five weeks ahead, and the participating units were due in the marshalling areas immediately after this exercise.

Bodies had to be quickly removed and there was simply no time or resources available to organize the correct identification procedure and transportation to a permanent military cemetery. The decision was taken, just as it had been after Exercise "Tiger" to bury the bodies locally, with the intention of later recovering them to a permanent cemetery.

Harold McAulley of the 479th Amphibious Truck Company was present at the mass gravesite and recognized one of the Ranger casualties as Joseph R.Trainor who was from the same hometown. This Ranger has a grave, block I, row 1, grave 32, in the American cemetery at Colleville, Normandy, France, with a date of death as 6th June 1944. The official explanation of his supposed interment in France is that his body drifted up the English Channel to the Pas de Calais and was buried in the military cemetery at St Andre and later removed to Colleville. But this does not explain why his official date of death is 6th June 1944.

But exercise "Fabius" continued. Personnel involved in transporting and burying the bodies went their very separate ways to war, some never to return.

Nineteen

Aftermath

AT 6.00 am on Friday 28th April Captain Tompkins, Admiral Moon's Chief of staff had left the USS Bayfield in an LCI to enquire into the E-Boat attack. News of the disaster of convoy T-4 was already flashing between Army and Navy departments with alarming speed and frequency. Commanders were demanding information and due to uncertainty of the number of casualties and LST commanders being pressured to give answers, their responses gave varying estimates until the US Navy could gain control of what was being said. The US navy already knew their record keeping and administration of the exercise was deficient, and they were very reluctant to divulge what scant details they had of the action at sea.

What they were certain of was that the disaster was of an unprecedented scale and the responsibility was theirs. Losses were of such an immense scale they could be sure of a deep seeking enquiry that would most certainly find the US Navy and many senior officers guilty, unless they could minimize their portion of the blame, or minimize the disaster itself.

The US Navy had three LSTs sunk. Aboard them were many army personnel that had been drowned or missing. The scale of the cover up was going to be immense requiring the closest liaison with the US Army and the Royal Navy at the very highest level, the alteration, falsification or destruction of relevant documents, and maintaining the silence of all survivors. Scapegoats had to be found, and most importantly, the deception required one trusted, man to organize and co-ordinate this complex task.

This man was not chosen by senior officers, he was already entwined in the intrigue having already arranged for the dummy attack on convoy

Commodore Virgil E. Korns.

T-4 by Free French MTBs. He was probably seeking a solution to his deep involvement, and seized the opportunity to vindicate himself using a much greater disaster to cover his own faults. Using his unique position within the navy's organizational hierarchy he was best placed to manage a cover up of the casualties and ships lost. This was Commodore Virgil Eben Korns. He had a Naval Intelligence background, had been a mathematics teacher, and knew in great detail all the preparations for "Tiger". But once he started manipulating reports and massaging casualty figures, he found himself compelled to continue, as one lie requires another to support it. He managed to distance himself from the documentary falsehoods by issuing obtuse recommendations that were interpreted by his subordinates to comply with his veiled intention. He also managed to avoid the arrows of blame, diverting each accusation to a superior or subordinate, and such was his eloquence and persuasive manner that he convinced the recipients they really were responsible for the catastrophe.

Those who suffered did so as an indirect result of Korn's manipulations, particularly the withholding of information in the immediate aftermath of the attack. Colonel Caffey of the 1st Engineer Special Brigade was relieved of his command. Admiral Wilkes was posted to the Pacific theatre of operations, and Admiral Moon allegedly committed suicide. Was the guilty knowledge of Exercise "Tiger" too much for Moon to bear, unable ever to reveal what he knew, forcing him to take his own life? Or had he let it be known that he intended to reveal the truth, and had to be silenced? Perhaps the truth was about to be revealed, and knowing his guilty part in the cover up, and unwilling to bear the blame, he did kill himself.

But first, officers participating in the exercise had to be briefed about what was to happen, and sworn to secrecy. At 9.19 am on Saturday 29th April, Captain M. T. Richardson, USN, commander of the Green Assault Group and officers of his staff arrived aboard USS Bayfield for conference with Admiral Moon. Three hours later Moon signaled that naval participation in Exercise "Tiger" had been completed, and at 1.00 pm Bayfield began preparations for getting under way from Slapton Sands. She anchored in Plymouth Sound at 5.03 pm and Admiral Moon immediately left for a meeting with British Admiral Leatham, C in C, Plymouth Command, Royal Navy, Rear Admiral Kirk, Rear Admiral Wilkes, and Rear Admiral Struble.

Admiral Sir Ralph Leatham – C in C Plymouth.

Plymouth Command could sense the Americans were looking for someone to blame, and were quick to advise them of what action they had taken on the E-Boat reports. They stated reports of E-Boat activity were first received from HMS "Onslow" at 12.11 am 28th April and re-broadcast by Plymouth on the area radio net at 12.39 am. Portsmouth Command had reported two groups of E-Boats south west of Portland Bill on the Port Wave radio frequency. The first unidentified radar plot from shore stations was received at Plymouth at 12.22 am and classified as hostile three minutes later. As more information came in, so Plymouth Command said, it was broadcast at intervals on both the Area net and Plymouth Port Wave. They suggested that the submarine periscope seen by a few of the LST crews was in fact a "foxer", a device towed with several hundred yards of cable behind a ship as a decoy for acoustic torpedoes. Although which ship would have deployed such a device during the action is not known.

C in C, Plymouth later offered several reasons for the mistakes made. Concurrently with the execution of Exercise Tiger, many urgent ship movements, planning and preparations were in progress for Exercise Fabius, scheduled to take place only a few days later. Additionally, a night action with enemy destroyers during the 25/26th April had prompted plans for another offensive on the night of 28th April. Both combined to severely stretch the capacity of his staff. Mention was also made of the late distribution of Exercise Tiger orders, and incompleteness of some of the sets supplied, giving very little time for their study and digestion. The Royal Navy was entirely to blame for the lack of escorts for convoy T-4 by initially keeping Scimitar in port, and they admitted it, with so much evidence against them they could do little else.

By early Saturday afternoon, 29th April, Admiral Moon had been presented with a few carefully selected pieces of information to make an early report to his commander-in-chief as to what had happened, as well as advising SHAEF. At 2.08 pm he sent a priority secret message ...

> "Convoy of 7 US LST's in command of Commander B J Scahill, USN, in force "U" Training Exercise TIGER attacked by hostile E-Boats April 280220B, 252 Degrees, Portland Bill 15 miles. Regret to report LST's 507, 531 loaded with estimated 744 Army and 282 Navy personnel sunk by torpedoes. Total known ambulatory survivors 257, litter cases 33. LST 289 received following torpedo damage wrecked steering gear and crew's quarters. Crack appearing amidships. 4 of crew dead, 9 missing, 18 wounded 1 critically, 4 Army personnel wounded. LST 289 towed to DARTMOUTH. LST 511, no damage, some Naval personnel wounded by gunfire. Number not yet reported. Have directed convoy Commander to forward required reports."

Moon was unwittingly suffering from an artificial famine of details his Chief of Staff had deliberately created through his policy of releasing as few details as possible until he could properly prepare the U.S. Navy's case. The US Army administration could only rely upon what they were told by the navy to form their own opinions and had no reason to suspect they were only being told what suited the US Navy. The only other source of information was from units aboard the convoy ships, but survivors were now scattered across the south west of England and in no position to make detailed reports.

One particular injustice resulting from this lack of information from the navy to the army was the fate of Colonel Eugene M. Caffey. As commander of the US 1st Engineer Special Brigade, his troops were mere passengers on the navy's ships, and had no control over events at sea, and as a result of the convoy T-4 disaster, he and his Brigade lost more than anyone. But his commander, General Lawton Collins had spoken to General Omar Bradley immediately after the exercise, both agreeing that the engineer organization had broken down. With no hard facts from the US Navy to say differently, Collins agreed with Bradley's suggestion that

Colonel Eugene M. Caffey – 1st Engineer Special Brigade.

Caffey should be replaced. Colonel Caffey was surprised when a few days later Collins relieved him of his command, giving no reason. Caffey didn't ask for reasons but meekly accepted the post of deputy commander and continued running the brigade as he always had. For seven years Caffey lived with the disgrace until prompted by reading General Omar N Bradley's memoirs to try and clear himself of any blame. [42]

On 3rd May 1944, Commander B.J. Skahill the T-4 convoy commander had collated all action reports from surviving LST commanders and submitted his own comprehensive report attaching them together with charts showing the convoy track. Under his heading of communications, Skahill's opening line is …

"No reports of the presence of enemy craft were received."

His recommendations highlight the problems that beset convoy T-4 right from the start and were probable causes for the scale of the disaster …

18 (a) Larger escort force, if available.

18 (b) Insure that vital information on enemy contacts is disseminated quickly.

18 (e) For short operating periods, carry only sufficient fuel for the operation. This would cut down on burnable material.

18 (k) Life preservers – from the number of dead bodies observed in the water, it is believed that the kapok jacket is more effective

for holding up the head of exhausted swimmers than the CO_2 inflated single belt type."

The following day Admiral R. Leatham sent a Top Secret letter to Admiral A. G. Kirk (Naval Commander Western Task Force). This was in reply to Kirk's letter of 1st May where Kirk advised Leatham that he was required to report to Commander in Chief, US Fleet furnishing information regarding the T4 convoy escort, protecting patrols and dissemination of enemy information. That letter had been loaded with obtuse accusations and had asked some very awkward and searching questions of Leatham and the Royal Navy. Leatham had to admit Azalea was on her own, and details what happened to HMS Scimitar from Plymouth Command's perspective ...

" For these mistakes I can only offer my profound regret ... "

By 6th May ETOUSA were now treating information fed to them by the US Navy with caution. This message to Commanding Officer, Southern Base Section in England illustrates that either the US Navy couldn't or wouldn't be accurate and specific about the number of US Army casualties, or they were limiting what information was released, even to the Army. Or they simply didn't know. So ETOUSA merely repeated what they were told ...

"The following information is available in this Headquarters on recent incident and loss by First Army thru enemy action during exercise "Tiger."

LST number 507 (Army serial number 496) assumed lost. Had following loading list:

Personnel from 478 Amphibian Truck Company,
557 Quartermaster Railhead Company,
33 Chemical Company;
1st Platoon 440 Engineer Company,
3891 Quartermaster Truck Company.

LST number 531 (Army serial number 495) assumed lost. Had following loading list:
Personnel from 462 Amphibian Truck Company,

3206 Quartermaster Service Company,

LST number 289 (Army serial number 501) damaged aft.
Had following loading list:
Personnel from 478 Amphibian Truck Company,
556 Quartermaster Railhead Company,
4th Medical Battalion.

Request list of major items of equipment actually lost or
damages beyond repair and advice as to your action being taken
to replace this material."

ETOUSA were clearly thinking ahead as each and every LST was vital to the D-Day plan and loss of equipment was critical. Whether a mix up at ETOUSA message center or incorrect information has resulted in this message transposing the LST and Army serial numbers for LSTs 531 and 289.

By the 6th of May 1944, Admiral Moon believed he had secured sufficient evidence to send his report of the incident to the Commander in chief, US Fleet. Enclosed with the report were transcripts of his interviews with the captains of HMS Azalea and Scimitar. The report opens with an outline of the exercise and vessels assigned to it by the Royal Navy commander in chief, Plymouth. It continues in paragraph 10 with Moon's actions upon receipt of news of the attack by sending USS "Tide", HMS "Dianthus" and HMS "Primrose" from screening the exercise area to screen the surviving LSTs of convoy T4, and to pick up survivors. He goes on to comment upon the LST commanders ...

"It may be noted that all LSTs of the subject convoy were newly
arrived in this theater, none having been in the United Kingdom
for more than a month ... All ships were newly commissioned,
their Commanding Officers being either ex-enlisted men with
from 12 to 16 years service, or reserve officers with from one
to two years active duty."

He also pointed out that many of the LSTs normally operated in other LST groups, and had never before acted together as a complete tactical group, stating there was evidence of considerable straggling prior to the attack.

Paragraph 12 is devoted to ...

"The danger from E boat attacks had been personally emphasized by CTF 125 (Moon) in a briefing conference of all Commanders two days before the exercise. Representatives of CinC Plymouth discussed E boat tactics at the same time."

His conclusions included the need for more escorts, suggesting four would have been sufficient. He went on to commend the captain of LST 289 for his handling of the vessel after the attack and bringing it safely back to port, and criticizing the convoy commander, Commander Skahill, for not terminating exercise conditions when flares were first seen. Rounding off the report with his recommendations, he was at pains to emphasize the need to counter E-Boat attacks, most of which pointed to the Royal Navy's lack of an effective defense. He also recommended the convoy and escort commanders check on means of communications with each other before leaving port.

The Commander in Chief, US Navy Fleet was beginning to sense he was not being told everything about the E-boat attack and called for more documents including the War diaries of LST 496 and LST 515, which were dispatched on 9th and 10th May 1944. Admiral Kirk forwarded his own memorandum and version of the action on 14th May, clearly suppressing his feelings in his report but emphasizing the Royal Navy were responsible for screening the exercise but the ships failed to intercept the E-Boats as they penetrated the screen, or upon their escape. He also draws attention to the fact that reports of the E-Boats approach were known to Azalea but were not passed on to the convoy, and neither did the convoy receive those reports directly. His conclusion was that ...

"Although risks in training had to be accepted, it is regretted that in this case there appear to have been incurred some risks that were preventable."

Paul ATKINS a navy crewman still on LST 511 at Falmouth, Cornwall records that on May 21st the ship received a new Executive Officer, Lieutenant J. F. Murdock from LST 507 who immediately ...

"took off the ship's records and logs."

This was a necessary afterthought to complete the documentary cover up by an officer who by now was deeply involved in the cover up.

By the middle of May 1944 interest in the disaster of Exercise "Tiger" had all but run its course. Royal Navy excuses had been accepted and the question of numbers of casualties had been successfully suppressed from further investigation. It was concluded by Admiral Stark's report of 19th May 1944, which was brief in conclusion but showed his belief that even if both escort vessels had been present, the escort would have been weak, and a much stronger escort could give no guarantee of immunity from attack. He did say that ...

"the provision of adequate escort has always been a matter of concern to the operating forces. It has been one of the hazards of war which had to be accepted."

His final paragraph refers to the dissemination of information received on enemy activity, and notes ...

"that in this case the information did not get through to all concerned."

D-Day, 6th June 1944 diverted attention away from Tiger, but the debate about casualties was to rumble on for decades provoked by several official quotes. On 5th August 1944 SHAEF made press release number 77 giving casualties of D-Day up to 20th July, and as a footnote added ...

"These figures include the following casualties sustained by the U.S. Army during pre-invasion exercise the latter part of April when enemy E-boats attacked a convoy."
Killed in action ...	*...*	*130*
Wounded in action	*...*	*41*
Missing in action	*...*	*312*

To reward those who masterminded the cover up it is ironic that Korns got Wilke's job. Korns had arrived in England on the 1st of September 1943 having been specifically requested as Chief of staff to Admiral Wilkes who was then Commander of US amphibious bases in the United Kingdom, and soon after Exercise "Tiger", Korns had his job commanding 1,500 officers and 30,000 men. Among other awards Korns received the British OBE ...

"for high endeavor and most successful co-operation in matters concerning the mutual naval interests of the USA and the UK

in the Plymouth Command, first as Chief of Staff and later as Commander, US Amphibious Bases, UK."

In July 1944 he was awarded the Legion of Merit by the Commander, US Naval Forces in Europe. Less than a year later he received a Gold Star in lieu of a second Legion of Merit for his work in connection with replacing vessels lost in the storm off Omaha beach in mid June 1944. Over the next few months he was awarded several high status medals including the French Legion of Honor, the French Croix de Guerre with Palm, the Belgian Order of Leopold and Croix de Guerre. Someone superior to Korns knew what he had done, and ensured he was handsomely rewarded for a job well done, and to ensure his continuing silence.

As part of a continuing campaign of dis-information, casualty figures were appearing in many official documents. One example is the "Final disposition of WWII dead 1945-1951" which states ...

" those buried in Brookwood Cemetery, south of London, and in Lisnabreeny, in North Ireland, were moved to Cambridge. Interments in the three temporary burial grounds in the United Kingdom totaled slightly more than 9,000. On 30 August 1948 permanent reinterments began. On 1 November 1948 a total of 3,113 permanent interments had been accomplished. By the end of 1948, an additional 370 remains rested at Cambridge. Reinterments ceased during February 1949. Most recent statistics reveal a total of 3,811 Americans resting in Cambridge."

It is now obvious that Lieutenant J F Murdock had been instrumental in the elaborate cover up, and continued to perpetuate the falsehoods at every opportunity, volunteering to be interviewed on the 16th August 1944 at the Office of Naval Record and Library to again put the official version on record. [43]

By August 1944 with the world's attention focused on the war racing across northern Europe, the exiled inhabitants of the Slapton Firing Range were preparing to return to their homes. Before they could be allowed to do so, a few final tasks had to be completed by the outgoing American military. Fields and villages had to be combed for any unexploded ordnance, and American bodies buried near Blackawton had to be removed.

43 See Appendix 43 – Lt. Murdock interview

They were quietly exhumed, loaded onto trucks and taken to Kingsbridge railway station. The station, yard and surrounding area had been cleared of all personnel except the stationmaster who for safety reasons had to receive and dispatch three "funeral" trains. For three days, trucks brought bodies in from the Blackawton field to the station to be loaded onto the trains destined for Greenock in Scotland where a railway signalman vividly remembers them arriving. The stationmaster estimated there were over a thousand bodies. All were in body bags and loaded onto the trains. He was convinced more were shipped across the Channel to France for burial there.

For many years acknowledged as the U.S. expert on Exercise "Tiger", Eugene E. Eckstam, M.D., had credibility on his side, claiming he was a survivor of LST 507, although some survivors say they never saw him on the ship. He adopted a helpful and sympathetic attitude to anyone who contacted him in search of the truth about Exercise "Tiger".

He was pleased to field questions from serious researchers, leading them towards the official version of events that were prepared in his own written account. Any difficult questions were responded to with snippets of documents that he rarely supplied as copies, just extracting relevant quotes or paragraphs and printing them in his replying correspondence. He was also nearly always present at reunions of "Tiger" survivors, and was a leading player in organizing survivors to re-visit Slapton Sands.

Eckstam was certainly in the survivor camp at Vicarage Barracks, Devonport, Plymouth, as he is in a group photograph of survivors of Exercise "Tiger". Also in that photograph is James Murdock. This photograph is the beginning of a series of remarkable coincidences suggesting that they, with others were briefed to perpetuate the cover up by promoting the official version of the events of Exercise "Tiger" at every opportunity.

The Wisconsin State Journal of 6th August 1944 carried an article entitled "Home from Normandy" as ...

> "Lieut. Eugene Eckstam ... is home on a 30-day survivors leave from the invasion action on the Normandy peninsula ... Several weeks before the invasion, the LST on which he was serving was torpedoed during maneuvers in the English Channel. He clung to a rubber life raft for many hours before being rescued."

His presence on "survivor's leave" is not remarkable as he was on his way to the Pacific Theatre, although he only got as far as the Californian coast before the war ended.

Coincidentally in the same newspaper on the same date was another article entitled "130 were killed in invasion drills" the source of this article is credited to SHAEF and very briefly repeats that ...

> *"during a rehearsal on April28 ... casualties occurred when German E-Boats darted through strong air and sea support ... cost American forces 483 casualties, of which 130 were killed, 41 wounded and 312 missing."*

Coincidence that an official story is released at the same time as Lieutenant Eckstam's homecoming is announced.

But Eckstam wasn't the only "Tiger" personality who had been shipped back to the United States at this time. Lieutenant J. F. Murdock who had removed the ship's logs and personnel records from LST 511 was giving the official story of the incident in an interview at the Office of Naval Record and Library - an opportunity to reinforce and perpetuate the cover up.

At the end of World War II, Colonel Whitney of the U.S. Army Graves Registration Service authored a document entitled "Passing in review" which gave a brief history of the service including Exercise "Tiger" where he quotes the official number of casualties at 284. It was another opportunity to promote the official story.

Twenty

D Day

EXERCISE "TIGER" had been a rehearsal for units that were to assault "Utah" beach in Normandy on D-Day, 6th June 1944. It was a true dry-run with every aspect of the exercise run in absolute parallel to the upcoming Operation "Overlord", right down to the codenaming of beaches. The infantry that was first to set foot on the French beaches on D-Day had been the first to be ashore at Slapton. The 1st and 2nd Battalions of the 8th Infantry Regiment took Slapton Sands just after dawn on 27th April 1944 and were reinforced an hour later by the 3rd Battalion, exactly as it was planned they would on D Day.

An LCVP approaches "Utah" beach.

But casualties of friendly fire in Exercise "Tiger" had critically depleted the 1st and 2nd Battalions to a point where the D-Day beach assault plan had to be re-written to take account of their losses. This adjustment is illustrated on the D-Day landing plan for "Utah" beach dated 24th May 1944 where the 1st and 2nd Battalions are shown as the first infantry assault waves just as they were in "Tiger", but the 3rd Battalion as first reinforcements are missing from the plan. The 1st and 2nd Battalions had been decimated by "defender's" fire as they stepped ashore at Slapton, and to replace those casualties at such short notice the 3rd Battalion was dissolved and those troops reassigned to the 1st and 2nd. It was a simple solution for there was no time to rebuild those battalions with fresh replacement troops, and the 3rd was already trained and immediately available. Reinforcing the re-vamped 1st and 2nd Battalions on "Utah" beach was now to be done by moving forward other battalions from other regiments to the 3rd Battalion's position in the invasion armada.

What still remained however was the thorny problem of how to account for the deaths at Slapton during "Tiger" and "Fabius". It could never be admitted that their bodies had been buried in peaceful, green Devonshire fields and would be secretly spirited away, yet those "lost" soldiers had to be accounted for in the mathematics of casualties.

The 4th Infantry Division achieved this by merely time-sliding their dates of death forward by a few weeks and labeling them as "missing in action". This satisfied the arithmetic of divisional losses and removed the problem of producing bodies for grieving families. But it is that false arithmetic that proves the lie in a document produced from G-1 reports of VII Corps battle casualties for the period 6th June to 1st July 1944. This states that during that period the 4th Infantry Division recorded 788 soldiers as "Missing in action". Yet the American Battle Monuments Commission commemorate at their cemeteries only 31, leaving 757 unaccounted for. As the ABMC record every casualty buried in their cemeteries and list all those missing in action, whether in combat or not, these 757 soldiers have simply disappeared from the records.

One officer serving with the intelligence section of the 4th Infantry Division has remarked that ... *"after Exercise "Tiger" we did notice some of our men weren't around."*

At last there is an indication of the number of men killed in Exercise "Tiger" buried in the field at Blackawton and later taken by train to Scotland. Their bodies could not be returned to the United States as they were now officially listed as "Missing in action" and while there is no record of their final destination, there is a very strong clue as to their disposal from John Cullen whose RML 532 had tried to tow a Rhino barge from Lyme Bay in April 1944. He remembers in late July just off Cherbourg, he again saw a Rhino barge. This time it carried a huge container and his vessel's task was to escort it out into the Atlantic. He asked the towing tugs captain what was in the container to be told it contained bodies of army personnel being repatriated to the United States. Repatriation however did not commence until 1947, and the military authorities could not possibly know after just one month of intense combat which families wanted the body of their loved one returned to the United States. This account has a chilling resemblance to stories told in Plymouth dockyards of bodies from Exercise "Tiger" and "Fabius" being loaded on barges that were towed into the Atlantic and deliberately sunk.

Those were the "Missing in action" of the 4th Infantry Division but the figure of those "Killed in action" during the same period must now be scrutinized. A total number of 844 is quoted, which compared with other units of VIIth Corps is remarkably high. Especially when the entire 4th Infantry Division suffered only 197 casualties during the actual landings on "Utah" beach, of which 60 were missing from the 29th Field Artillery Battalion, and the deadly "Battle of the hedgerows" that was to claim hundreds of lives had not yet begun. [44]

An official document entitled "Battle deaths of the 4th Infantry Division", dated 30th June 1947 lists all fatal casualties including the 8th Infantry Regiment, and among that list are some suspicious entries.

There are names with service numbers that were not issued - names with the wrong service numbers. Soldiers listed as "Killed in action" or "Died of wounds" when in fact they were "Missing in action". There are far too many irregularities to assign to typographical errors or simple mistakes. This document has been written to deceive.

According to this list Paul R. Belli a Private in 8th Infantry Regiment, service number 36675446 was killed in action on June 6th 1944. The American Battle Monuments Commission does not record his burial which may suggest his body was repatriated, but this service number is untraceable and Paul Belli was issued with service number 32665910 when he enlisted.

Thomas F. Bowden service number 32278641, a Private First Class in 8th Infantry Regiment is listed as killed in action on 24th June 1944. This service number was not issued and Bowden had been assigned service number 33450864.

Rangers lost during Exercise "Fabius" have simply been swallowed into the appalling statistics of D-Day deaths raising suspicions that not every grave in Normandy contains a body, and not every burial casket repatriated to America contained the correct remains, or any remains at all.

One puzzling official document has come to light in response to an enquiry with the American Battle Monuments Commission as to how many infantrymen were lost in exercise "Tiger". The details speak for themselves to reach a total of 1,405 casualties, almost twice the number that has been officially designated as the correct casualty figure, and this document includes "unspecified units" which must be counted as infantrymen. Another revelation within the same document is that over 500 bodies are buried at "various sites" other than Brookwood.

EXERCISE TIGER PERSONNEL ACCOUNTING

A	B 1st Eng Sp Bde	C 35th Sig Bn	D U.S. Navy	E Sub-Total	F Unspec-ified Units	G Grand Total
1 Buried At Brookwood	142	2	34	178	82	260
2 Various Sites	271	17	84	372	156	528
3 Bodies Recovered Total	413	19	118	550	238	788
4 Missing	334	9	80	423	193	616
5 Total Dead And Missing	747	28	198	973	431	1405
6 Rescued	191	4	122	317	110	427
7 Total Aboard	938	32	320	1290	542	1832

Documentation Cell #

B1 Brigade Kia per neptune: training for and mounting the attack, Page 259, by C.L.Jones
B2 Brigade Mia same above
B3 Brigade total killed and missing same above
C1 Non-Brig (35th Sig Const Bn) at Cambridge
C2 Non-Brig graves at Cambridge
C4 Army total 441 less 413 less non-brig at Cambridge 19
D1 Navy grave sites at Cambridge
D3 Bodies recovered per navy list of casualties
D4 Missing per navy list of casualties
G1 Buried at brookwood per "passing in review" page 3 chapter 26 y col. l.r.talbot
C6 Sig const bn per lst 531 survivors list

Appendix 1

PROPOSED
BATTALION LANDING TEAM (ASSAULT)
REGIMENTAL LANDING TEAM (ASSAULT)
T / O 7-15 modified

	T / O	Near Atchd	Shore	Afloat
Hq	4	)		(3
Hq Co	108	)		(59
Rifle Co (Assault)	192	)		(187
Rifle Co (Assault)	192	) 227		(187
Rifle Co (Assault)	192	)		(187
Hv Wpns Co	162	)		(0
Subtotal	850		227	623
Med Det	23			23
Engrs, 2 plat	90			90
Shore Fire Control Party	10	1		11
Art Obs Party	12			12
Tank Co		85		85
Chemical Sqds (48)		73		73
Total Bn Lndg Team	985	159	227	917

TRANSPORT

	T / O	Near Atchd	Shore	Afloat
Tlr, 1-ton	1		1	
Trk, 1/4 –ton	11		11	
Trk, amph, ¼-ton	1	1		2
Trk, ¾-ton wpn carr	5		4	1
Trk, 1 1/2-ton	12		12	

LANDING CRAFT

	T / O	Near Atchd	Shore	Afloat
LCVP		33	33	
LCM		19*	19*	
Engineers		(2)	(2)	

ARMAMENT

MG, light, cal. 30	9	8	5	12
MG, cal. 30	8	6	8	6
MG, cal. 50, HB	7	2	6	3
Multiple gun, M15, 37/50		3		3
Gun, 37mm, towed	3	3	0	
Launcher, rocket, AT	24	18	18	24
Mortar, 60mm	9	6	3	12
Mortar, 81mm	6	6	6	6
Flame thrower		18		18
Mortar, chem., 4.2"		8		8
Tank, medium		17		17

16 LCM's for tanks may be replaced by 4 LCT(5)'s
2 LCM's for Engrs may be replaced by 4 LCVP's

U. S. Assault Training Center
18 September 1943

Appendix 2

SECRET   (D.25-550) 28-2-44

PLYMOUTH COMMAND WAR ORDERS
Short Title: "P. C. W. 0."

Section 5 – OPERATIONS

138   CONTROL OF FORCES ESCORTING AND COVERING U.S. TASK FORCES DURING AMPHIBIOUS EXERCISES

Information to be passed

Information of enemy activity of any nature in the vicinity of ships at sea is passed by the Commander-in-Chief, Plymouth, or the Naval Officer-in-Charge, Dartmouth, as soon as known. In the case of task forces the address of the signal will include the commanding officer of the task group and senior officer of the close escort.

Control of covering forces

2. Allied surface patrols and covering forces will be controlled in the normal manner by the Commander-in-Chief, Plymouth, or as directed by him (e.g. the Flag Officer-in-charge, Falmouth, or the Naval Officer-in-Charge, Dartmouth).

Control of task force and close escort

3. The control of the task force and close escort will be carried out by the senior officer present whether British or American. The Commander-in-Chief, Plymouth, may, however, suggest a course of action to the senior officer, task force, in the light of information at his disposal (from radar surface and air plots, etc.).

4. Assuming that the senior officer, task force, is the senior officer, the close escort remains under his orders unless or until released by him.

Courses of action

5. There are two conditions
    (a) When the task force is on passage.
    (b) When the task force is actually conducting an exercise at the Slapton Assault Training Area between Dartmouth and Start Point.

Case (a)

6. The senior officer, task force, is responsible for ordering the movements of the task force and the close escort as may be necessary. He will give due weight to advice received from the Commander-in-Chief, Plymouth (see para. 3 above).

Case (b)

7. In the event of enemy surface or submarine activity the senior officer, task force, will take his force as close inshore as possible, and will beach landing craft at his discretion if conditions are suitable.
8. He will form the close escort on a close screen round the task force.
9. Units of the task force and close escort will **not** proceed to seaward of QZS 440 and 416 unless in contact with enemy forces.
10. Units of covering forces will **not** proceed inshore of QZS 440 and 416 unless in contact with enemy forces.

Conduct of close escort

11. In both cases (a) and (b) the close escort remains under the orders of the senior officer, task force, until released by him. Should, however, the senior officer, task force, decide to detach any of the close escort (e.g. destroyers) in pursuit of the enemy or to effect an interception he should immediately place such vessels under the control of the Commander-in-Chief, Plymouth. In the case of coastal craft being detached from the close escort they are to be set W/T watch in accordance with D.C.O. 15, para. 14(b), and thereafter may be controlled by the Kingswear shore control station to intercept and attack.

Appendix 3

Slapton Battle Area Map

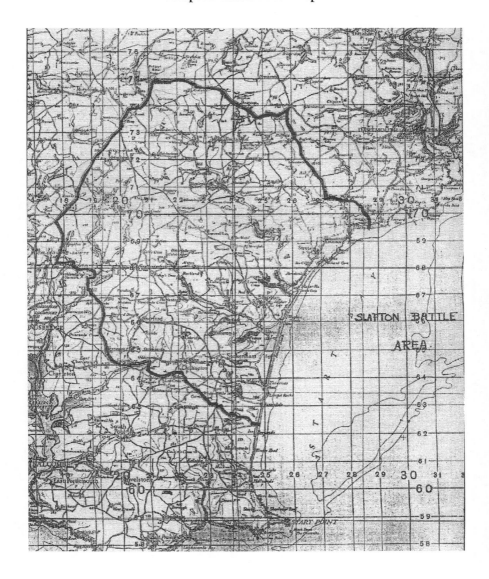

Appendix 4

> SECRET
> Auth: CG, First US Army
> Date: 21 Mar 44
> Initials

HEADQUARTERS
FIRST UNITED STATES ARMY
APO 230
Register No PG-1503

Copy **No. 14** of 26 copies.
353 [C]   21 March 1944

SUBJECT: Amphibious Exercise TIGER

TO: Commanding General, VII Corps

1. Information.
In preparation for forthcoming operations, Force "U" will conduct an amphibious training exercise during the period 26 – 30 April 1944. The exercise will be known as TIGER and will be held on the SLAPTON SANDS Training Area.

2. Purpose.
The purpose of Exercise TIGER is to conduct a rehearsal of Force "U", Operation Overlord, in which actual plans, formations and conditions are adhered to as closely as limitations of equjpment and maintenance will permit. Emphasis is to be placed on the establishment and maintenance of communication between all supported and supporting forces. Camouflage discipline will be stressed in the concentration areas and during the exercise proper.

3. Scope.
The exercise will be conducted to include the following operations:

a. Accomplishment of all pertinent instructions contained in Section, "Preparation for Movement" of ETO-POM-SSV dated 10 January 1944 (corrected).
b. Processing of all participating troops through concentration and marshalling areas.
c. Embarkation at proper scales.
d. Movement overseas under control of US Navy.
e. Execution of prearranged Naval Fire Support Plan and Air Support Plan.
f. Debarkation and assault of SLAPTON SANDS beaches.

(3) **Phase III** – Operations during this phase will include consolidation and extension of the beach head line, concentration of forces involved in preparation for return movement to home stations or marshalling areas as ordered by T/C, SOS.
(4) **Phase IV** – Completion of unloading and continuation of operation of beach maintenance area.
    b. **Phase I.** Operations during Phase I will be conducted under the supervision of the SOS.

(1) **Preparation for movement.**
(a) Movement to the concentration area will be governed by movement instructions to be issued by the Transportation Corps, SOS, based on VII Corps Plan
(b) Prior to departure from home stations all units will comply with par. 107, POM-ETO-SSV, dated 10 January 1944 (revised).

(2) **Concentration and Embarkation.**
(a) Concentration will take place in the Dartmouth, Plymouth East Area. Embarkation will be out of Dartmou,th, Brixham, Torquay and Plymouth East.
(b) Details for the concentration and embarkation of Forces "U" will be determined by the SOS in conjunction with the CG, VII Corps and appropriate US Naval and British authorities.

© Unit overstrength and residual personne1 will be handled in accordance with paras. 70, 71, and 73, ETO-POM-SSV.

Phase II.

(1) CG, VII Corps will prepare and submit to this headquarters by 7 April 1944, a tactical exercise on SLAPTON SANDS Training Area for Phase II. This exercise will approximate the Force "U" assault plan for Operation OVERLORD as closely as the area will permit and will include participation by elements of the 101st A/B Division. In the event it is considered impractical to drop these elements they will be moved into position by motor. Position areas selected should be on the western edge of the Slapton sands AREA OUT OF THE impact area.

(2) Emphasis will be placed on the establishment, maintenance and testing of all means and channels of communication.

(3) Service ammunition will be fired.

(4)

Appendix 5

VII Corps

4th Inf Div:
1-7 Arty Firing by Div Arty — Merrivale Range
1-10 Arty Firing — Exmoor Range
6-7 Arty Firing — Okehampton Range
8-10 Combined Inf-Arty Exercise with Corps Arty. Okehampton and Merrivale Ranges

9th Inf Div:
9-11 Exercise "Agua Caliente" with Corps Arty — Imber & Westdown Ranges
4-8 Combined Inf-Arty Firing — Imber & Westdown Ranges
20-22 Infantry Combat Firing — Slapton Sands

Corps Troops:

4th Cav Group:
15-18 AFV Firing — Q-5130
20-23 AFV and Anti-tank Firing — Q-9416

188th FA Group:
13-14 Arty Firing — Q-9024
19-20 Arty Firing — Q-9024

1st TD Group:
17-30 Anti-tank Firing — R-4835
27-30 AFV Firing — Kimmeridge Range

Corps Arty:
9-11 Exercise "Agua Caliente" — Imber & Westdown Ranges

Corps Exercise:
26-29 Exercise "Tiger" — Slapton Sands

XIX Corps

2nd Armd Div:
6-12 AFV Firing — Castle Martin Range
13-19 AFV Firing — Castle Martin Range
20-21 Arty Problems — 'L6876
22-24 AFV Firing — Minehead Range
24-30 Experts Test for 60 & 81mm Mortars — Beaches Barn Range
24 OC Firing Problems — Imber Range
25-30 AFV Firing — Minehead Range
27-30 Arty Firing with Corps Arty — Imber & Westdown Ranges

3rd Armd Div:
4-6 Division Field Exercise — U-3258
13-19 Combined Inf-Armd Tng with 30th Inf Div — U-3258
17-21 AFV Firing — Minehead Range
21-22 Arty Firing — Imber Range
24-27 Arty Firing with Corps Arty — Imber & Westdown Ranges
25-30 Combined Inf-Armd Exercises with 30th Inf Div — U-3258
Imber Range

Appendix 6

WAR DIARY

Commander Group TWO, Eleventh Amphibious Force

April, 1944

1

Commander Task Force 122's operation plan 1-44 became effective at 0000, 1 April 1944.

LST 531 arrived in Plymouth, bringing 10 enlisted men and substantial supplies from Norfolk, Va.

7th Corps, USA, conducted Army's critique on Exercise BEAVER at Exeter, the discussion lasting throughout the morning and early afternoon. Com Group TWO, accompanied by Lt. Col. Greear and Major Meese, attended.

2

An all-day critique on Beaver was held at Hamoaze conducted by Capt. Moran. It was attended by Commander 11th Amphibious Force (Rear Admiral J.L.Hall, Jr.), Major General J. Lawton Collins of the 7th Corps, and most of the staff officers and unit commanders of Group TWO.

3

Admiral Moon and Capt. Moran outlined plans for the next exercise, TIGER, to senior members of the staff.

4

Com Group TWO, Capt. Moran, Lt. Col Greear, Major Meese, and Lieut. Gorcyzk attended a conference at Paignton with the 7th Corps Maneuvers Directors Group. Col. Young discussed gunfire, targets, objectives, and safety precautions. It was agreed that the plan for Exercise TIGER, to be held 27 April, should be completed and distributed by 18 April. Comdr. Lowe (MC) went to Bristol for a conference with medical officers of the First Army, 7th Corps, 4th Division, and 1st Engineers Shore Battalion.

5

A staff planning conference was held on TIGER. Those present were Capt. Tompkins, chief of staff, Capt. Moran (operations), Lt. Colonel Greear (Army liaison), Comdr. Lowe (medical), Comdr. Moreno, (air), Lt. Comdr. Thayer, (intelligence), Lt. Comdr. Staudt (logistics), Lt. Comdr. Braue, (communications), Lt. Comdr. Jahncke (movement), Major King, (Assault), Major Meese (loading and demolitions), Lieut. Wheatley (supply), Lieut. Hamilton, flag secretary, and Lt. (jg) Lee, flag lieutenant.

6

Another planning conference on TIGER, with special reference to the Far Shore Service. Capt. Percifield and Capt. Arnold, who is to be NOIC for Group TWO's beach attended.

At 1145 Rear Admiral Hall came aboard to call on Admiral Moon.

7

Admiral Moon, accompanied by Capt. Moran departed from Plymouth at 1230 and arrived at London at 1730. They stayed at Dorchester House.

The Chief of Staff held a planning conference on TIGER.

8

Admiral Moon conferred with Commander Task Force 122 (Rear Admiral Kirk) and the Naval Commander Allied Expeditionary Forces, Admiral Bertram Ramsay, RN.

9

Admiral Moon and Capt. Moran flew back to Plymouth, leaving Hendon Field at 1648 and arriving at Harrow Beer Field, Plymouth, at 1735.

10

Air raid alert from 0155 to 0235. No damage or casualties. Sir David Petrie, in charge of security for United Kingdom, conferred with Com Group TWO, while the latter was calling on Admiral Hall aboard ANCON.

11

Comdr. Lowe (MC), attended Exercise SPLINT, a medical demonstration of handling casualties by LST's, at Fowey.

A combined operations meeting was held at the headquarters of commander in Chief Plymouth (Admiral Leatham, RN).

12
A letter from Commander Task Force 123 (Commander 11th Amphibious Force) to all holders of Com TF 123's operation plan B-44 (revised 20 March 1944) discusses operation plan B-44 in the light in the light of Commander Task Force 122's Operation Plan 1-44 effective 1 April 1944. It states in part: "Operating Forces U (Group 2, 11th Phib —-TF125) and B (Transports, 11th Phib. - TF 126), as such, are directly under the command of Commander Task Force 122. Administrative command of units of these forces which are listed in the Task Organization of my Operation Plan B-44 is exercised as therein indicated. The Force Commander (Commander 11th Amphibious Force) does not desire to restrict or to interfere in any way with the exercise of operational command, including training and active preparations for active operations, by the Commanders of Forces U and B. Commanders of ships and of units of the 11th Amphibious Force herein assigned to Forces U and B may expect instructions directly from their Operating Force Commanders, but in the absence of any special instructions will continue their intensive training and preparation for amphibious operations under existing directives of the Commander 11th Amphibious Force and the Commander Landing Craft and Bases."

Capt. Glover, of the staff of the Commander in Chief United States Fleet, had luncheon with Admiral Moon.

13
Lt. Comdr. Braue, Communications Officer, proceeded to London for conference with staffs of TF 122 and ComNavEu.

Demolition exercises were conducted at Pentewan at 1430 by demolition units of 2nd Beach Battalion under the supervision of Lt. R.C. Smith, USNR. Admiral Moon, Major General Collins and members of their staffs attended.

14
Planning for Exercise TIGER continued.

15
Admiral Moon went aboard ANCON at 1000 for a conference with Commander 11th Amphibious Force (Rear Admiral Hall).

Lieut. John M. Schiff, D-V(S), reported for duty.

16

Work on TIGER plans continued.

17

Admiral Moon attended a combined operations meeting at CinC, PlyWouth, headquarters.

18

Planning conference as usual at 0900.

TIGER Operation Order was issued on the date contemplated.

19

Staff intelligence officers began briefing of small craft officers for TIGER.

Restudy of operation order resulted in the discovery of some errors and contradictions which had to be corrected by amendment.

20

Staff was engaged in making fipal revisions on TIGER plan.

21

7th Corps conference on Exercise TIGER was held at 0900 in Royal Marine Barracks, Plymouth. Admiral Moon, Major General Collins, and Major General Barton attended.

Lieut. Thomas J. Hughes, I-V(S), Lt. (jg) Harold X McGowan, I-V(S), and Lt. (jg) Richard B. Tucker, I-(S), reported for duty.

22

The 7th Corps' briefing of unit commanders was held at South Brent. It was conducted by Major General R.O. Barton, commanding general of the 4th Infantry Division. Lt. Col. Greear represented Com Group TWO.

Commodore Caslon, chief of staff of CINC Plymouth, and Capt. Gandell, deputy chief of staff, had lunch with Com Group TWO.

23 (Sunday)

Dry-run for Force briefing conference was held in the afternoon. Annex F (movement of ships and craft from hards to beach) finally was completed. Com Group T_ conferred with Brigadier General Quesada, commanding general of the 9th Air Support Command.

24

Briefing conference on TIGER was held at the Royal Marine Barracks Theatre, Plymouth, and lasted throughout the morning and most of the afternoon. Capt. Moran conducted the explanation and discussion. Rear Admiral Moon, Rear Admiral Hall, Major General Collins, Major General Barton and many Army and Navy staff officers participated.

25

During the morning officers and men of his staff began arriving on board BAYFIEI in preparation for Exercise TIGER (D-day, 27 April: H-hour, 0730). At 1430 BAYFIELD' boats commenced embarking troops, vehicles and supplies. At 1900 Com Group TWO came
aboard and his flag was flown as Commander, Operating Force "U". Western Naval Task Force, Allied Expeditionary Force.

Operating Order No. 2-44 of this command (Task Force 125), dated 18 April 1944, Plymouth, Devon, SECRET-TIGER, file no. 2GIIPhib/A4-3, Serial: 0075, provided that "this force will firmly establish 7th Corps in position north of Start Point in order (1) to ensure the capture of Okehampton with minimum delay, and (2) to assist in securing a lodgement area as a base for further operations leading to capture of the Devonshire southern coast ports.

The order stated further: "Attack by enemy aircraft, submarines, and E-boats may be expected en route to and in exercise area. Friendly aircraft will fly over exercise area in operational flights. Units from 101st Airborne Division will participate by simulating landing west of Slapton Sands Range area at about H-4 hours ... The 9th Air Force Support Command will provide direct air support ... The covering force consists of the Tribal destroyers HMS HAIDA, HMS HURON, HMS ASHANTI, HMS ATHABASKAN, and coastal forces of Plymouth Command ... This operation plan effective 0800, 24 April, 1944 ... Com TF 125 in BAYFIELD. Second in Command Capt. Richardson in LCH-95. Commanding Generals 7th Corps, 4th Infantry Division in BAYFIELD".

This was the first major exercise in which the searched channels were purposely extended and complicated in order better to simulate operational conflicts, and in which several "build-up" convoys were scheduled to follow the assault phase.

Lt. (jg) Milton E. Mermelsteinm C-V(S), reported for duty.

26
In Plymouth there was an air raid alert at 0821, followed by the all clear at 0839.

Appendix 7

S E C R E T

Adv Hq VII Corps
DEVONPORT 8876, ENGLAND
15 Apr 44

FO 1

Maps: GSGS No. 3907, 1/63,360, Sheets 137, 138, 144, 145.
      Overlay.

1.   a.   Int Annex..

     b.   (1)   Group 2, 11th Amphibious Force Navy, provides lift, protection at sea, and support.

          (2)   Ninth Air Force supports operation. (ADGB through C-in-C PLYMOUTH provides air cover during Exercise TIGER).

2.   a.   VII Corps attacks SLAPTON SANDS and captures OKEHAMPTON 0216 with minimum delay.(See Annex No.1 - Operations Overlay).

3.   a.   lOlst A/B Div (herein designated 1st TD Gp) (-): Arrives east of KINGSBRIDGE 1665 beginning approximately H-5 hour, D-day, with principal mission of assisting landing of 4*th* Div by seizing high ground west of beach. Seizes for our use road-center MOUNTS 1870, crossings of R. AVON at NEW BR. 1469 and south of AVETON GIFFORD 1269 and seizes the exits of SALCOMBE 1660 and HOPE 1061 along the general line: MARLBOROUGH 1361 - GALMPTON ll62 so as to protect the south flank of the VII Corps. After elements are relieved in zone of 4th Div, seizes the road centers at ST ANN's CHAPEL 0969 and contacts the 142nd FA Gp at SEQUERS BR 0673. Thereafter, protects Corps south flank between START POINT 2558 and ERME RIVER.

b. 4th Inf Div:
    (1) Lands and attacks SLAPTON SANDS H-hour, D-day; seizes D-day objective by dark D-day. Relieves 1st TD Gp elements in 4th Div zone as soon as practicable. Continues attack to seize the Corps Inter- mediate Objective preparatory to advance on OKEHAMPTON 0216.

    (2) Co F, 24th Cav Sq reconnoiters 142d FA Gp Operations Zone, blocks LEE MILL BR and YEALMBRIDGE on YEALM R until relieved by 142d FA Gp; pushes reconnaissance to PLYM R. RCT 359 90th Inf Div attached upon landing D+1 day for operations east of R. DART.

    (2) The 4th Div will be prepared to advance and seize OKEHAMPTON without delaying on intermediate objectives, if the tactical situation permits.

c. 82d A/B Div (herein designated 142d FA Gp) (-): Arrives (simulated) west of ERMINGTON before dawn D+l day. Prevents enemy reinforcements advancing east of YEALM RIVER. Blocks crossings YEALM R. between CORNWOOD 0381 and YEALMPTON 0073, inclusive. Protects Corps south flank west of the ERME RIVER.

d. 90th Inf Div (-): Lands (simulated) D+l and D+2 on, SLAPTON SANDS, advances north on right of 4th Div, Assists 4th Div to seize OKEHAMPTON. Resumes command of RTC 359 when established ashore.

e. 1st Engr Spec Brig: Supports assault landing VII Corps, organizes and operates all shore installations necessary for debarkation, supply, evacuation, and local security in order to ensure expeditious movement across beaches.

f. Composite Force: Consisting of;
        87th Armd FA Bn
        Tr B, 4th Cav Sq
        Co C, 746th Tk Bn
        3809th QM Trk Co
    prepares to move afternoon Dtl day to reinforce 142d FA Gp.

g.   11th AAA Gp: Protects beach, beach exits, and beach maintenance area SLAPTON SANDS area; and airfield and air strips in VII Corps zone.

x.   (1) Safety Orders for Exercise TIGER issued by Director Headquarters govern firing of live ammunition and explosives.

4.   Adm O 1.

5.   a.   (1) Sig Annex and current VII Corps SOl amended by special exercise items.

(2) Radio silence: Sig Annex.

(3) See Annex No. 11 - Special Secrecy Instructions. No message will indicate in anyway the presence or designation of airborne units.

b.   (1) CP's: VII Corps afloat: USS BAYFIELD.
VII Corps ashore: SHEPLEGH COURT 237l.
4th Div: Vicinity MERRIFIELD 2468.
1st TD Gp: To be reported.
142d FA Gp: To be reported.
90th Div: GALMPTON 3177.

(2) Ax Sig Com:

VII Corps:	USS BAYFIELD - SHEPLEGH COURT 2371 – BORESTON 1975 – DIPTFORD – 1578 – BUCKFASTLEIGH 1687.
4th Inf Div:	USS BAYFIELD – MERRIFIELD 2468 – HALWELL 2074 — DIPTFORD 1578 — BUCKFASTLEIGH 1687.
90th Inf Div:	GALMPTON 3177 – MARLDON 2985 – NEWTON ABBOT 2993.

COLLINS
CG

Annexes:

No. 1 -   0pns Overlay .

No. 2 -   Troop List.

No. 3 –   Intelligence Plan.

No. 4 -   Loading Tables (separately issued).

No. 5 -   Artillery and Naval Fire Support Plan separately issued).

No. 6 –   Air Support Plan (separately issued).

No. 7 -   AAA Defense Plan.

No. 8 -   Engineer Operations Plan.

No. 9 -   Signal Communications Plan.

No.10 -   Civil Affairs Plan.

No.11 -   Special Secrecy Instructions.

DISTRIBUTION: "Special"

Appendix 8

Army LST Landing Table

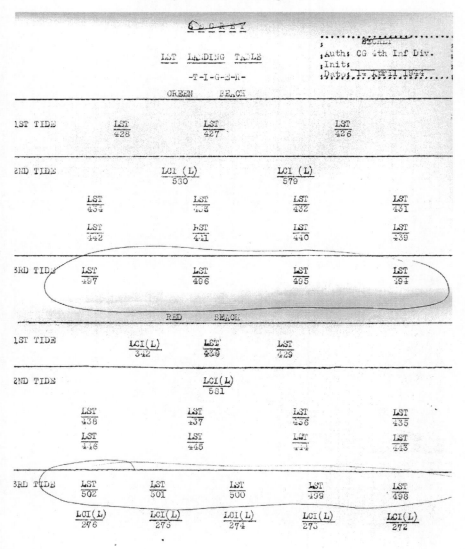

LST LANDING TABLE

-T-I-G-E-R-

GREEN BEACH

1ST TIDE	$\frac{LST}{428}$	$\frac{LST}{427}$		$\frac{LST}{426}$
2ND TIDE		$\frac{LCI\ (L)}{530}$	$\frac{LCI\ (L)}{579}$	
	$\frac{LST}{434}$	$\frac{LST}{433}$	$\frac{LST}{432}$	$\frac{LST}{431}$
	$\frac{LST}{442}$	$\frac{LST}{441}$	$\frac{LST}{440}$	$\frac{LST}{439}$
3RD TIDE	$\frac{LST}{497}$	$\frac{LST}{496}$	$\frac{LST}{495}$	$\frac{LST}{494}$

RED BEACH

1ST TIDE	$\frac{LCI(L)}{342}$	$\frac{LST}{430}$	$\frac{LST}{429}$		
2ND TIDE		$\frac{LCI(L)}{581}$			
	$\frac{LST}{438}$	$\frac{LST}{437}$	$\frac{LST}{436}$	$\frac{LST}{435}$	
	$\frac{LST}{446}$	$\frac{LST}{445}$	$\frac{LST}{444}$	$\frac{LST}{443}$	
3RD TIDE	$\frac{LST}{502}$	$\frac{LST}{501}$	$\frac{LST}{500}$	$\frac{LST}{499}$	$\frac{LST}{498}$
	$\frac{LCI(L)}{276}$	$\frac{LCI(L)}{275}$	$\frac{LCI(L)}{274}$	$\frac{LCI(L)}{273}$	$\frac{LCI(L)}{272}$

Appendix 9

SHAEF/23036/8/Trg   19 April 1944.

Subject: Exercise Tiger.

To:

    1. Exercise TIGER will involve the concentration, marshalling and embarkation of troops in the TOR BAY – PLYMOUTH area, and a short movement by sea under the control of the U.S. Navy, disembarkation with Naval and Air support at SLAPTON SANDS, a beach assault using service ammunition, the securing of a beachhead and a rapid advance inland.

    2. Major troop units are the VII Corps Troops, 4th Infantry Division, the 101st and 82nd Airborne Divisions, 1st Engineer Special brigade, Force "U" and supporting Air Force units.

    3. During the period H-60 to H-45 minutes, fighter-bombers attack inland targets on call from the 101st AB Div and medium bombers attack three targets along the beach. Additional targets will be bombed by both fighter-bombers and medium bombers on call from ground units. Simulated missions will also be flown with the target areas marked by smoke pots.

    4. Naval vessels fire upon beach obstacles from H-50 to H-hour. Smoke may be used during the latter part of the naval bombardment both from naval craft by 4.2" chemical mortars and at H-hour by planes, if weather conditions are favourable. Naval fire ceases at H-hour.

    5. The schedule of the exercise is as follows:

        22 April   Move to marshalling area commences.

    D-Day 27 April   101st AB Div simulates landing. Preparatory bombardment by air and navy. Assault landing and advance of 4th Div.

        28-29 April   Advance of 4th Div & 101st AB Div continues. 82nd AB Div simulates landing, secures and holds objective.

        (Exercise terminates on 29 April)

    6. Joining instructions will be issued later.

                        W. R. PIERCE,
                        Colonel, G.S.C.,,
        TOP SECRET   Chief, Training, Sub-Section.

9

Appendix 10

ANNEX NO.2 to FIELD ORDER NO. 1, VII Corps

TROOP LIST

4th 1nf Div

4th Inf Hq
* Various Special G-Z Teams
*2 Air Support Parties
*9 Shore Fire Control Parties
4th Med Bn
4th Engr C Bn
4th QM Co
4th Sig Co
4th Rcn Trp M
4th Div Arty Hq & Hq Btry
8th Inf Regt
12th Inf Regt
22nd Inf Regt
20th FA Bn
29th FA Bn
42nd FA Bn
44th FA Bn
704th Ord LM Co
*165th Signal Photo Co, Det "G"
*65th Armd FA Bn
*70th Tank Bn
*746th Tank Bn
*Btry "B", 980th FA Bn
*2nd Platoon, 603rd QM GR Co

*13th FA Obsn Bn
*1106th Engr Gp
    *49th Engr C Bn
    *237th Engr C Bn
    *238th Engr C Bn
    *612th Engr L Equip Co
    *50lst Engr L Pont Co
    *991st Engr Trdwy Br Co
    *582nd Engr Dump Trk Co
*Co "F", 24th Cav Sq
*87th Cml Bn (Mtz)
*2nd Plat, 3891st QM Trk Co
*87th Armd FA Bn (To be atohd to 142nd FA Gp later)

90th Inf Div
    359th RCT (Regt & 4 Bn CPs)

142nd FA Gp (CP only)
*87th Armd FA Bn (To be attaohed to 4th Inf Div initia1ly)
*Co "A", 294th Engr C Bn   )
*Co "C", 746th Tank Bn   )   To be attached upon landing
*Tr "B", 4th Cav Sq.   )

1st TD Gp and included elements
    *3807th QM Trk Co

1st Engr SP Brig
    Hq & Hq Co, 1st Engr Sp Brig
        *Det "E", 165th Sig Photo Co
    531st Engr Sh Regt
    *2nd Naval Beavh Bn
    *lst Plat, 440th Engr Depot Co
*1605th Engr Map Sec
*Det, 8th Air Force Intransit Depot Gp
261st Med Bn
*6 Teams, 3rd Aux Surg Gp

Hq & Hq Det, 191st Ord Bn (w/atchd Med)
                3497th Ord MAM Co (Det "A", "B", "C")
                625th.Ord Am Co

        *23rd Ord Bomb disp Sqd
        33rd Cml Decon Co
Hq & Hq Det, 306th QM Bn
        3206th QM Sv Co
        3207th QM Sv Co
        4144th QM Sv Co
        *1st Plat, 607th QM GR Co
Hq & Hq Det, 306th QM Bn
        556th QM RHD Co
        557th QM RHD Co
        3939th QM Gas Supply Co
286th Joint Assault Sig Co
    *Det, 980th Sig Sv Co AGR
*Det, 175th Sig Repair Co
*Det, 215th Sig Depot Co
449th MP Co
Hq & Hq Det, 24th Amph Trk Bn
    462nd Amph Trk Co
    478th Amph Trk Co
    479th Amph Trk Co
*490th TC Port Bn (Hq Det)
    *227th TC Port Co
*Navy Underwater Demolition Teams

VII Corps Troops
Hq & Hq Co, VII Corps
        Hq & Hq Btry, VII Corps Artillery
        MP Platoon, VII Corps
        Co "B", 507th MP Bn
        1st Plat, 506th QM Car Co
        *VII Corps Special G-2 Teams
        *VII Corps Air Support Team
        *385th QM Trk Co
        109th AAA Gp
        *Det "B", 165th Sig Photo Co
*1120th Engr Gp, Hq & Hq Co
50th Sig Bn
        *Det, 35th Sig Construction Bn
        *175th Sig Repair Co

*11th AAA Gp
        *474th AAA AW Bn (SP)
        *116th AAA Gun Bn (M)
        *535th AAA AW Bn (M)
        *Btries "D", "E", "F", 1st TD Gp
        *Ntry "C", 320th AAA Bln Bn

Air Force Elements
    Co "A", 819th Avn Engr Bn
    47th Ord Bomb Disp Sqd
    2062nd Engr FF Platoon
    187th Avn Med Disp

*Indicates attached units.

OFFICIAL:

                                    COLLINS

Appendix 11

SECRET   **4th INFANTRY DIVISION**
ANNEX No 3   **LANDING DIAGRAM**
To FO No 1   **TIGER**

Wave No.	Time	No and Type of Craft	Unit	Uncle Red Beach											
0	H-40	11 LCVP	NAVY DEMOLITION		V 11	V 10		V 9		V 8		V 7		V 6	
0	H-3	8 LCT(6)s	Co B 70 Tk Bn			T6s 158		T6s 157			T6s 156		T6s 155		
1	H	20 LCVP	2 Bn 8 Inf		V 31	V 30	V 29	V 28	V 27	V 26	V 25	V 24	V 23	V 22	
2	H+7	10 LCVP	2 Bn 8 Inf			V 41	V 40		V 39		V 36		V 37		
3	H+15	8 LCT(5a)	70 Tk Bn			T5A 166		T5A 165			T5A 164		T5A 163		
4	H+25	14 LCVP	2 Bn 8 Inf & Co C 237 Engrs		V 55	V 54	V 53		V 52		V 51	V 50	V 49		
5	H+40	16 LCVP	2 Bn 8 Inf & Co C 237 Engrs		V 71	V 70	V 69			V 68	V 67	V 66	V 65	V Free Boat 64	
6	H+50	16 LCVP	Co G 87			V 87	V 86	V 85	V 84	V 83	V 82	V 81	V 80		
7	H+60	12 LCVP	1 ESB		V 99	V 98	V 97	V 96	V 95	V 94	26 persons 1106 Rcn GR				
8	H+75	20 LCVP	3 Bn 8 Inf		V* 119	V* 118	V* 117	V* 116	V* 115	V* 114	V* 113	V* 112	V* 111	V* 110	
9	H+85	24 LCVP	3 Bn 8 Inf	V* 143	V* 142	V* 141	V* 140	V* 139	V* 138	V* 137	V* 136	V* 135	V* 134	V* 133	V* 132
10	H+95	8 LCT (4) 12 LCT (3) 2 LCT (6) Total 18 LCT	65th F A Bn		T5* 181	T5* 180	T5 179	T5 178	T5 177	T5 176	T5 175	T5 174			
11	H+115	1 LCT (6) 14 LCVP	237 Eng Bn 1 Bn 8 Inf	T6 Free boat 182	V* 157	V* 156	V* 155		V* 154	V* 153	V* 152	V* 151			V* Free boat 150
12	H+125	16 LCVP	Co G 87			V* 173	V* 172	V* 171	V* 170	V* 169	V* 168	V* 167	V* 166		
13	H+135	7 LCVP													
14	H+135	10 LCT	531st ESR(A) 204 MP Co 81 Eng Av Bn 43 Engr Co		T6* 156		T6* 155		T6* 184		T6* 158			T6* 157	

Appendix 12

S E C R E T
BOAT ASSIGNMENT TABLE

LST Craft Serial Number	TROOP UNITS	No. of Personnel	Total Vehicles and Types
426 LST 282	Co "A" 4th Engr Combat Bn Hq Co	96 119 215	6 - 1/4T, 2 Air compressors 1 - Angledozer, 7 - 2 1/2T Dump, 1 - 4T Cargo, 1 - 1 1/2T, 5 - 3/4T W/C, 6 - 2 1/2T (LWB) 1 - 4T Wkr,1 - Tlr, welding 6 - 1T Tlr, 1 - Tlr pole type
427 LST 281	Co "B" 4th Engr Combat Bn	54	2 - 1/4T, 1 - 2 1/2T Air compressor 1 - R-4 Angledozer, 8 – 2 1/2T Dump
428 LST 230	Co "C" 4th Engr Combat Bn	54	8 - 2 1/2T Dump,2 - 1/4T 4x4 1 - 2 1/2T Air Comp,1 – R4 Angle-dozer
429 LST 47	Hq Btry 13th FA Obsn Bn (F&S) Serv Btry 44th FA Bn	77 2 79	4 - 1/4T, 7 - 3/4T, 3 – 2 1/2T
430 LST 48	Btry "B" 13th FA Obsn Bn (F&S) Med Det 13th ...... 4th Div Hq Co Serv Btry 29th FA Bn Serv Btry 42nd FA Bn	95 17 6 4 4 126	3 - 1/4T, 7 - 3/4T W/C 1 - 3/4T C/R, 4 - 2 1/2T 6 - DUKW, 2 - 21/2T LWB
431 LST 46	Co "A" 22nd Infantry Co "B" .. .. Co "C" .. .. Co "D" .. .. Co "E" .. .. Co "F" .. .. Co "G" .. .. Co "H" .. .. Co "I" .. .. Co "K" .. .. Co "L" .. .. Co "M" .. .. Hq Co 1st Bn 22nd Inf Hq Co 2nd Bn .. .. Hq Co 3rd Bn .. .. Hq Co 22nd Inf Serv Co	2 2 2 8 2 2 2 8 2 2 2 8 12 12 12 67 56	7 - 2 1/2T 7 - 3/4T 59 - 1/4T 24 - 1/4T Tlr 4 - 2 1/2T

	Cannon Co 22nd Inf	42			
	AT Co 22nd Inf	38			
	Serv Btry 44th FA Bn	16			
	Btry "A"	25			
	Btry "B"	25			
	Btry "C"	25			
	Hq Btry	25			
		397			
432	Co "C" 4th Engr Combat Bn	65	3 - 1/4T, 1 - 3/4T C/R		
LST 400	Hq Det & Co "C" 4th Med Bn	50	1 - 2 1/2T Dump,		
		116	2 - 2 1/2T		
			2 - 2 1/2T Tlr pole type,		
			1 - 1T Tlr		
			1 - 4T Cargo,		
			2 - 3/4 T W/C 5 – 3/4T Amb.		
433	Co "A" 12th Infantry	2	69 - 1/4T		26
LST 54	Co "B"	2	- 1/4T Tlr		10
	Co "C"	2	- 3/4T		7 –
	Co "D"	8	2 1/2T		
	Co "E"	2			
	Co "F"	2			
	Co "G"	2			
	Co "H"	8			
	Co "I"	2			
	Co "K"	2			
	Co "L"	2			
	Co "M"	8			
	Hq Co 1st Bn 12th Inf	12			
	.. .. 2nd	12			
	.. .. 3rd	12			
	Hq Co 12th Inf	67			
	Serv Co	56			
	Cannon Co 12th Inf	42			
	AT Co 12th Inf	38			
	Serv Btry 42nd FA Bn	16			
	Btry "A"	25			
	Btry "B"	25			
	Btry "C"	25			
	Hq Btry	26			
		391			
434	Co "B" 4th Engr Combat Bn	110	1 - 2 1/2T Dump		
LST 501	Co "B" & Hq Det 4th Med Bn	50	2 - 2 1/2T 6x6		
	Co "D" 12th Inf	3	2 - 2 1/2T Pole Tlr		
	Co "H" 12th Inf	2	1 - 4T Cargo		
	Co "M" 12th Inf	2	1 - 1T Tlr		
		167	10 - 1/4T 4x4		
Army 434 = LST 231 on LST plan			1 - 3/4T C&R		
LST 501 = Army 427 on LST plan			2 - 3/4T 4x4		
			5 - 3/4T Amb		
			7 - 1/4T Tlr		

LST Craft Serial Number	TROOP UNITS	No. of Personnel	Total Vehicles and Types
435 LST 311	Co "A" 4th Engr Combat Bn Co "A" & "D" 4th Med Bn	68 50 118	1 - 2 1/2T Dump 2 - 2 1/2T 6x6 1 - 3/4T C&R 2 - 2 1/2T Tlr Pole 3 - 1/4T 4x4 2 - 1T Tlr 5 - 3/4T Amb 2 - 3/4T W/C
436 LST 371	Co "A" 8th Infantry Co "B" .. .. Co "C" .. .. Co "D" .. .. Co "E" .. .. Co "F" .. .. Co "G" .. .. Co "H" .. .. Co "I" .. .. Co "K" .. .. Co "L" .. .. Co "M" .. .. Hq Co 1st Bn 8th Inf Hq Co 8th Inf Serv Co 8th Inf Cannon Co 8th Inf AT Co 8th Inf Serv Btry 29th FA Bn Battery "A" 29th FA Bn .. "B" .. .. .. "C" .. .. Hq Btry 29th FA Bn	1 1 1 5 1 1 1 5 1 1 1 5 5 12 8 8 4 16 25 25 25 21 180	59 - 1/4T 4x4 24 - 1/4T Tlr 4 - 3/4T 4x4 12 - 2 1/2T 6x6 3 - 3/4T W/C
437 LST 380	Hq Btry 20th FA Bn Btry "A" .. .. .. Btry "B" .. .. .. Serv Btry 20th FA Bn	65 101 101 37 304	9 - 1/4T 4x4 10 - 3/4T 4x4 11 - 2 1/2T 6x6 11 - 4T 8 - 155mm How 6 - M-10 Tlr 1 - 1T Tlr
438 LST 382	Hq Btry 20th FA Bn Btry "C" 20th FA Bn Serv Btry 20th FA Bn Co "F" 24th Rcn Sq (Cav)	58 101 35 6 200	8 - 1/4T 4x4 8 - 3/4T 4x4 8 - 2 1/2T 6x6 5 - 4T 4 - 155mm How 2 - M-10 Tlr 0 - 1T Tlr 1 - AT M2

439 LST 491	Missing on sheet		
440 LST 491	Co "C" 70th Tank Bn	30	6 - Tanks M-4
441 LST 50	Co "D" 4th ?? Bn Serv Co 70th Tank Bn	140 88 228	17 - 2 1/2T 6x6 1 - 10T Wkr 4 - M-10Tlr 3 - HT M3 3 - HT M21 4 - 1/4T 4x4 3 - 3/4T 6x6 9 - 1T Tlr 2 - 250 gal. Water Tlr 2 - 1 1/2T
442 LST 492	4th Signal Co 4th MP Plat 4th QM Co 4th Div Hq Co (CIC Det) 44th FA Bn Div Arty Hq & Hq Btry 6th Armd Gp Hq & Hq Co	82 21 2 3 2 66 15 188	18 - 1/4T 4x4 12 - 3/4T 6 - 1 1/2T 11 - 2 1/2T 6x6 3 - T4 Med 4 - 1/4T Tlr 7 - 1T Tlr 1 - Airplane
443 LST 55	Fwd Ech Div Hq Div Arty Hq Liaison 4th QM Co 704th Ord L Maint Co Engr Shore Brigade Air Support Party 1106th Engr Group 70th Tank Bn 746th Tank Bn 65th Armd FA Bn 101st Airborne Div	236 3 3 2 2 8 3 3 3 3 2 268	40 - 1/4T 14 - 3/4T 4 - 1 1/2T 6 - 2 1/2T 3 - 1T Tlr 1 - 1/4T Tlr 1 - M8
444 LST 346	Hq Co 4th Inf Div 4th MP Platoon 4th Signal Company	36 50 15 101	1 - 1/4 T 6 - 1 1/2 T 4 - 2 1/2 T 5 - 1T Tlr 3 - 57mm 2 - 2 1/2T DUKW
445 LST 283	Serv Co 746th Tk Bn	163	4 - 1/4T 3 - HT M3 3 - HT M21 6 - 2 1/2T 4 - Ammo Tlr, 1 - Hvy Wkr

LST Craft Serial Number	TROOP UNITS	No. of Personnel	Total Vehicles and Types
494 LST 499	Co "M" 12th Inf Co "H" 12th Inf Co "D" 12th Inf Cannon Co 12th Inf	6 6 5 2 19	17 - 1/4T 2 - 2 1/2T 8 - 1/4 Tlr 2 - 1 T
495 LST 289	4th Medical Bn	60	
496 LST 507	**Missing on sheet**		
497	4th QM Co	40	51 - 1/4T
LST 508	Cannon Co 8th Inf Cannon Co 22nd Inf Co "D" 8th Inf Co "H" .. .. Co "L" .. .. Co "D" 22nd Inf Co "H" .. .. Co "M" .. .. Co "A" 8th Infantry Co "B" .. .. Co "C" .. .. Co "E" .. .. Co "F" .. .. Co "G" .. .. Co "I" .. .. Co "I" .. .. Co "K" .. .. Co "L" .. .. 1st Bn Hq Co 8th Inf 2nd Bn .. .. .. 3rd Bn .. .. .. Hq Co 8th Inf Serv Co 8th Inf AT Co 8th Inf	4 4 8 8 8 8 8 8 20 20 20 20 20 20 20 20 20 20 16 16 16 10 4 7 345	1 - 3/4T 13 - 2 1/2T 12 - 1T Tlr 30 - 1/4T Tlr
498 LST 515	4th QM Co Hq Btry 44th FA Bn	129 8 137	3 - 1/4T 4x4 1 - 3/4T 32 - 2 1/2T 32 - 1T Tlr
499 LST 496	704th Ord L Maint Co 4th QM Co 4th Rcn Tr Mecz Co "L" 746th Tank Bn Hq Btry 42nd FA Bn	143 8 14 72 14 251	6 - 1/4T 5 - 3/4T 18 - 2 1/2T 2 - 4T Wkr 1 - 10T Wkr 17 - 1T Tlr 18 - Tks M5 2 - 57mm

Appendix 13

BOAT ASSIGNMENT TABLES
A P A

Name of Ship	TROOP UNITS	Number of Personnel	Number and Type of Vehicles
USS DICKMAN	1st Bn 8th Infantry 29th FA battalion 237th Engr Combat Bn Co "A" 87th Chemical Battalion Shore Fire Control Party, 286th Signal Company	763 12 90 102 6 973	18 - 1/4 T 4x4
USS BARNETT	2nd Bn 8th Infantry 87th Chemical SFCP 286th Sig Co 29th FA Bn Co "C" 237th Engr Combat Bn	724 101 12 9 90 936	20 - 1/4 T 4x4 *Incorrect total*
USS BAYFIELD	3rd Bn 22nd Infantry 44th FA Bn Co "C" 4th Engr Combat Bn 87th Chemical Bn SFCP, 286th Sig Co	699 12 45 108 6 870	20 - 1/4 T 4x4
HMS EMPIRE GAUNTLET	3rd Bn 8th Infantry 29th FA Battalion 237th Engr Combat Bn 87th Chemical Bn	879 6 90 86 1061	None

SHIP SHEET

	CRAFT	NAVY		VEHICLES					PASS	ZONE 67		
SERIAL NO	NO.	CRAFT NO.	UNIT	PERS	NO.	TYPE	SY EC-2	ROUTE	TF	ADR	DEP	ARRIVE
	APA/DICKMAN		8th Inf, 1st Bn	763	2	1/4 Ton		Marching Units				
			29th F A Bn	12	0			route will be				
			Co C 237th Engr C Bn	93	0			provided by TC				
			87th Cml Bn	157	16	1/4 Ton		X Camp follow				
			Ship Fire Control Party	61	0			TC Signs				
			474th A M Bn	6	0			55 to 57 R on 57				
				152	18			to ECRP 68 L on				
			Details & Stragglers	5	8			TC to Hard 67				
T-4			MU/9	7	8		0915			0730	0809	C
T-5			MU/10	70	8		0730			0745	0824	C
T-6			MU/11	200	2		0745			0800	0839	C
			MU/12	20	0		0800					C
			MU/13	20	0		0825					C
			MU/14	200	0		0830					

SPEED: Average 10 MPH, Maximum 25 MPH.
DENSITY: 35 yds between vehicles during movement and halts.
CAMOUFLAGE: Camouflage measures will be taken during all halts exceeding two minutes.

Appendix 15

Series NO   07-1

Date of Movement 24th April 1944

UNIT SCHY

CONVOY NO.	CRAFT SERIAL NO.	NAVY CRAFT NO.	UNIT	PERS	VEHICLES			DEPART MA		ROUTE	PASS TP	RCRP 67	
					NO.	TYPE		SP	R3			ARR	DEP
●	APA BARNETT		2nd Bn 6th Inf	724	4	1/4 T	(Shiphay)						
			87th Chem Bn	101	16	1/4 T							
			Shore Fire Control	12	0								
			29th FA Bn	9	0								
			Co A 237th Engr C Bn	90	0								
			Co C 237th Engr C Bn	90	0								
			Hq 1106th Engr Gp	5	0								
			49th Engr C Bn	6	0								
			991st Engr Trdwy Br	1	0								
			81st A/B AA Bn	66	0								
			Co A 531 Engr S.R.	118	*0								
			3/4 Plat Co B Navy Beach Co.	53	*0			See next Page for details and breaks					
			Det 286th Sig Co	10	*0								
			1st Plat 33rd Chem Co	14	*0								
			1st Plat 449th MP Co	23	*0								
			Hq 1st Bn 531 Engr Sh Reg	19	*0								
●			Co C 531st Engr Sh Reg	41	*0			*Does not include total craft load but contains that portion of the total comprised of troops Engr Sp Brig.					
			D-6 Plat Co B 2nd Navy Beach	13	*0								
			Det 286th Sig Co.	10	*0								
				1403	20								

SPEED: Average 10 MPH, Maximum 25 MPH.
DENSITY: 35 yds between vehicles during movement and halts.
CAMOUFLAGE: Camouflage measures will be taken during all halts exceeding ten minutes.

S E C R E T

Appendix 16

EXERCISE "TIC

CRAFT SERIAL NO.	CRAFT NO.	UNIT	PERS	VEHICLES HO	TYPE	DEPART MA SF CO	ROUTE	PASS TP	RCRP JET DEP	ARRIVE HARI COMMENCE LC
67	Gauntlet	8th Inf 3rd Bn	879	0		(Shiphay)	Marching units			
		29th Fd Bn	6	0			route will be			
		237th Engr C Bn	90	0			provided by TC			
		87th Chem Bn	86	0			at Camp. Follow			
		81st A/B AA Bn	65	0			"E t" signs			
		Co A 237th Engr C Bn	45	0						
		Co C 237th Engr C Bn	45	0						
		Plat, 3207 QM Co (SV)	100	0						
			1316							
		Details and Breakdown is follows:								
		MU/15	240			0915				101
		MU/16	240			0930				103
		MU/17	240			0945				104
		MU/18	240			1000				110
		MU/19	240			1015				111
		MU/20	116			1030				113

SPEED: Average 10 MPH, Maximum 25 MPH.
DENSITY: 35 yds between vehicles during movement and halts.
CAMOUFLAGE: Camouflage measures will be taken during all halts exceeding ten minutes.

196

Appendix 17

SECRET

ROAD OR RAIL MOVEMENT TABLE

Date of Movement 23 Apr 1944

CRAFT NO	CONVOY NO	UNIT NAME	STRENGTH		HOME STA	FUP		HOME STA	PASS EXETER RJ353107	PASS TP306
			PERS	VEH		ARRIVE	DEPART			
APA HMS EMPIRE GAUNTLET	SH-1	3rd Bn 8th Inf 29th F A Bn 1 Plat Co C 237th Engr Bn 1 Plat Co A 237th Engr Bn	679 6 45 45	5880S	Honiton (T5921)		0810	81 Exeter By Pass L 31 to RJ 33 L TP 306 L 35 to Dest	100	1130
APA USS BARNETT	SH-7	2nd Bn 8th Inf Shore Fire Control Party 29th F A Bn Co A 237th Engr C Bn(-1Plat)	724 12 9 90	4 4980S	Seaton (T6911)		0915	To RJ A35, Exeter By Pass, 31 to RJ 33 L to TP 306, L on 35 to Dest	1115	1245
APA DICKMAN	SH-12	1st Bn 8th Inf 29th F A Bn Co C 237th Engr C Bn(-1Plat)	763 12 90	2 5180S	Honiton (T5921)		1015	81 Exeter By Pass, 31 to RJ 33, L to TP 306 L 35 to Dest	1200	1330

SPEED: Average 10 MPH, Maximum 25 MPH

DENSITY: 60 yds. Between vehicles during movements and at halts.

MARKING: Convoy numbers must be shown on the first vehicle of each serial and on rear of the last vehicle of the convoy in lettering.

HALTS: 10 minute halt every two hours at ten minutes before the even hour. Long halts of 1 hour will be made during marches exceeding

Camouflage measures will be taken during all halts exceeding 10 minutes.

* Will move by organic transporation to Honiton to arrive two (2) hours prior to time of deoparture. Plat Ldr will report to CO 3rd Bn

SECRET
S E C R E T

HQ 4TH INF DIV
18 April 1944
APO 4, U S Army

SUPPLEMENT #1 to APPENDIX #2 to
ANNEX #4 to FO #1 (TIGER)

Units listed below are responsible for furnishing CO of troops and TQM's for craft as indicated:

LST NO.	UNIT FURNISHING CO OF TROOPS AND TQM
426	4th Engr Combat Bn.
427	Hq Btry, 11th AA Gr.
428	Hq & Hq Co, 1st Bn, 401st Glider Inf.
429	Hq 101st A/B Div.
430	Co A, 401st Glider Inf.
431	Hq Co, 22d Inf.
432	Btry D, 116th AA Gun Bn.
433	Hq Co, 12th Inf.
434	Btry C, 116th AA Gun Bn.
435	Hq Co, 327th Glider Inf.
436	Hq Co, 8th Inf.
437	20th FA Bn.
438	20th FA Bn.
439	Hq & Hq Co, 3d Bn, 531st Engr, Shore Regt.
440	Btry B, 980th FA Bn.
441	Co G, 327th Glider Inf.
442	Hq Btry, 4th Div Arty.
443	Hq Co, 4th Inf Div.
444	4th Sig Co.
445	746th Tank Bn.
446	479th Amph Truck Co.
494	Btry D, 535th AA AW Bn.
495	478th Amph Truck Co.
496	557th QM Co (Rhd).
497	Hq Co, 8th Inf.
498	4th QM Co.
499	704th Ord Co.
500	462d TC Amph Truck Co.
501	3206th QM Co (Sv).
502	Det Hq & Hq Co, 50th Sig Co.

MARR
G-4

SECRET
S E C R E T

Appendix 19

BRIXHAM

	UNIT	LOCATION		Total No. of Personnel	NO. OF VEHICLES					No. Pers. Not carried on Org. Transp.	REMARKS
		Place	Coord		1/4T	3/4T	1 1/2T	2 1/2T			
497	4th QM Co	Exeter	T 3515	40	3	1		9	8	0	8 1-T trlrs
	Cannon Co 8th I	Honiton	T 5921	4				2	2	0	2 1-T ..
	.. ..	..	..	4				2	2	0	2 1-T ..
	Co D, 6th Inf	..	..	8	8				5	0	5 1/4T trlrs
	Co H, ...	..	..	8	8				5	0	5 1/4T trlrs
	Co M, ...	..	..	8	8				5	0	5 1/4T trlrs
	Co D, 22d Inf	South Bre	Y 1382	8	8				5	0	5 1/4T trlrs
	Co H, 22d Inf	..	..	8	8				5	0	5 1/4T trlrs
	Co M, ...	..	..	8	8				5	0	5 1/4T trlrs
	Co A, 8th Inf	Honiton	T 5921	20						20	
	Co B, ...	..	..	20						20	
	Co C, ...	..	..	20						20	
	Co E, ...	..	..	20						20	
	Co F, ...	..	..	20						20	
	Co G, ...	..	..	20						20	
	Co I, ...	..	..	20						20	
	Co K, ...	..	..	20						20	
	Co L, ...	..	..	20						20	
	1st Bn Hq, 8th	..	..	16						16	
	2d Bn Hq, 8th I	..	..	16						16	
	3d Bn Hq, 8th I	..	..	16						16	
	Hq Co, 8th Inf	..	..	10						10	
	Serv Co, 8th In	..	..	4						4	
	AT Co, 8th Inf	..	..	7						7	
				345						249	

Appendix 20

SE*RET-TIGER

ANNEX FOX to
OPERATION ORDER
  No. 2-44

Serial: 0075

TASK ORGANIZATION - (PRE-ASSAULT PHASE)

    (x) REFERENCE VESSELS

        SCIMITAR, AZALEA, ML 214

(a) CONVOY T-1A - Captain G. E. Maynard, USN, in BARNETT

      CONVOY - Captain G. E. Maynard, USN, in BARNETT

      BARNETT (F), EMPIRE GAUNTLET, BAYFIELD (FF), DICKMAN, LCH 86, 95

      ESCORT - Captain J. A. McCoy, RN in ONSLOW

      ONSLOW, OPPORTUNE, ONSLAUGHT, ORIBI, OFFA
      PCs - 1261, 484, 1176
        (1) PLYMOUTH SECTION - Captain L. Spencer, USCG, in BAYFIELD

          CONVOY - Captain L. Spencer, USCG, in BAYFIELD
          BAYFIELD (FF), LCH 86, 95

          ESCORT - Captain J. A. McCoy, RN, in ONSLOW
          ONSLOW, OPPORTUNE

        (2) TOR BAY SECTION - Captain G. E. Maynard, USN, in BARNETT

          CONVOY - Captain G. E. Maynard, USN, in BARNETT
          BARNETT (F), EMPIRE GAUNTLET, DICKMAN

          ESCORT - Comdr., W. H. Selby, DSC, RN, in ONSLAUGHT
          ONSLAUGHT, OFFA, ORIBI
          PCs - 1261, 484, 1176

(b) CONVOY T-1B - Commander J. S. Bresnan, USCG, in LCI(L) 321

      CONVOY - Commander J. S. Bresnan, USCG, in LCI(L) 321
      31 LCI(L)s - 350, 326, 324, 96, 411, 325, 412, 349, 522, 409, 524, 410,
      521, 553, 523, 408, 322, 321 (F), 517, 319, 516, 320, 514, 323, 515,
      527, 525, 528, 526, 529, 551.

      ESCORT -
      MLs - 193, 191.

        (1) SALCOMBE CONVOY - Lt.(jg), W. Allison, USCGR, in LCI(L) 326
          LCI(L)s - 350, 326(F), 324, 96, 411, 325, 412, 349, 522, 409, 524,
          410, 521, 553, 408, 523.

              - 1 -   TASK ORGANIZATION

ANNEX FOX to
OPERATION ORDER   18 April 1944
   No. 2-44.

Serial: 0075

           ESCORT -
           ML 193

   (2) BRIXHAM CONVOY - Comdr. J.S. Bresnan, USCG, in LCI(L) 321
       LCI(L)s 322, 321(F), 517, 319, 516, 320, 514, 323, 515, 527, 525,
       528, 526, 529, 551.

           ESCORT -
           ML 191

   (c) CONVOY T - 2A1 - Captain J.E. Arnold, USNR, in LCI(L) 401

       CONVOY - Captain J.E. Arnold, USNR, in LCI(L) 401.
         LCI(L) - 401, 552
         LCTs - 592, 596, 593, 597, 594, 531, 595, 510, 244, 7, 703, 22,
         616, 25, 294, 199, 415, 200, 970, 201, 542, 532, 526, 533, 534,
         543, 645, 758, 691, 967, 794, 954, 797, 756, 801, 512, 824, 965,
         539, 544, 537, 800, 833, 538.
         LCT(A) - 2478, 2124, 2301, 2227, 2309, 2273, 2454, 2275.
         LCG(L) - 426, 449,   811, 893.
         LCFs - 18, 27, 22, 31.
         LCT(R)s - 366, 368
         3 LCMs (Salvage Unit #1) and 3 LCMs (Salvage Unit #3)
         42 LCMs
         LCCs 60, 70, 80, 90
         16 LCP(L)

           ESCORT - Comdr. B.J. St.Croix, RN in TANATSIDE
           SALADIN, TANATSIDE.
           ML 118, 153, 155, 163, 187, 230, 304.

   (1) SALCOMBE SECTION - Lt.Comdr. L.E. Hart, USNR, in LCI(L) 552

       CONVOY - Lt. Comdr. L.E. Hart, USNR, in LCI(L) 552
       LCI(L) - 552
       LCT(A)s - 2478, 2124, 2301, 2227, 2309, 2273, 2454, 2275.
       LCTs - 532, 526, 533, 534.
       LCGs - 426, 449, 893, 811
       LCFs - 18, 27, 22, 31
       LCT(R)s - 366, 368.
       30 LCM(3)s
       3 LCMs (Salvage Unit #1) and 3 LCMs (Salvage Unit #3)
       16 LCP(L)

           ESCORT - Comdr. B.J. St Croix in TANATSIDE
           SALADIN, TANATSIDE
           ML 118, 153

                          - 2 -   ANNEX FOX.

CONFI-ENTIAL

ANNEX FOX to   18 April 1944
OPERATION ORDER
   No. 2-44

Serial: 0075

    (2) <u>DARTMOUTH SECTION</u> - Captain J.E. Arnold, USNR, in LCI(L) 401

       <u>CONVOY</u> - Captain J.E. Arnold, USNR, in LCI(L) 401
       LCI(L) 401
       LCTs - 592, 596, 593, 597, 594, 531, 595, 510, 244, 7, 703, 22,
       616, 25, 294, 199, 415, 200, 970, 201, 542
       LCC - 60, 70 80, 90

           <u>ESCORT</u> - S.O. in ML 163
           MLs - 155, 163(S.O.) 187

    (3) <u>BRIXHAM SECTION</u> - Lt.Comdr. Armstrong, RN in ML 230

       <u>CONVOY</u> - Lt.Comdr. Armstring, RN in ML 230
       LCTs - 543, 645, 758, 691, 967, 794, 954, 797, 756, 801, 512,
       824, 965, 539, 544, 537, 800, 833, 538.

           <u>ESCORT</u> - S.O. in ML 230
           MLs - 230, 304.

    (4) <u>TEIGNMOUTH SECTION</u> - Lieutenant Orr, USNR
       12 LCMs

  (d) <u>CONVOY T-2A-2</u> - Captain E. C. Kline, USNR, in LCI(L) 513.

      <u>CONVOY</u> - Captain E. C. Kline, USNR, In LCI(L) 513
       LCI(L) 513
       LCTs - 27, 147, 540, 541, 153, 583, 195, 584, 271, 585, 305, 642,
       519, 644, 516, 517, 520, 836, 527, 528, 3, 362, 476, 920, 492,
       511, 443, 474, 447, 529, 975, 956, 974, 522, 524, 532, 526, 533,
       534, 460, 545, 546, 30, 413, 332, 547, 548, 580, 475, 581, 525,
       766, 777, 663, 809, 486, 489, 495, 456, 457, 459, 497.
       3 LCM Salvage Unit #3

      <u>ESCORT</u> - Lieut., R. F. Pembry, RNR, in HMS PRIMROSE
      LINCOLNSHIRE, PRIMROSE, NEAVE
      MLs - 189, 194, 195

    (1) <u>DARTMOUTH SECTION</u> - Captain E. C. Kline, USNR, in LCI(L) 513

       <u>CONVOY</u> - Captain E. C. Kline, USNR, in CLI(L) 513
        LCI(L) 513
        LCTs - 27, 147, 540, 541, 153, 527, 528, 3, 362, 476, 920, 511,
        443, 474, 447, 529, 975, 974, 522, 524, 460, 545, 546, 30, 413,
        525, 766, 777, 663, 809, 486, 489, 495, 456, 492.

       <u>ESCORT</u> - Lt., R. F. Pembry, RNR, in PRIMROSE
       PRIMROSE, NEAVE, ML 189
                 - 3 -   ANNEX FOX

S·A·...-......
·A·
ANNEX FOX to   18 April 1944
OPERATION ORDER
   No. 2-44

Serial: 0075

        (2) BRIXHAM SECTION - Lt.(jg) J.E. Spainhour, USNR.

        .   LCT's - 583, 195, 584, 271, 585, 395, 642, 519, 644, 516, 517, 520,
            836, 956, 532, 526, 533, 534, 332, 547, 548, 580, 475, 581, 457, 459,
            497.
            3 LCM Salvage Unit #3.

            ESCORT - Skipper Lt. S.L. Larner, RNR, in LINCOLNSHIRE.
            LINCOLNSHIRE, ML 194, 195

    (e) CONVOY T-2B - Lt. J. L. Chadwick, USNR in LST 48

            CONVOY - Lt. J. L. Chadwick, USNR in LST 48
            LST 48 towing RHF 20
            LST 47 towing RHF 21
            LST 230 towing RHF 11
            LST 281 towing RHF 13
            LST 282 towing RHF 19

            ESCORT - Lt. Comdr. P. C. Moore, RNVR, in ROWAN
            ROWAN, GANILLY

    (f) CONVOY T-3 - Comdr. J.C. Guillot, USN, in LST 491

            CONVOY - Comdr. J.C. Guillot, USN, in LST 491
            LST's - 284, 371, 380, 382, 346, 55, 283, 311, 491, 49, 50, 400, 46,
            492, 501, 54,
            RHF's - 22, 24, 23, 25,
            COASTERS - LILEIA, BIRKER

            ESCORT - Lt. The Hon. D.D.E. Vivian, RN, in BRISSENDEN
            BRISSENDEN, KRAKOWIAK, DIANTHUS, LORD ESSENDEN, CAIDY

        (1) PLYMOUTH CONVOY - Commander J. C. Guillot, USN, in LST 491

            CONVOY - Commander J. C. Guillot, USN, in LST 491
            LST's - 491, 284, 49, 50, 400,
            COASTERS - LILEIA, BIRKER

            ESCORT - Lt. The Hon. D.D.E. Vivian, RN, in BRISSENDEN
            BRISSENDEN, KRAKOWIAK, DIANTHUS.

        (2) DARTMOUTH CONVOY - Lt. Comdr. S. B. Purdie, USNR, in LST 311.

            CONVOY - Lt. Comdr. S.B. Purdie, USNR, in LST 311
            LST's - 46, 501, 283, 311, 54,
            RHF's - 22, 23, 24, 25.

                            - 4 -   ANNEX FOX

ANNEX FOX to   18 April 1944
OPERATION ORDER
   No. 2-44

Serial: 0075

        ESCORT - Lt. G. C. Cowley, RNVR, in CALDY
        LORD ESSENDEN, CALDY
    BRIXHAM CONVOY - see page 5(a) following.
(g) CONVOY T-4 - Commander B. J. Skahill, USN, in LST 515.

      CONVOY - Commander B. J. Skahill, USN, in LST 515.
      LST's - 515, 496, 511, 531, 58, 499, 289, 507, 508.
      2 Pontoon Causeways

      ESCORT - Lt. Comdr. P.G.C. King, RNVR, in SALADIN
      SALADIN, AZALEA

      (1) PLYMOUTH SECTION - Commander B. J. Skahill, USN, in LST 515

          CONVOY - Commander B. J. Skahill, USN, in LST 515.
          LST's - 515, 496, 511, 531, 58.
          2 Pontoon Causeways

          ESCORT - Lt. Comdr. P.G.C. King, RNVR, in SALADIN
          SALADIN, AZALEA

      (2) BRIXHAM SECTION - Lt. E. F. Witte, USN, in LST 499.

          CONVOY - Lt. E. F. Witte, USN, in LST 499
          LST's - 499, 289, 507, 508.

          ESCORT - NONE

(h) CONVOY TM-4 - Lt. Comdr. L. J. McMillan, RNVR, in ALVISTA

      CONVOY - Lt. Comdr. L. J. McMillan, RNVR, in ALVISTA
      ALVISTA
      LBV's - 1, 2, 3, 4, 5, 6, 7, 8, 9, 16, 24, 25, 26, 27, 28, 29, 30, 31.
      LBO's - 11, 12, 13, 18, 19, 20, 21.
      LBE's - 10, 14, 17, 22,
      LBW's - 15, 23;
      Fueling Trawlers: FRENTONIAN, ROMAN, BEN BREAC.

      (1) EXMOUTH SECTION - Lt. Comdr. L. J. McMillan, RNVR, in ALVISTA
          ALVISTA
          LBV's - 1, 2, 3, 4, 5, 6, 7, 8, 9, 16, 24, 25, 26, 27, 28, 29,
          30, 31.
          LBO's - 11, 12, 13, 18, 19, 20, 21.
          LBE's - 10, 14, 17, 22,
          LBW's - 15, 23.

      (2) DARTMOUTH SECTION -
          3 Fueling Trawlers: BEN BREAC, ROMAN, FRENTONIAN

ANNEX FOX

SECRET-TIGER

ANNEX FOX to
OPERATION ORDER
No. 2-44

18 April 1944

Serial: 0075

(f)　　(3) BRIXHAM CONVOY -
　　　　　LST's - 371, 380, 382, 346, 55, 492.

- 5a -　　　　ANNEX FOX

SECRET - TIGER

APPENDIX THREE to ANNEX FOX to
OPERATION ORDER
   No. 2-44

18 April 1944

Serial: 0075

(SAILING DIRECTIONS - CONVOY T-4)
(TO BE USED WITH CONVOY DIAGRAM T - 4)

1. **PLYMOUTH SORTIE:**

  (a) **CONVOY:** LST's 515(GF), 496, 511, 531, 58

     (1)   Sortie from PLYMOUTH in column in order indicated, convoy commander and guide in LST 515, pass boom gate at 0950B 27 April, other ships at four minute intervals. Speed of guide will be six (6) knots.

     (2)   LST 58, last ship in column, will tow two sections of pontoon causeway which must be delivered and connected sufficiently early to permit sortie with other LST's.

     (3)   On clearing channel, when signal "HOW VICTOR ONE pennant" is executed, close up into positions indicated in Formation #1, Convoy T-4 Diagram.

     (4)   After rendezvous with Brixham Section, convoy commander and guide of combined convoy will continue to be in LST 491.

  (b) **ESCORT:** AZALEA, SCIMITAR

             *SCIMITAR JOIN CONVOY T-4 OFF PLYMOUTH BOOM-GATE & REPORT TO G**
             B OF CONVOY T-4 AS SCREENING VESSEL.
     (1)   ~~Sortie from PLYMOUTH prior to 0920B 27 April; conduct A/S patrol off entrance; cover sortie and screen ahead of convoy.~~
     (2) AZALEA JOIN OFF POINT A & REPORT AS SCREENING VESSEL.

2. **BRIXHAM SORTIE AND RENDEZVOUS:**

  (a) **CONVOY:** LST's 499, 289, 507, 508

     (1)   Sortie from BRIXHAM in column, in order indicated, convoy commander and guide in LST 499, pass breakwater at 1815B 27 April, other ships at four minute intervals. Speed of guide will be six (6) knots.

     (2)   On clearing channel close to distance 400 yards and proceed via Point E2 to rendezvous with PLYMOUTH SECTION of convoy in Point E at 1930B 27 April.

     (3)   At Point E maneuver into positions in column astern of PLYMOUTH SECTION as shown in Formation #1 Convoy Diagram T-4.

-1-   APPENDIX 3 to ANNEX FOX

167

SECRET - TIGER

18 April 1944.

APPENDIX THREE to ANNEX FOX to
OPERATION ORDER
    No. 2-44

Serial: 0075   (SAILING DIRECTIONS - CONVOY T-4)

    (4) LST 499 keep 350 yards open water astern of rear pontoon
        causeway towed by LST 58.

  (b) ESCORT: NONE.

3. PASSAGE

    (a)   Proceed via prescribed convoy route as shown in MINESWEEPING
               OVERLAY, Appendix 1 to Annex F through Points A, B, C, D, E,
               and searched channel.

    (b)   PLYMOUTH SECTION adjust speed to arrive at Point E at 1930B
               27 April to rendezvous with BRIXHAM SECTION.

    (c)   When crossing boat lanes, during passage from Point C to D,
               at about 1700B 27 April, keep particularly alert and maneuver
               as necessary to keep clear of traffic between Transport Area
               and beaches.

    (d)   After passing Point E, keep to LEFT of searched channel
               shown in MINESWEEPING OVERLAY, Appendix 1 to Annex F.

    (e)   Approach Transport Area via Swept Channel #2, keeping to
               RIGHT of mid-channel marker buoys.

    (f)   Adjust speed to arrive at Point K2 at 0730B 28 April.

    (g)   On approaching Point K2, report to NOIC SLAPTON and Com-
               mander Force "U".

    (h)   Proceed in accordance with instructions of NOIC SLAPTON.

4. CHANGE OF SCREEN FORMATION:

    (a)   On approaching Point I2, escorts reduce front to remain with-
               in swept channel; AZALEA remain ahead of convoy, SCIMITAR
               take station astern.

    (b)   Continue screening Convoy T-4 until the convoy is within
               established area screens.

    (c)   Report arrival to Area Screen Commander, and proceed as
               directed by him.

169

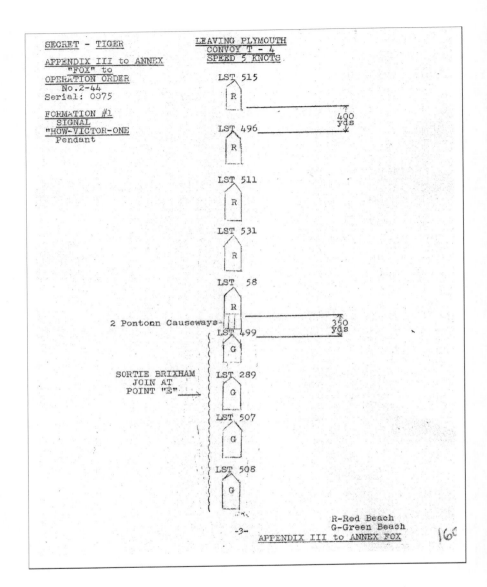

APPENDIX III to ANNEX
"FOX" to
OPERATION ORDER
No.2-44
Serial: 0075

FORMATION #1
SIGNAL
"HOW-VICTOR-ONE
Pendant

LEAVING PLYMOUTH
CONVOY T - 4
SPEED 5 KNOTS

LST 515
R

400 yds

LST 496
R

LST 511
R

LST 531
R

LST 58
R

2 Pontoon Causeways

350 yds

LST 499
G

SORTIE BRIXHAM
JOIN AT
POINT "E"

LST 289
G

LST 507
G

LST 508
G

R-Red Beach
G-Green Beach

-3-

APPENDIX III to ANNEX FOX

160

Appendix 22

Serial : 00885
LOADING ORDER NO. 5-44
S E C R E T   TIGER
L.S.T. LOADING PLAN
21 April 1944.

Date	Ship No.	Hard No.	Berth No.	Div Ser	Sos Load	Pers Lift	Vehicle	Berthing	Loaded
April	Dartmouth		Pc3/63						
24	48	PC3/63	A	430				0900	1500
24	47	PC3/63	B	429				0900	1500
24	230	PC3/63	A	428				1500	2200
24	501	PC3/63	B	427				1500	2200
24	282	PC3/63	A	426				2200	0300
24	46	PC3/63	B	431				2200	0300
25	283	PC3/63	A	432				0300	0900
25	54	PC3/63	B	433				0300	0900
25	231	PC3/63	A	434				0900	1500
25	311	PC3/63	B	435				0900	1500
BRIXHAM			PU/64						
24	499	PU/64	A	494				0900	1500
24	289	PU/64	C	495				0900	1500
24	507	PU/64	B	496				1500	2200
24	508	PU/64	D	497				1500	2200
24	382	PU/64	A	438				2200	0300
24	371	PU/64	C	435				2200	0300
25	380	PU/64	B	437				0300	0900
25	492	PU/64	D	447				0300	0900
25	55	PU/64	A	443				0900	1500
25	346	PU/64	C	444				0900	1500
PLYMOUTH			PK/39						
24	515	PK/39	A	498				0900	1500
24	496	PK/39	B	499				0900	1500
24	511	PK/39	A	500				1500	2200
24	531	PK/39	B	501				1500	2200
24	50	PK/39	A	441				2200	0300
24	49	PK/39	B	440				2200	0300
25	491	PK/39	A	439				0300	0900
25	58	PK/39	B	502				0300	0900
25	400	PK/39	A	445				0900	1500
25	284	PK/39	B	446				0900	1500

Appendix 23

NAME	Army serial No	Convoy	SECTION	ROLE	SHIP COMMANDER
USS Barnett	LSI(L)	T1A	Torbay		Capt G E Maynard USN Ship commander Commander S S Reynolds USN
USS Bayfield		T1A	Plymouth		Capt Lynden Spencer USCG
USS Joseph T Dickman		T1A	Torbay		Capt R T Mauerman USCG
USS Maloy					Lt Kellogg USN
HMS Alvista		TM4	Exmouth	Ferry control Assault phase	Lt Comdr L J McMillan RNVR
HMS Ashanti					
HMS Athabaskan					
HMS Azalea		T4		Escort	
Ben Breac		TM4	Dartmouth		
Birker		T3	Plymouth		
HMS Brissenden		T3	Plymouth	Escort	Lt The Hon D D E Vivian RN
HMS Caldy		T3	Dartmouth	Escort	Lt G C Cowley RNVR
HMS Celandine					
HMS Dianthus		T3	Plymouth	Escort	
HMS Empire Gauntlet		T1A	Torbay		Capt Jeffers Merchant Navy (SNOP Lt C E M Thorncraft RN)
HMS Enterprise		TC	Cruiser	Fire support unit	Capt H T W Grant DSO RCN
Frentonian		TM4	Dartmouth		
HMS Ganilly		T2B			
HMS Haida					
HMS Hawkins		TC	Cruiser	Fire support unit	Capt J W Josselyn RN
HMS Huron					
HMS Krakowiak		T3	Plymouth	Escort	
Lileia		T3	Plymouth		
HMS Lincolnshire		T2A2	Brixham	Escort	Lt S L Larner RNR
HMS Lord Essenden		T3	Dartmouth	Escort	
HMS Neave		T2A2	Dartmouth	Escort	
HMS Obedient				Screen	Lt Cdr H Unwin DSC RN
HMS Offa		T1A	Torbay	Escort	Lt Cdr R F Leonard RN
HMS Onslaught		T1A	Torbay	Escort	Comdr W H Selby DSC RN
HMS Onslow		T1A	Plymouth	Escort & Screen	Capt J A McCOY DSO RN
HMS Opportune		T1A	Plymouth	Screen	Comdr J Lee Barber DSO RN
HMS Oribi		T1A	Torbay	Escort	Lt Cdr J C A Ingram DSC RN
HMS Orwell				Screen	Lt Cdr J M Hodges DSO RN
HMS Primrose		T2A2	Dartmouth	Escort	Lt R F Pembry RNR
Roman		TM4	Dartmouth		
HMS Romney			Sweeper unit #1	14th M/S Flotilla commander	Comdr G W A T Irvine RNR
HMS Rowan		T2B			Lt Comdr P O Moore RNVR
HMS Saladin		T2A1 & T4		Escort	Lt Comdr P G C King RNVR
HMS Scimitar		T4		Escort	
HMS Settsu				Net Unit	Comdr C R Ryman RN
HMS Shippigan			Sweeper unit #2		Comdr M H Brown RN
HMS Tadoussac				16th M/S Flotilla commander	Comdr J P Apps RN
HMS Tanatside		T2A1		Escort	Comdr B J St Croix RN
LBE 10		TM4	Exmouth		

TIGER UNIT	BEACH	TIDE	LOADED	NOTES
Convoy commander & Flagship & Torbay Section commander				
Task Force commander's flagship & Plymouth section commander				
USN observer Commodore C D Edgar USN				
"Convoy commander & Section commander 36 LBVs, 20 LCMs"				
Covering force				
Covering force				
Close Escort Group				
Fuelling trawler				
Coaster				
Close Escort Group				
Close Escort Group				
Close Escort Group				Deleted from Op Order
Close Escort Group				
Red AP Unit				
Gunfire Support Group				
Fuelling trawler				
Close Escort Group				Sunk Channel 5 Jul 44
Covering force				
Gunfire Support Group Unit commander				
Covering force				Replaced HMS Skate in Op Order
Close Escort Group				
Coaster				
Close Escort Group				
Close Escort Group				Replaced HMS Rowan in Op Order itself replaced by HMS Skonner in Op Order
Gunfire Support Group				
Gunfire Support Group				
Gunfire Support Group				
Gunfire Support Group Escort commander				
Gunfire Support Group Join at Point I				
Gunfire Support Group				
Gunfire Support Group				
Close Escort Group				
Fuelling trawler				
"Plus 11 minesweepers Vegreville, Seaham, Kenova, Guysborough, Poole, Rye, Whitehaven, Peterhead, Sir Galahad, Sir Lancelot"				
				Replaced by HMS Neave in Op Order
Close Escort Group				
Close Escort Group				
Net unit commander				
M/S group commander				
" Plus 10 minesweepers Beaumaris, Dornoch, Ilfracombe, Parsboro, Qualicum, Shippigan, Wedgeport, Blyth, Kings Grey, Commander Evans"				
Close Escort Group Commander				

LBE 14		TM4	Exmouth		
LBE 17		TM4	Exmouth		
LBE 22		TM4	Exmouth		
LBE 41		TM5	Exmouth		
LBE 45		TM5	Exmouth		
LBE 48		TM5	Exmouth		
LBE 52		TM5	Exmouth		
LBO 11		TM4	Exmouth		
LBO 12		TM4	Exmouth		
LBO 13		TM4	Exmouth		
LBO 18		TM4	Exmouth		
LBO 19		TM4	Exmouth		
LBO 20		TM4	Exmouth		
LBO 21		TM4	Exmouth		
LBO 42		TM5	Exmouth		
LBO 43		TM5	Exmouth		
LBO 44		TM5	Exmouth		
LBO 46		TM5	Exmouth		
LBO 49		TM5	Exmouth		
LBO 50		TM5	Exmouth		
LBO 51		TM5	Exmouth		
LBV 1		TM4	Exmouth		
LBV 2		TM4	Exmouth		
LBV 3		TM4	Exmouth		
LBV 4		TM4	Exmouth		
LBV 5		TM4	Exmouth		
LBV 6		TM4	Exmouth		
LBV 7		TM4	Exmouth		
LBV 8		TM4	Exmouth		
LBV 9		TM4	Exmouth		
LBV 16		TM4	Exmouth		
LBV 24		TM4	Exmouth		
LBV 25		TM4	Exmouth		
LBV 26		TM4	Exmouth		
LBV 27		TM4	Exmouth		
LBV 28		TM4	Exmouth		
LBV 29		TM4	Exmouth		
LBV 30		TM4	Exmouth		
LBV 31		TM4	Exmouth		
LBV 32		TM5	Exmouth		
LBV 33		TM5	Exmouth		
LBV 34		TM5	Exmouth		
LBV 35		TM5	Exmouth		
LBV 36		TM5	Exmouth		
LBV 37		TM5	Exmouth		
LBV 38		TM5	Exmouth		
LBV 39		TM5	Exmouth		
LBV 40		TM5	Exmouth		
LBV 47		TM5	Exmouth		
LBV 54		TM5	Exmouth		
LBV 55		TM5	Exmouth		
LBV 56		TM5	Exmouth		
LBV 57		TM5	Exmouth		
LBV 58		TM5	Exmouth		
LBV 59		TM5	Exmouth		
LBV 60		TM5	Exmouth		
LBV 61		TM5	Exmouth		
LBW 15		TM4	Exmouth		
LBW 23		TM4	Exmouth		
LBW 53		TM5	Exmouth		
LCC 60		T2A1	Dartmouth		
LCC 70		T2A1	Dartmouth		
LCC 80		T2A1	Dartmouth		
LCC 90		T2A1	Dartmouth		

Secondary Control vessel LCM Unit				
Tertiary Control vessel LCM Unit				
Secondary Control vessel LCM unit				Listed in Annex Fox but not in Op Order
Tertiary Control vessel LCM unit				Listed in Annex Fox but not in Op Order

LCF 18		T2A1	Salcombe		
LCF 27		T2A1	Salcombe		
LCF 22		T2A1	Salcombe		
LCF 31		T2A1	Salcombe		
LCG 426		T2A1	Salcombe		
LCG 449		T2A1	Salcombe		
LCG 893		T2A1	Salcombe		
LCG 811		T2A1	Salcombe		
LCH 86		T1A	Plymouth		Capt M T Richardson USN
LCH 95		T1A	Plymouth		Comdr A L Warburton USN (originally in LCH 86 in Op Order)
LCI(L) 96		T1B	Salcombe		
LCI(L) 319		T1B	Brixham		
LCI(L) 320		T1B	Brixham		
LCI(L) 321		T1B	Brixham		Comdr J S Bresnan USCG
LCI(L) 322		T1B	Brixham	Red beach salvage unit #3 (3 LCMs)	
LCI(L) 323		T1B	Brixham		
LCI(L) 324		T1B	Salcombe		
LCI(L) 325		T1B	Salcombe		
LCI(L) 326		T1B	Salcombe		Lt(jg) W Allison USCGR
LCI(L) 349		T1B	Salcombe		
LCI(L) 350		T1B	Salcombe		
LCI(L) 401		T2A1	Dartmouth		Capt J E Arnold USNR
LCI(L) 408		T1B	Salcombe		
LCI(L) 409		T1B	Salcombe		
LCI(L) 410		T1B	Salcombe		Commander J A Bresnan USCG Green LCI(L) Unit commander
LCI(L) 411		T1B	Salcombe		
LCI(L) 412		T1B	Salcombe		
LCI(L) 513		T2A2	Dartmouth		Capt E C Kline USNR
LCI(L) 514		T1B	Brixham		
LCI(L) 515		T1B	Brixham		
LCI(L) 516		T1B	Brixham		
LCI(L) 517		T1B	Brixham		Lt Cdr J Capponi USNR
LCI(L) 521		T1B	Salcombe		
LCI(L) 522		T1B	Salcombe		
LCI(L) 523		T1B	Salcombe		
LCI(L) 524		T1B	Salcombe		
LCI(L) 525		T1B	Brixham		
LCI(L) 526		T1B	Brixham		
LCI(L) 527		T1B	Brixham		
LCI(L) 528		T1B	Brixham		
LCI(L) 529		T1B	Brixham		
LCI(L) 551		T1B	Brixham		
LCI(L) 552		T2A1	Salcombe		Lt Comdr L E Hart USNR
LCI(L) 553		T1B	Salcombe		
LCM					Lt C J Alfke USNR
LCM(3)		T2A1	Salcombe		
LCM		T2A1	Teignmouth		Lt Orr USNR
LCM		T2A2	Brixham	Salvage unit #3	
LCM		TM5	Teignmouth	Section commander	Ens K J Lang USNR (flagship not indicated)
LCM					Lt (jg) J R Edith USNR
LCP(L)		T2A1	Salcombe	Smokers	

Support Craft Group				
Support Craft Group				
Support Craft Group				
Support Craft Group				
Support Craft Group				
Support Craft Group				Op Order - 424 substitutes if 449 not available
Support Craft Group				
Support Craft Group				
Red Assault Group				See LCH 95
Red Assault Group				Green Assault Group commander in original Op Order - replaced by LCH 86 - 8th RCT & 22nd RCT commanders aboard
Red LCI(L) Unit				
Red LCI(L) Unit Green Beach Salvage Unit after				
Red LCI(L) Unit				
Red LCI(L) Unit Convoy commander Towing RHF 20				
Red LCI(L) Unit				
Red LCI(L) Unit				
Red LCI(L) Unit				
Red LCI(L) Unit				
Red LCI(L) Unit Section commander				
Red LCI(L) Unit				
Red LCI(L) Unit				
Convoy commander & Dartmouth section commander Slapton Shore Service Group				
Green LCI(L) Unit				
Green LCI(L) Unit				
Green LCI(L) Unit				
Green LCI(L) Unit				
Green LCI(L) Unit				
Shuttle Control Group Convoy commander & Section commander				
Red LCI(L) Unit				
Red LCI(L) Unit				
Red LCI(L) Unit				
Red LCI(L) Unit commander				Sunk Jun 44 Normandy (classed as LCI(S) when sunk)
Green LCI(L) Unit				
Green LCI(L) Unit				
Green LCI(L) Unit				
				Listed in Annex Fox but not in Op Order Sunk Jun 44 Normandy (classed as LCI(S) when sunk)
Green LCI(L) Unit				
Green LCI(L) Unit				
Green LCI(L) Unit				
Green LCI(L) Unit				
Green LCI(L) Unit				
Green LCI(L) Unit				
Green LCI(L) Unit Section commander & Support craft group commander				
Green LCI(L) Unit				
Green LCM unit commander (20 LCMs)				
Thirty (30)				
Twelve (12)				
Three (3)				
Eighteen (18)				
Twenty (20) Red LCM Unit				
"Sixteen (16) 85,86,88,95,97,98,118,137,145,1 46,149,150,240,245,246,269"				

LCT (R) 366		T2A1	Salcombe	Green LST unit 1 commander (3 LSTs)	
LCT (R) 368		T2A1	Salcombe		
LCT 3	260	T2A2	Dartmouth		
LCT 7		T2A1	Dartmouth		
LCT 22		T2A1	Dartmouth		
LCT 25		T2A1	Dartmouth		
LCT 27		T2A2	Dartmouth		
LCT 30		T2A2	Dartmouth		
LCT 147		T2A2	Dartmouth		
LCT 153		T2A2	Dartmouth		
LCT 195		T2A2	Brixham		
LCT 199		T2A1	Dartmouth		
LCT 200		T2A1	Dartmouth		
LCT 201		T2A1	Dartmouth		
LCT 244		T2A1	Dartmouth		
LCT 271		T2A2	Brixham		
LCT 294		T2A1	Dartmouth		
LCT 305		T2A2	Brixham		
LCT 332		T2A2	Brixham		
LCT 362		T2A2	Dartmouth		
LCT 413		T2A2	Dartmouth		
LCT 415		T2A1	Dartmouth		
LCT 443		T2A2	Dartmouth		
LCT 447		T2A2	Dartmouth		
LCT 456		T2A2	Dartmouth		
LCT 457		T2A2	Brixham		
LCT 459	265	T2A2	Brixham		
LCT 460		T2A2	Dartmouth		
LCT 474		T2A2	Dartmouth		
LCT 475		T2A2	Brixham		
LCT 476		T2A2	Dartmouth		
LCT 486		T2A2	Dartmouth		
LCT 489		T2A2	Dartmouth		
LCT 492		T2A2	Dartmouth		
LCT 495		T2A2	Dartmouth		
LCT 497		T2A2	Brixham		
LCT 510		T2A1	Dartmouth		
LCT 511		T2A2	Dartmouth		
LCT 512		T2A1	Brixham		
LCT 516		T2A2	Brixham		
LCT 517		T2A2	Brixham		
LCT 519		T2A2	Brixham		
LCT 520		T2A2	Brixham		
LCT 522		T2A2	Dartmouth		
LCT 524		T2A2	Dartmouth		
LCT 525		T2A2	Dartmouth		
LCT 526		T2A1	Salcombe		
LCT 527		T2A2	Dartmouth		
LCT 528		T2A2	Dartmouth		
LCT 529		T2A2	Dartmouth		
LCT 531		T2A1	Dartmouth		
LCT 532		T2A1	Salcombe		
LCT 533		T2A1	Salcombe		
LCT 534		T2A1	Salcombe		
LCT 537		T2A1	Brixham		
LCT 538		T2A1	Brixham		
LCT 539		T2A1	Brixham		
LCT 540		T2A2	Dartmouth		
LCT 541		T2A2	Dartmouth		
LCT 542		T2A1	Dartmouth		
LCT 543		T2A1	Brixham		

Support Craft Group				
Support Craft Group				
Red LCT Unit				
Red LCT Unit				
Red LCT Unit				
Red LCT Unit				Sunk Normandy 6 Jun 44
Red LCT Unit				Sunk N France 6 Jun 44
Green LCT Unit				Sunk N France 6 Jun 44
Red LCT Unit				Sunk N France Jun 44
Red LCT Unit				
Red LCT Unit				
Red LCT Unit				Sunk N France Jun 44
Red LCT Unit				
Green LCT Unit				Sunk Normandy 6 Jun 44
Red LCT Unit				
Green LCT Unit				Sunk Normandy 6 Jun 44
Red LCT Unit				Sunk N France 6 Jun 44
Green LCT Unit				Sunk N France 6 Jun 44
Red LCT Unit				Sunk N France 6 Jun 44
Green LCT Unit				
Green LCT Unit				Sunk N France 6 Jun 44
Red LCT Unit				
Red LCT Unit				
Green LCT Unit				
Green LCT Unit				
Green LCT Unit				Sunk W France 9 Oct 44
Green LCT Unit				
Red LCT Unit				
Green LCT Unit				
Red LCT Unit				
Green LCT Unit				Sunk N France 7 Jun 44
Green LCT Unit				
Red LCT Unit				
Green LCT Unit				
				12 RCT reserve commander aboard
Red LCT Unit				
Red LCT Unit				
Red LCT Unit				Replaced LCT 755 on Op Order
Red LCT Unit				
Red LCT Unit				
Red LCT Unit				
Red LCT Unit				
Red LCT Unit				
				Sunk Jun 44 Assault area
Green LCT Unit				
Red LCT Unit				Listed in Annex Fox but not in Op Order. Also shown as Convoy T2A2 Brixham section.
Red LCT Unit				
Red LCT Unit				
Red LCT Unit				Listed in Annex Fox but not in Op Order
Red LCT Unit				Listed in Annex Fox but not in Op Order. Also shown as Convoy T2A2 Brixham section.
Red LCT Unit				Listed in Annex Fox but not in Op Order. Also shown as Convoy T2A2 Brixham section.
Red LCT Unit				Listed in Annex Fox but not in Op Order. Also shown as Convoy T2A2 Brixham section.
Red LCT Unit				
Red LCT Unit				
Red LCT Unit				Sunk N France 6 Jun 44
Red LCT Unit				
Red LCT Unit				
				Listed in Annex Fox but not in Op Order
Green LCT Unit				

LCT 544		T2A1	Brixham		
LCT 545		T2A2	Dartmouth		
LCT 546		T2A2	Dartmouth		
LCT 547		T2A2	Brixham		
LCT 548		T2A2	Brixham		
LCT 580		T2A2	Brixham		
LCT 581		T2A2	Brixham		
LCT 583		T2A2	Brixham		
LCT 584		T2A2	Brixham		
LCT 585		T2A2	Brixham		
LCT 592	In Op Order	T2A1	Dartmouth		
LCT 593	In Op Order				
LCT 594					
LCT 595		T2A1	Dartmouth		
LCT 596		T2A1	Dartmouth		
LCT 597		T2A1	Dartmouth		
LCT 616		T2A1	Dartmouth	Red beach salvage unit (4 LCTs)	
LCT 642		T2A2	Brixham		
LCT 644		T2A2	Brixham		
LCT 645		T2A1	Brixham		
LCT 663		T2A2	Dartmouth		
LCT 691		T2A1	Brixham		
LCT 703		T2A1	Dartmouth		
LCT 756		T2A1	Brixham		
LCT 758		T2A1	Brixham		
LCT 766		T2A2	Dartmouth		
LCT 777		T2A2	Dartmouth		
LCT 794		T2A1	Brixham	Green beach salvage unit (4 LCTs)	
LCT 797		T2A1	Brixham		
LCT 800		T2A1	Brixham		
LCT 801		T2A1	Brixham		
LCT 809		T2A2	Dartmouth		
LCT 824		T2A1	Brixham		
LCT 833		T2A1	Brixham		
LCT 836		T2A2	Brixham		
LCT 851					
LCT 920		T2A2	Dartmouth		
LCT 954		T2A1	Brixham		
LCT 956		T2A2	Brixham		
LCT 965		T2A1	Brixham		
LCT 967		T2A1	Brixham		
LCT 970		T2A1	Salcombe (Dartmouth)	Salvage unit #1 commander until LCI 319 reports	
LCT 974		T2A2	Dartmouth		
LCT 975		T2A2	Dartmouth		
LCT(A) 2124		T2A1	Salcombe		
LCT(A) 2227		T2A1	Salcombe		
LCT(A) 2273		T2A1	Salcombe		
LCT(A) 2275		T2A1	Salcombe		
LCT(A) 2301		T2A1	Salcombe		
LCT(A) 2309		T2A1	Salcombe		
LCT(A) 2454		T2A1	Salcombe		
LCT(A) 2478		T2A1	Salcombe		
LST 46	431	T3	Dartmouth		
LST 47	429	T2B			
LST 48	430	T2B			Lt J L Chadwick USNR
LST 49	440	T3	Plymouth		
LST 50	441	T3	Plymouth		

Unit	Beach	Wave	Convoy	Notes
Green LCT Unit				
Green LCT Unit				
Green LCT Unit				
Green LCT Unit				
Green LCT Unit				Sunk Portsmouth Nov 44
Green LCT Unit				
Green LCT Unit				
Red LCT Unit Section commander Lt(jg) J E Spainhour USNR				
Red LCT Unit				
Red LCT Unit				
Green LCT Unit				
Green LCT Unit				
Green LCT Unit				
Green LCT Unit				
Red LCT Unit				
Red LCT Unit				Green LCT Unit in Op Order
Red LCT Unit				
Red LCT Unit				
Green LCT Unit				
Green LCT Unit				
Green LCT Unit				
Green LCT Unit				
Red LCT Unit				
Red LCT Unit				Replaced LCT 969 on Op Order
Green LCT Unit				
Green LCT Unit				Sunk N France 6 Jun 44
Green LCT Unit				
Green LCT Unit				
Red LCT Unit				
Green LCT Unit				
Green LCT Unit				Sunk June - Assault area
Green LCT Unit				
Green LCT Unit				
Green LCT Unit				
Red LCT Unit				Replaced by LCT 642
Green LCT Unit				
Red LCT Unit				
Green LCT Unit				
Red LCT Unit				
Red LCT Unit				
Green Beach Salvage Unit				Listed twice in Op Order. Salcombe and Dartmouth sections. Green Beach Salvage Unit and Red LCT Unit.
Green LCT Unit				
Green LCT Unit				
Support Craft Group				
Support Craft Group				
Support Craft Group				
Support Craft Group				
Support Craft Group				
Support Craft Group				
Support Craft Group				
Support Craft Group			7	
Green LST Unit 2	Tare Green	Second	Dartmouth PC3/63 24 Apr 44	
Red LST Unit 1 towing RHF 21 (Red RHF Unit)	Uncle Red	First	Dartmouth PC3/63 24 Apr 44	Discrepancy of Army units loaded between Navy and Army
Convoy commander Red LST Unit 1 commander Towing RHF 20 (Red RHF Unit)	Uncle Red	First	Dartmouth PC3/63 24 Apr 44	Discrepancy of Army units loaded between Navy and Army
Green LST Unit 2	Tare Green	Second	Plymouth PK/39 24 Apr 44	
Green LST Unit 2	Tare Green	Second	Plymouth PK/39 24 Apr 44	

LST 54	433	T3			
LST 55	443	T3	Brixham		
LST 58	502	T4	Plymouth		
LST 230	428	T2B			
LST 281	427	T2B			
LST 282	426	T2B			Comdr L E Gilbert USNR
LST 283	445	T3			
LST 284	446	T3	Plymouth		
LST 289	495	T4	Brixham		
LST 311	435	T3			Lt Comdr S B Purdie USNR
LST 346	444	T3	Brixham		
LST 371	436	T3	Brixham		
LST 380	437	T3	Brixham		
LST 382	438	T3	Brixham		
LST 400	432	T3	Plymouth		
LST 491	439	T3			Comdr J C Guillot USN
LST 492	442	T3	Brixham		
LST 496	499	T4	Plymouth		Lt (jg) Grode
LST 499	494	T4	Brixham		Lt E F Witte USN
LST 501	434	T3	Dartmouth		
LST 507	496	T4	Brixham		Lt J S Swarts USNR
LST 508	497	T4	Brixham		
LST 511	500	T4	Plymouth		6/6 Force B Division 61 Comdr B J Skahill USN
LST 515	498	T4	Plymouth		
LST 531	501	T4	Plymouth		
2 Pontoon causeways		T4	Plymouth		
ML Flotilla				M/S Unit 5	
ML 118		T2A1	Salcombe	Escort	
ML 153		T2A1	Salcombe	Escort	
ML 155		T2A1	Dartmouth	Escort	
ML 163		T2A1	Dartmouth	Escort	
ML 187		T2A1	Dartmouth	Escort	
ML 189		T2A2	Dartmouth	Escort	

Green LST Unit 2	Tare Green	Second	Dartmouth PC3/63 25 Apr 44	
Red LST unit # 2	Uncle Red	Second	Brixham PU/64 25 Apr 44	
Red LST unit # 3	Uncle red	Third	Plymouth PK/39 25 Apr 44	
Green LST Unit 1 towing RHF 11	Tare Green	First	Dartmouth PC3/63 24 Apr 44	Discrepancy of Army units loaded between Navy and Army
281 Green LST Unit 1 towing RHF 13	Tare Green	First	Dartmouth PC3/63 25 Apr 44	427 is Army serial number for LST 501 Discrepancy of Army units loaded between Navy and Army
Green LST Unit 1 commander towing RHF 19	Tare Green	First	Dartmouth PC3/63 24 Apr 44	Sunk S Farnce 15 Aug 44 Discrepancy of Army units loaded between Navy and Army
Red LST unit # 2	Uncle Red	Second	Dartmouth PC3/63 25 Apr 44	Navy Op Order lists LST 283 as Army Serial 432 Personnel total altered
Red LST unit # 2	Uncle Red	Second	Plymouth PK/39 25 Apr 44	
Green LST Unit 3	Tare Green	Third	Brixham PU/64 24 Apr 44	Damaged 28 Apr 44
Red LST unit #2	Uncle Red	Second	Dartmouth PC3/63 25 Apr 44	
Red LST unit # 2	Uncle Red	Second	Brixham PU/64 25 Apr 44	
Red LST unit # 2	Uncle Red	Second	Brixham PU/64 24 Apr 44	
Red LST unit # 2	Uncle Red	Second	Brixham PU/64 25 Apr 44	
Red LST unit # 2	Uncle Red	Second	Brixham PU/64 24 Apr 44	
Green LST Unit 2	Tare Green	Second	Plymouth PK/39 25 Apr 44	Serial 445 on Army Loading plan
Green LST Unit 2 Follow up Convoy Group Convoy commander & Section commander	Tare Green	Second	Plymouth PK/39 25 Apr 44	
Green LST Unit 2	Tare Green	Second	Brixham PU/64 25 Apr 44	Serial 447 on Navy Loading plan
Red LST unit # 3	Uncle red	Third	Plymouth PK/39 24 Apr 44	Sunk N France 11 Jun 44
Section commander Green LST unit #3	Tare Green	Third	Brixham PU/64 24 Apr 44	Sunk N France 8 Jun 44
Green LST Unit 2 Follow up Convoy Group Convoy commander & Section commander Listed in Annex Fox but not Op Order	Tare Green	Second	Dartmouth PC3/63 24 Apr 44	LST 501 is shown as Serial number 427 on Army loading plan LST 231 is shown as Serial number 434 on Army loading plan
Green LST unit # 3	Tare Green	Third	Brixham PU/64 24 Apr 44	Sunk 28 Apr 44
Green LST unit # 3	Tare Green		Brixham PU/64 24 Apr 44	
Red LST unit # 3	Uncle red	Third	Plymouth PK/39 24 Apr 44	
Convoy commander & Section commander & Red LST unit #3	Uncle red	Third	Plymouth PK/39 24 Apr 44	
Red LST unit # 3	Uncle red	Third	Plymouth PK/39 24 Apr 44	Sunk 28 Apr 44
"ML 142, 255, 257, 275"				
Close Escort Group				
Close Escort Group				
serve flagship (Bayfield)				
Close Escort Group Section escort commander				
Dispatch craft - Slapton shore service group				
Dispatch craft - Slapton shore service group				

ML 193		T1B	Salcombe	Escort	
ML 194		T2A2	Brixham	Escort & reserve flagship	
ML 195		T2A2	Brixham	Escort	
ML 214		TM5	Exmouth	Escort	Lt C H Adlitt RNVR
ML 230		T2A1	Brixham	Escort & Green unit LCT commander	Lt Comdr Armstrong RN
ML 304		T2A1	Brixham	Escort	
ML 491		T1B	Salcombe	Escort	Lt Comdr A Luddlow RNVR
MMS 261			Sweeper unit #3	132nd M/S Flotilla	
PC 80					
PC 90					
PC 484		T1A	Torbay	Escort	
PC 1176		T1A	Torbay	Escort	Lt (jg) J B Ricker USNR
PC 1261		T1A	Torbay	Escort	Lt Floyd Sewell USNR PrimaryControl Officer
RHF		T3	Dartmouth		
Shore Party					Col E J Caffey 1st Engr Sp Bde
USN 2nd Beach Bn					Comdr J F Curtin USNR
YMS Flotilla				M/S Unit 4	

Red Assault Group Relief & Dispatch craft				in Op Order - replaced by ML 491
Close Escort Group	serve flagship (Bayfield)			
Close Escort Group	serve flagship (Bayfield)			
Close Escort Group Convoy commander (after reaching sortie point) - serve flagship				
Section commander - serve flagship(Bayfield)				
Close Escort Group				
Red Assault Group				replaced ML 193
"8 Motor minesweepers MMS229, 233, 236, 274, 277, 293, 302"				
Red LCG Secondary Control Craft				
Red LCG Tertiary Control Craft				
Close Escort Group				
Green Primary control craft commander				
Red P:rimary Control Craft				
"22,23,24 & 25"				

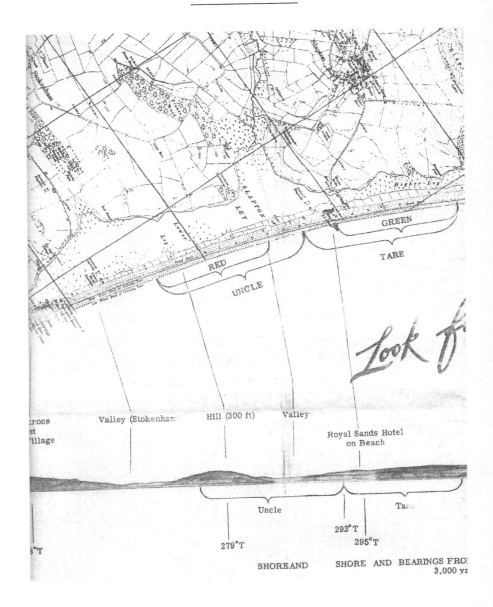

GREEN

TARE

RED

UNCLE

look f

cross
nt
illage

Valley (Stokenha...   Hill (300 ft)   Valley

Royal Sands Hotel
on Beach

Uncle   Tar...

293° T

295° T

279° T

...° T

SHORE AND   SHORE AND BEARINGS FRO...
3,000 y...

Appendix 25

ANNEX GEORGE to
OPERATION ORDER
No. 2-44

18 April 1944

Serial: 0075

LCVP ASSIGNMENT TABLE - BEACH TARE GREEN

Army Serial	Navy Serial	Troop Unit	Boat Spaces	Transport	Land
24	11TG	Co. A, 8th·Inf. SFCP Bty A 29th FA	25	DICKMAN	H -hour
25	12TG	Co. B, 8th Inf. Det Bty A 29th FA	19		
23	13TG	Co. A 8th Inf.	31		
26	14TG	Co. B 8th Inf.	31		
22	15TG	Co. A 8th Inf.	31		
27	16TG	Co. B 8th Inf.	31		
21	17TG	Co. A 8th Inf.	31		
28	18TG	Co. B 9th Inf.	31		
20	19TG	Co. A 8th Inf.	33		
29	1-10TG	Co. B 8th Inf.	33		
42	21TG	Co. C 8th Inf.	31	DICKMAN	H ≠ 7
43	22TG	Co. C 8th Inf.	31		
41	23TG	Co. C 8th Inf.	31		
44	24TG	Co. C 8th Inf. HQ Co. 1st Bn.	17		
40	25TG	Co. C 8th Inf.	33		
61	41TG	Co. D 8th Inf; Co. B 8th Inf.	31	DICKMAN	H ≠ 25
62	42TG	Co. D 8th Inf. Co. C 8th Inf.	31		
60	43TG	Co. D 8th Inf. Co. B 8th Inf.	31		
63	44TG	Co. D 8th Inf. Co. C 8th Inf.	31		
59	45TG	Co. D 8th Inf. Co. A 8th Inf.	31		
64	46TG	Co. D 8th Inf.	18		
58	47TG	Co. D 8th Inf. Co. A 8th Inf.	31		
75	51TG	1st Plat. Co. A 237 Eng.	22	DICKMAN	H ≠ 40
76	52TG	1st Plat Co. A 237 Eng.	23		
74	53TG	HQ Co. 1st Bn 8th Inf.	28		
77	54TG	2d Plat. Co. A 237 Eng.	22		
73	55TG	HQ Co. 1st Bn 8th Inf	10		
78	56TG	2d Plat, Co. A, 237th Eng.	23		
72	57TG	HQ Co 1st Bn 8th Inf	15		
79	Free	HQ Btry 29th FA; HQ 1s Bn 8th Inf.	16	On order	

Appendix 26

18 April 1944

ENCLOSURES EASY to
APPENDIX TWO to ANNEX GEORGE to
OPERATION ORDER
   No. 2-44

Serial 0075

LCVP ASSIGNMENT TABLE - BEACH UNCLE RED

Army Serial	Navy Wave	Troop Unit	Boat Spaces	Transport	Land
34	11UR	Co E 8th Inf, SFCP	25	BARNETT	H-Hour
35	12UR	Co F 8th Inf, SFCP	25		
33	13UR	Co E 8th Inf	30		
36	14UR	Co F, 8th Inf	31		
32	15UR	Co E 8th Inf	31		
37	16UR	Co F, 8th Inf	31		
31	17UR	Co E 8th Inf	31		
38	18UR	Co f, 8th Inf	31		
30	19UR	Co E, 8th Inf	33		
39	1-10UR	Co F, 8th Inf	33		
47	21UR	Co G, 8th Inf	31	BARNETT	H / 7
48	22UR	Co G, 8th Inf	31		
46	23UR	Co G, 8th Inf	31		
49	24UR	Co G, 8th Inf	33		
45	25URr	Co G, 8th Inf, HQ 2d Bn 8th Inf	17		
68	41UR	Co H, 8th Inf, Co F 8th Inf	31	BARNETT	H / 25
69	42UR	Co H 8th Inf, Co G 8th Inf	31		
67	43UR	Co H. 8th Inf, Co F, 8th Inf	31		
70	44UR	Co H, 8th Inf, Co G, 8th Inf	31		
66	45UR	Co H, 8th Inf, Co E, 8th Inf	31		
71	46UR	Co H, 8th Inf,	18		
65	47UR	Co H, 8th Inf, Co E, 8th Inf	31		
84	51UR	Co C, 237th Eng C Bn	23	BARNETT	H / 40
85	52UR	HQ Co 2d Bn, Med Det	15		
83	53UR	Co C, 237th Eng C Bn	22		
86	54UR	HQ Co 2d Bn; Med Sect	15		
82	55UR	Co C, 237th Eng	23		
87	56UR	HQ Co 2d Bn 8th Inf	28		
81	57UR	Co C, 237th Eng Bn	22		
80	Free	HQ Co 2d Bn 8th Inf; HQ 29 FA Bn	16	BARNETT	On order

ENCLOSURE EASY To
APPENDIX TWO to ANNEX GEORGE

18 April 1944

ENCLOSURES EASY to
APPENDIX TWO to ANNEX GEORGE to
OPERATION ORDER
   No. 2-44

Serial 0075

LCVP ASSIGNMENT TABLE - BEACH UNCLE RED

Army Serial	Navy Wave	Troop Unit	Boat Spaces	Transport	Land
34	11UR	Co E 8th Inf, SFCP	25	BARNETT	H-Hour
35	12UR	Co F 8th Inf, SFCP	25		
33	13UR	Co E 8th Inf	30		
36	14UR	Co F, 8th Inf	31		
32	15UR	Co E 8th Inf	31		
37	16UR	Co F, 8th Inf	31		
31	17UR	Co E 8th Inf	31		
38	18UR	Co f, 8th Inf	31		
30	19UR	Co E, 8th Inf	33		
39	1-10UR	Co F, 8th Inf	33		
47	21UR	Co G, 8th Inf	31	BARNETT	H / 7
48	22UR	Co G, 8th Inf	31		
46	23UR	Co G, 8th Inf	31		
49	24UR	Co G, 8th Inf	33		
45	25URr	Co G, 8th Inf, HQ 2d Bn 8th Inf	17		
68	41UR	Co H, 8th Inf, C_o F 8th Inf	31	BARNETT	H / 25
69	42UR	Co H 8th Inf, C_o G 8th Inf	31		
67	43UR	Co H. 8th Inf, C_o F, 8th Inf	31		
70	44UR	Co H, 8th Inf, Co G, 8th Inf	31		
66	45UR	Co H, 8th Inf, Co E, 8th Inf	31		
71	46UR	Co H, 8th Inf,	18		
65	47UR	Co H, 8th Inf, Co E, 8th Inf	31		
84	51UR	Co C, 237th Eng C Bn	23	BARNETT	H / 40
85	52UR	HQ Co 2d Bn, Med Det	15		
83	53UR	Co C, 237th Eng C Bn	22		
86	54UR	HQ Co 2d Bn; Med Sect	15		
82	55UR	Co C, 237th Eng	23		
87	56UR	HQ Co 2d Bn 8th Inf	28		
81	57UR	Co C, 237th Eng Bn	22		
80	Free	HQ Co 2d Bn 8th Inf; HQ 29 FA Bn	16	BARNETT	On order

-16-

ENCLOSURE EASY To
APPENDIX TWO to ANNEX GEORGE

Appendix 27

APPENDIX TWO to ANNEX NAN to   18 April 1944
OPERATION ORDER
   NO. 2-44

Serial: 0075

MEDICAL PLAN FOR HANDLING AND DISPOSING OF SIMULATED CASUALTIES.

  1.   Simulated casualties will be designated through Exercise TIGER from
D day to midafternoon of D plus 1. Designation of casualties will be by Army
Umpires who will affix tags indicating the type of injury. These simulated
casualties are to be handled as realistically as possible and in accordance
with the VII Corps and Task Force 125 Operation TIGER Medical Plans.

  2.   Army Umpires will correlate simulated personnel casualties with
simulated or actual material casualties.

  3.   Casualty tags will be furnished by the Army.

  4.   Litters and blankets employed in TIGER will be furnished by the
Army.

  5.   Property exchange as outlined in Paragraph 4 - SUPPLIES of Navy
Medical Plan will not be carried out, but blankets, litters, and splints will
be handled as follows:

        (a) Army medical units will furnish litters, blankets, and splints
            normally.
        (b) 2nd Beach Battalion Medical Platoons will furnish litters,
            blankets, and splints, normally.
        (c) Exchange Unit of medical supplies will be furnished LST No. 47
            to be landed by the Engineer Special Brigade in accordance with
            Paragraph 4(c) of Medical Plan.
        (d) All simulated casualties will be charged with returning to the
            beach Medical Property used on them.

  6.   Beach Battalion will disperse the simulated casualties to as many
ships as practical in order to give as many as possible practice in casualty
handling.

  7.   As soon as casualties are handled through the casualty evacuation
ships, they will be returned to the beach with the medical gear they brought
with them to the ship. The medical gear will be deposited in dumps established
at the Aid Stations for collection by the 261st Medical Battalion. The simulated
casualties will be turned over to the 649th Clearing Company for messing, quarter-
ing, and return to their various organizations. These Army personnel must be
returned to the beach as rapidly as possible and in any case before the ships
depart the area.

  8.   The medical property used in this exercise is not practice equipment,
but must be used in actual operation. To that end, care must be employed in
using it, and every effort must be made to see that it is returned properly and
promptly to the units to whom it belongs.

                              -1-   APPENDIX TWO to ANNEX NAN

Appendix 28

DATE ... 29th April 1944

To ... THE FLAG OFFICER IN CHARGE, PORTLAND,
(Copies to :- The Commander in Chief, Plymouth.

COM 11th PHIB
CONGROUP TWO 11th PHIB
Captain (D), Plymouth.)

The following survivors were picked up by ONSLOW on 28th April, 1944.

2.

Name	Rank	Number	Unit
Leonard F BICKFORD	Pte	39540356	462 A.T. Compy
George C GRADY Tech:Cpl:5		31383637	.. .. ..
Narion BRITT	Pte	37626348	607 G.R. Com:
Walter A. BORKONSKI	H.A.1	8135891	U.S.N.R.
Walter J. WIDIUK	Sea:1	7066002	..
Joseph W. Holland Motor Mach.1,		7617339	..
Wendall JONES	Sea:2	6374342	..
Edgar W. DORTCH	First:Lt.	0-1584149	3206 Q.M. Service Com. 1st Engineers Special Brigade.
James RILEY	Private	37504720	.. ..
Siden STRICKER	Sgt	37502527	.. ..
Marion P. HARRISON	Cpl.	37503225	.. ..
Eugene DALE	Pte.	37504135	.. ..
Earl PICHT	Pte.	37503275	.. ..
Laurence A. RIDER	Pte	39144508	607 Q.M. Copps. 531 Div
Hartly W. WAGNER	Sea.	856289	U.S.N.R.
Henry L. SHREWDER	G.M.3.	65048	..
William W. DONEY	Sig 3.	7626344	..
George WYVILLE	Ships Ck.3	7091520	..
Robert NOWLAN	Pte.	13121100	531 Engineering Shore Regiment H.Q. Coy. 1st Batt
Harry BEAVER	Pte.	35290951	.. ..
Raymond A. GOSSELIN	Ensign.	313876	U.S.N.R.
Eugene T. HOCH	Ensign.	189642	..
Douglas HARLANDER	Ensign	224045	..
Maynard P. KLOSSNER	Sea,1.	6656725	..
* Donald R. POST		8083120	..
Theodore JACHOWEZ	Pte.	39011337	3206 Q.M. Service Comm. 1st Engineers Special Brigade
George WHEELER	Pte.	37413584	..
Harvey HARDINGE	Pte.	35748956	..
Lloyd R. MANN	Fire 2.	80596	U.S.N.R.
Arthur DECKELMAN	MM2.	7505824	..
James BROWN	GM3.	8171133	..
Issidore F. KATTRUSZ Sea.2		24618908	..
William B. HICKS	SF3.	8681818	..
Victor A. RACCI	Pte.	31229646	35th Signal Construction Batt.
John HENLEY.	Sea.2.	8031132	U.S.N.R.

Man under Morphia, full details could not be obtained.

ALL SURVIVORS WERE FROM U.S. L.S.T. 531
The following dead men were also picked up. (See * below).

	HARTZ ?		Lieutenant, Signal Corps ?	
	Walter BURGFELD	37411567		T.43 43AP
	L. H. LEVY.		? Lieutenant U.S.N.R. ?	
*	Lindsay PETERS, Jnr.	01584731		T.42 43A.
*	Lester WRIGHT	01641083		T.42 43.
	VENDERLAND		Seaman 1st Cl. ?	?

* The identity discs of these men were taken from them. The bodies had to be left in the water.

For CAPTAIN

FROM. . The Commanding Officer,

H.M.S. "Obedient".

DATE . . 28th April, 1944.   No. 680/900

TO . . . The Flag Officer-in-Charge,

Portland.

(Copies to:- The Commander-in-Chief

Plymouth.
COM 11th PHIB.
COMGROUP TWO 11th

The following survivors were
Picked up by "Obedient" on 28th April, 1944.

Cecil L. Huston,   Cpl. 38046842,   1605 Engineers, Map Depot Detachment.

Thomas J. DeLucan, Sergt.   32318553, 3206 Q.M. Service Com. 1st Engineers Special
                                                   Brigade.

Both men were from U.S. L.S.T. 507 and both retained their personal belongings.

Lieutenant Commander
In Command

COPY

To: F.O.I.C. PORTLAND.   FROM: ONSLOW.
          (R) CINC PLYMOUTH, COM 11TH PHIB,
          COM GROUP 2 11TH PHIB,
          CAPTAIN (D) PLYMOUTH.

My letter of 28th April, re survivors. Add to paragraph 2
Repeat 2 :-

John P. BROWN M.	M.M.2.	8350996	U.S.N.R.
John SCHULASKI	Fireman 1	8124951	U.S.N.R.

T.O.O. 281315B.

Appendix 29

SECRET - TIGER

APPENDIX ONE to ANNEX NAN to   18 April 1944
OPERATION ORDER
No. 2-44

Serial: 0075

MEDICAL PLAN FOR ACTUAL CASUALTIES

Actual casualties occurring in this operation will be taken care of as follows:

1. Navy

    (a) Injured - to limits of capacity of medical facilities of ship on which injury occurs or is brought. If beyond the capacity of the ship, transfer to any APA or to USN Dispensary, Dartmouth.

    (b) Dead - In accordance with ComLanCrabEu order #42, subject "Death of U.S. Naval Personnel, Procedure following".

2. Army

    (a) Injured - To capacity of ship in which injury occurs or to which patient is brought. If beyond capacity of ship's medical facilities, transfer to any APA or to Army facilities in accordance with wishes of cognizant Senior Army Officer present

    NOTE - VII Corps, U.S. Army, will establish a static collecting station for actual casualties in the vicinity of POUNDHOUSE (Y-294709) which will take care of actual casualties.

    (b) Dead - Hold for Army Graves Registration Service or release to Army in accordance to wishes of cognizant Senior Army Officer present.

Appendix 30

Name	Service No.	Rank	Organization	Burial Dy M Yr	A B M C	N A R A	Reburied
MUZA, Earl V.	869-53-48	S2/c	USNR	2 May 44	no trace		WISC
ROBERTS, Clifford L.	875-50-78	QM2/c	USNR	2 May 44	no trace		
SHIPP, John L. Jr.	659-79-04	S1/c	USNR	2 May 44	no trace		Hampton, VA
NEFF, Harold A.	942-98-57	S2/c	USNR	2 May 44	no trace		
GRIFFIN, Joseph W.	607-66-80	SK2/c	USNR	2 May 44			Cambridge
MACDONALD, Lawrence E.	35388045	S/Sgt	3206 Q.M. Serv. Co.	4 May 44	no trace	19181585	MINN
LAMBERT, Douglas L.	35444446	Pfc	557 Q.M. Railhead Co.	1 May 44	no trace		W VA
BOHL, Jacob A.	36821790	Pvt	557 Q.M. Railhead Co.	1 May 44	no trace		Cambridge
MORANG, Robert C.	31217684	Pfc	557 Q.M. Railhead Co.	1 May 44	no trace		MAINE
HANKS, John P.	34763923	Pfc	557 Q.M. Railhead Co.	1 May 44	no trace		?
WEST, Chalcie G.	34438934	Pvt	557 Q.M. Railhead Co.	1 May 44	no trace		N CAR
MARCUM, Glenn R.	20518566	Pvt	557 Q.M. Railhead Co.	1 May 44			Cambridge
YANARELLO, Dominick	42035605	Pvt	557 Q.M. Railhead Co.	1 May 44	no trace		NY
BROWN, George E.	39396010	T/5	557 Q.M. Railhead Co.	1 May 44			Cambridge
MITCHELL, James C.	38119032	S/Sgt	557 Q.M. Railhead Co.	1 May 44	no trace		TX
BLAKE, Floyd E.	35410567	T/4	557 Q.M. Railhead Co.	1 May 44	35410567		35410567-OHIO
BLAKE, Floyd E.	33271593						
MARINO J.A.	32220065	Pvt	557 Q.M. Railhead Co.	1 May 44	Joseph		Cambridge
ZEMPEL, Lawrence C.	36266902	Pfc	557 Q.M. Railhead Co.	1 May 44			Cambridge
GONSHIRSKI, John J.	35511468	Pvt	557 Q.M. Railhead Co.	1 May 44	no trace		OHIO
HOGLAND, Alvie M.	34390350	Pfc	557 Q.M. Railhead Co.	1 May 44	no trace		MISS
SCHWARTZ. Stephen G.	32337843	Pfc	557 Q.M. Railhead Co.	1 May 44	no trace		Gettysburg, PA
EINTRACHT, Herman	33328846	Pvt	557 Q.M. Railhead Co.	1 May 44			Cambridge
NATHAN, Hyman	32821535	Pvt	557 Q.M. Railhead Co.	1 May 44			Cambridge
SILVERSMITH, Samuel	42035925	Pvt	557 Q.M. Railhead Co.	1 May 44	no trace		?
TYSON, Ernest	32802841	Pvt	557 Q.M. Railhead Co.	1 May 44	no trace		?
SWEENEY, Myles E	42030843	Pvt	557 Q.M. Railhead Co.	1 May 44			Cambridge
DYE, Quong, Jee	32596619	Pfc	557 Q.M. Railhead Co.	1 May 44	no trace		?
MORSE, Erwin F.	31206069	Pfc	557 Q.M. Railhead Co.	1 May 44			Cambridge
PRITT, Isaac W.	35444182	Pfc	557 Q.M. Railhead Co.	1 May 44	no trace		?
MARINO, Patty	32538043	Pfc	557 Q.M. Railhead Co.	1 May 44	no trace		Long Island, NY
GODSEY, Shirley C.	35444544	T/5	557 Q.M. Railhead Co.	1 May 44			Cambridge
HAYNES, Ernest P.	32716315	Pvt	557 Q.M. Railhead Co.	1 May 44	no trace		?
METHNER, Paul H.	36712742	Pfc	557 Q.M. Railhead Co.	1 May 44			Cambridge
GLASS, John P.	35416769	T/5	557 Q.M. Railhead Co.	1 May 44	no trace		?
PENTECOST, Curtis	14041607	Pfc	557 Q.M. Railhead Co.	1 May 44	no trace		?
MORGENSTERN, A.G.	35605272	Pfc	557 Q.M. Railhead Co.	1 May 44	Aloysius		Cambridge
WILLIS, Obie D.	34575369	T/5	557 Q.M. Railhead Co.	1 May 44			?
VEENBAAS, John C.	37448967	Pvt	557 Q.M. Railhead Co.	1 May 44			Cambridge
VONWALD, Richard F.	36251672	S/Sgt	557 Q.M. Railhead Co.	1 May 44			Cambridge
CAVANAGH, James P.	32808444	Pvt	557 Q.M. Railhead Co.	1 May 44	no trace		Long Island, NY
CAMPBELL, William M.	34425815	Pfc	557 Q.M. Railhead Co.	1 May 44			Cambridge
BATTLE, William R.	36875514	Pvt	557 Q.M. Railhead Co.	1 May 44			Cambridge
VIEIRA, Manuel	31137027	Pvt	557 Q.M. Railhead Co.	1 May 44	no trace		?
DE LEON, Anastacio	32108629	Pfc	557 Q.M. Railhead Co.	1 May 44	no trace		Long Island, NY

Name	Service No.	Rank	Organization	Burial Dy M Yr	ABMC	NARA	Reburied
OLSEN, John A.	32860180	Pfc	557 Q.M. Railhead Co.	1 May 44			Cambridge
FOLLMER, William J.	35472974	Pfc	557 Q.M. Railhead Co.	1 May 44			Cambridge
WRIGHT, Joseph O.	32732324	Pvt	557 Q.M. Railhead Co.	1 May 44			Cambridge
BARRETT, Chester	32506520	S/Sgt	557 Q.M. Railhead Co.	1 May 44			Cambridge
ALEXANDER, Walter	32420064	Pvt	557 Q.M. Railhead Co.	1 May 44			Cambridge
BLOND, William	35545484	Pvt	557 Q.M. Railhead Co.	1 May 44	no trace		?
SEIBERT, Ray E.	0-1580301	Capt	557 Q.M. Railhead Co.	2 May 44	no trace		?
TOMBERLIN, Clarence H.	0-1576749	1st Lt	557 Q.M. Railhead Co.	2 May 44	no trace		Marietta, GA
CRAWFORD, P.D. Jr.	38205141	Pfc	557 Q.M. Railhead Co.	1 May 44	Poindexter		Cambridge
MONK, Clarence	34440548	Pfc	557 Q.M. Railhead Co.	1 May 44			Cambridge
DI PASQUALE, Michael J.	0-1585368	2nd Lt	557 Q.M. Railhead Co.	2 May 44			Cambridge
SWANSON, Richard E.	19016503	T/Sgt	1605 Engr Map Depot Det.	1 May 44	no trace		?
WALSH, Joseph J.	33099540	T/3	1605 Engr Map Depot Det.	1 May 44	no trace		?
HOOPS, George E.	39312785	Pvt	1605 Engr Map Depot Det.	1 May 44	no trace		
EDWARDS, John J	35377891	Pfc	531 Engr Shore Regt.	1 May 44			Cambridge
PARK, Clifford F.	32899794	Pvt	531 Engr Shore Regt.	1 May 44	no trace		Cypress Hills, NY
SIMMONS, Leland	39237054	Pfc	531 Engr Shore Regt.	1 May 44			Cambridge
STEEN, George W.	32950816	Pvt	531 Engr Shore Regt.	1 May 44			Cambridge
BORCHERS, Harvey J.	39308563	Pfc	531 Engr Shore Regt.	1 May 44			Cambridge
BISAILLON, Martial J.	31053434	T/5	531 Engr Shore Regt.	1 May 44			Cambridge
LILLO, Rocco F.	32926865	Pvt	531 Engr Shore Regt.	1 May 44			Cambridge
STEVENS, Marshall J.	31102109	Pfc	531 Engr Shore Regt.	1 May 44	no trace		?
ELLIOTT, William R.	35377903	Pfc	Hq Co 2nd Bn 531 Engr Shore Regt	2 May 44			Cambridge
SUESSE, Ralph A.	0-1035021	Capt	33rd Chem. Deco. Co.	1 May 44			Cambridge
SIGMAN, Charles W.	34443424	Pvt	33rd Chem. Deco. Co.	1 May 44	no trace		Long Island, NY
CLAYTON, Kenneth	37408572	Pvt	33rd Chem. Deco. Co.	1 May 44	no trace		?
STRAPP, John W.	35505209	T/4	33rd Chem. Deco. Co.	1 May 44	no trace		?
BERTINI, Nilo V.	33322366	Pfc	33rd Chem. Deco. Co.	1 May 44			Cambridge
BERNARDO, John	32409916	Pfc	33rd Chem. Deco. Co.	1 May 44	no trace		?
JOHNSON, Horace	34514719	Pvt	33rd Chem. Deco. Co.	1 May 44			Cambridge
ROSOWSKI, A.J.	33587420	Pvt	33rd Chem. Deco. Co.	1 May 44			?
STOKES, Oris A.	31110688	Pvt	33rd Chem. Deco. Co.	1 May 44	no trace		?
MIECZKOWSKI, Harry	36510674	T/5	33rd Chem. Deco. Co.	1 May 44	no trace		Camp Butler, ILL
NIEDERMEIER, C.C.	38377638	Sgt	607 QM GRS Co	1 May 44	no trace		?
CARACCIOLO, Dominick	32194654	Pfc	607 QM GRS Co	1 May 44	no trace		DoD 5Apr44
SANDERS, E.J.	35098574	Pfc	607 QM GRS Co	1 May 44	no trace		?
GREVON, John C.	39285912	S/Sgt	607 QM GRS Co	1 May 44			Cambridge
WARD, Luther T.	34168137	Pfc	607 QM GRS Co	1 May 44	no trace		?
DAKIS, Nick C.	36666554	Pvt	607 QM GRS Co	1 May 44	initial G	no trace	Cambridge
WAUGH, J.N.	827-91-88	S1/c	U.S. Navy	1 May 44	James		Cambridge
VANNATTA, Raul J.	35573665	Pvt	35th Constr.Bn.(Signal)	1 May 44	no trace	Paul	?
NELSON, Hollis L.	34447215	T/4	35th Constr.Bn.(Signal)	1 May 44	no trace		MISP
McCLATCHEY, Evert M.	38230181	T/5	35th Constr.Bn.(Signal)	1 May 44			Cambridge
WILSON, Kenneth P.	15324742	T/5	35th Constr.Bn.(Signal)	1 May 44			Cambridge
WRIGHT, Lester	0-1641083	2nd Lt	35th Constr.Bn.(Signal)	2 May 44	no trace	no trace	?
VAN ESS, Simon	36463730	T/5	462 Amph.Trk.Co.	1 May 44			Cambridge
SCHULTHEIS, C.L.	35756590	Pvt	462 Amph.Trk.Co.	1 May 44	Carl L.		Cambridge
VAN NOSTRAND, C.M.	32858037	T/5	462 Amph.Trk.Co.	1 May 44	Clarence		Cambridge
HOBBS, Charles W.	0-1315688	2nd Lt	462 Amph.Trk.Co.	2 May 44	no trace		?
CONKLIN, Robert J.	32918383	T/5	462 Amph.Trk.Co.	2 May 44	no trace		?

Name	Service No.	Rank	Organization	Burial Dy M Yr	ABMC	NARA	Reburied
GOODHUE, Elmer J.	31215043	Cpl	3891st Q.M. Truck Co.	1 May 44			Cambridge
MISCIAGNO, Christian	32682571	T/5	3891st Q.M. Truck Co.	1 May 44			Cambridge
KREUTZ, Harold E.	0-1591251	2nd Lt	3891st Q.M. Truck Co.	2 May 44	no trace		?
GRAHAM, Thomas D. Jr.	34655706	T/5	3021 Q.M. Bakery	1 May 44			Cambridge
OCCHIPINTI, Joseph	32890847	Pvt	557 Q.M. Railhead Co.	6 May 44			Cambridge
JOYAL, Raymond O.	11031014	T/5	478 Amph.Truck Co	1 May 44			Cambridge
OGUREK, M.A.	32108130	Cpl	478 Amph.Truck Co	1 May 44	Michael		Cambridge
CATMAN, Ulysses J.	32858792	Pvt	478 Amph.Truck Co	1 May 44	no trace		Long Island, NY
SCANLON, Edward T.	36007782	T/5	478 Amph.Truck Co	1 May 44	no trace		?
SOUTHCOTT, Herbert A.	32032890	T/5	478 Amph.Truck Co	1 May 44	no trace		Rochester, NY
DINDINO, Paul J.	33311953	T/5	478 Amph.Truck Co	1 May 44			Cambridge
MIGLIONICO, John A.	32108038	T/5	478 Amph.Truck Co	1 May 44	no trace		Long Island, NY
MASSA, Charles F.	6912640	Pfc	478 Amph.Truck Co	1 May 44			Cambridge
LEE, Harold E.	35004178	T/4	478 Amph.Truck Co	1 May 44			Cambridge
BROWN, John B.	34776588	Pvt	478 Amph.Truck Co	1 May 44	no trace		?
MLAKAR, Albert	33032707	S/Sgt	478 Amph.Truck Co	1 May 44			Cambridge
HUMBLE, Merle B.	33102342	T/5	478 Amph.Truck Co	1 May 44	no trace		?
GRIGSBY, Roy B.	34801109	Pvt	478 Amph.Truck Co	1 May 44			Cambridge
POWELL, Herrel K.	0-324403	1st Lt	478 Amph.Truck Co	1 May 44			Cambridge
ARCURI, Sam S.	32035938	T/5	478 Amph.Truck Co	1 May 44	no trace		?
HARRISON, Frank G. Jr.	35596178	T/4	625 Ord. Amm. Co.	1 May 44	no trace		Cambridge
FRANKS, Richard L.	35595949	Pvt	625 Ord. Amm. Co.	1 May 44	no trace		?
PENALVER, Joe V.	18012028	Pvt	3206 Q.M. Serv. Co.	1 May 44	no trace		Ft Sam Houston, TX
MEURER, Lawrence L.	37416408	Pfc	3206 Q.M. Serv. Co.	1 May 44			Cambridge
WILSON, Paul W.	38185187	Pfc	3206 Q.M. Serv. Co.	1 May 44			Cambridge
THOMAS, Fay E.	37504430	Pfc	3206 Q.M. Serv. Co.	1 May 44	no trace	2 service numbers	
NAGEL, Curtis A.	37502727	Pfc	3206 Q.M. Serv. Co.	1 May 44			Cambridge
CLARK, Herman D.	37503147	Pfc	3206 Q.M. Serv. Co.	1 May 44	no trace		Springfield, MO
POPE, Edgar F.	32554089	T/4	3206 Q.M. Serv. Co.	1 May 44	no trace		?
SPURLING, James W.	37416680	Pfc	3206 Q.M. Serv. Co.	1 May 44			Cambridge
BRYSON, Ernest C.	37415508	Pvt	3206 Q.M. Serv. Co.	1 May 44	no trace		?
REESE, William R.	35003973	1st Sgt	3206 Q.M. Serv. Co.	1 May 44			Cambridge
BOYLES, Hoy F.	37503191	Pvt	3206 Q.M. Serv. Co.	1 May 44	no trace		?
KLOBE, John T.	37415642	Cpl	3206 Q.M. Serv. Co.	1 May 44	no trace		?
CICCIO, Joseph	37501145	Cpl	3206 Q.M. Serv. Co.	1 May 44			Cambridge
BUTRY, Metro	33604511	Pvt	3206 Q.M. Serv. Co.	1 May 44			Cambridge
GUFFIN, Dale E.	37503381	Cpl	3206 Q.M. Serv. Co.	1 May 44			Cambridge
WINTJEN, Floyd E.	37416334	Pfc	3206 Q.M. Serv. Co.	1 May 44			Cambridge
GROVES, Marvin W.	37659918	T/5	3206 Q.M. Serv. Co.	1 May 44	no trace		?
MORGAN, Alvin G.	37504065	Pfc	3206 Q.M. Serv. Co.	1 May 44	no trace		?
FLOYD, Charles R.	37659872	Pvt	3206 Q.M. Serv. Co.	1 May 44			Cambridge
GOSS, Dennie	37416264	Pvt	3206 Q.M. Serv. Co.	1 May 44			Cambridge
BURGFELD, Walter	37415567	Pvt	3206 Q.M. Serv. Co.	1 May 44	no trace		Russell Heights, Missouri
HUMPHREY William L.	37504138	Pfc	3206 Q.M. Serv. Co.	1 May 44			Cambridge
CALLAHAN, John H.	37416192	Pfc	3206 Q.M. Serv. Co.	1 May 44			Cambridge
SNYDER, Wallace F.	0-258951	Capt	3206 Q.M. Serv. Co.	1 May 44	no trace		?
COPE, C.J.	37504179	Pfc	3206 Q.M. Serv. Co.	1 May 44	no trace	Christopher T	?
MATHEWSON, John I.	0-418809	Capt	3206 Q.M. Serv. Co.	1 May 44	no trace		Golden Gate, CA
LAIACONA, Salvatore	0-357935	1st Lt	3206 Q.M. Serv. Co.	1 May 44	no trace		?
KREISS, Ezra F.	33188497	S/Sgt	3206 Q.M. Serv. Co.	1 May 44			Cambridge

Name	Service No.	Rank	Organization	Burial Dy M Yr	ABMC NARA	Reburied
HOLLON, Otis L.	37498733	Pfc	3206 Q.M. Serv. Co.	1 May 44	no trace	White Oak, MO
KAY, William M.	37415554	Pfc	3206 Q.M. Serv. Co.	1 May 44	no trace	?
CESARO, Libro C.	42002642	Pvt	3206 Q.M. Serv. Co.	1 May 44		Cambridge
WILLIAMS, Horace S.	38393615	Cpl	3206 Q.M. Serv. Co.	1 May 44	no trace	?
LOUDER, Blaine L.	37503238	Pfc	3206 Q.M. Serv. Co.	1 May 44	no trace	Springfield, MO
BRECHEISEN, Calvin	37503150	T/5	3206 Q.M. Serv. Co.	1 May 44	no trace	?
GOLFINOPULOS, Louis	37415686	Pfc	3206 Q.M. Serv. Co.	1 May 44	no trace	Jefferson Barracks, MO
CHAMBERS, Robert G	37502173	Pvt	3206 Q.M. Serv. Co.	1 May 44	no trace	?
WRIGHT, Myron A. Jr.	37502117	Pfc	3206 Q.M. Serv. Co.	1 May 44	no trace	Cambridge
HAILE, Francis L.	37503825	Pfc	3206 Q.M. Serv. Co.	1 May 44	no trace	?
BLEVINS, Harley E.	37504160	Pfc	3206 Q.M. Serv. Co.	1 May 44		Cambridge
SHARFF, Willard C.	37659948	Cpl	3206 Q.M. Serv. Co.	1 May 44		Cambridge
ROBERSON, Melvin A. **	37416153	Pvt	3206 Q.M. Serv. Co.	1 May 44	no trace	?
HACKES, Mike G.	712-01-76	S2/c	LST 289 U.S. Navy	2 May 44		Cambridge
HARVIE, James H.	806-02-82	S2/c	LST 289 U.S. Navy	2 May 44		Cambridge
KORTENHORN, Herman R.	868-31-11	F1/c	LST 289 U.S. Navy	2 May 44		Cambridge
BROSKE, Mitchell	807-27-14	GM3/c	LST 289 U.S. Navy	3 May 44	no trace	
MAY, Robert M.	657-87-98	S2/c	LST 289 U.S. Navy	3 May 44	no trace	Raleigh, NC
HILL, John H.	363-969	Lt(jg) EVS	LST 531 U.S. Navy	2 May 44	no trace	
HURLEY, James W.	834-88-54	HA2/c	LST 531 U.S. Navy	2 May 44		Cambridge
COYLE, Michael J.	245-67-29	Bkr3/c	LST 531 U.S. Navy	2 May 44		Cambridge
BROCK, Norris G.	825-08-32	S1/c	LST 531 U.S. Navy	2 May 44	no trace	
KESSINGER, Mark F.	895-33-32	S2/c	LST 531 U.S. Navy	2 May 44	no trace	Mountain View, WVA
LAND, Charles G.	867-76-58	S2/c	LST 531 U.S. Navy	2 May 44	no trace	KY
LOCKLEAR, Melvin L.	341-72-16	CCS	LST 531 U.S. Navy	2 May 44	no trace	
HAYTH, Eugene N.	612-46-06	SF2/c	LST 531 U.S. Navy	2 May 44	no trace	
EDSON, Richard W.	800-88-96	S2/c	LST 531 U.S. Navy	2 May 44	no trace	
KUHNS, Harold D.	805-57-59	S2/c	LST 531 U.S. Navy	3 May 44	no trace	
PEAR, William	647-48-20	EM3/c	LST 531 U.S. Navy	3 May 44	no trace	
KIRKWOOD, R.	855-93-04	F2/c	LST 531 U.S. Navy	3 May 44	Ralph A	Cambridge
KRIZANOSKY, A.	249-52-60	F2/c	LST 531 U.S. Navy	3 May 44	no trace	
HOLMES, Samuel D.	83-27-30	MoMM2/c	LST 531 U.S. Navy	3 May 44	Jr	Cambridge
PARKER, Cornelius J.	843-60-94	MoMM2/c	LST 531 U.S. Navy	3 May 44	no trace	
UNGER, A.C.	821-30-84	SK3/c	LST 531 U.S. Navy	3 May 44	no trace	
BOLLING, Floyd H.	832-77-42	S2/c	LST 531 U.S. Navy	3 May 44	no trace	
HAUBER, Bernard A.	629-00-91	EM2/c	LST 531 U.S. Navy	3 May 44	no trace	
MONTGOMERY, Doyle D.	656-18-11	Y1/c	LST 531 U.S. Navy	3 May 44	no trace	
WENDELAND, Albert J.	857-79-69	S1/c	LST 531 U.S. Navy	3 May 44	no trace	
GALLAGHER, J. J.	313847	Ensign DVG	LST 531 U.S. Navy	3 May 44		Cambridge
ACKMAN, Walter P.	267-163	Ens. VVG	LST 531 U.S. Navy	3 May 44	Jr	Cambridge
LEVY, L.H.	247575	Lt DVS	LST 531 U.S. Navy	3 May 44	no trace	
MANNING, Tiffany J.	132268	Lt (jg) MC	LST 531 U.S. Navy	3 May 44	Tiffany V	Cambridge
PETCAVAGE, William J.	820-95-96	S1/c	LST 531 U.S. Navy	3 May 44		Cambridge
ACHEY, Allen O. Jr.	832-41-77	MoMM3/c	LST 531 U.S. Navy	2 May 44	no trace	
ACQUES, Edmond J.	823-92-33	S2/c	LST 531 U.S. Navy	2 May 44	Edmond Leopo	823-92-38 Cambridge
KELLY, Ford H.	851-79-75	S2/c	LST 531 U.S. Navy	2 May 44	no trace	
MILLER, Ralph R.	249-87-62	Cox	LST 531 U.S. Navy	2 May 44	no trace	
SOLOMON, William	872-68-77	HA1/c	LST 531 U.S. Navy	2 May 44	no trace	Beverley, NJ
BAUGHER, Ellis W.	864-47-68	HA2/c	LST 531 U.S. Navy	3 May 44	no trace	
DAWSON, Glenn H.	263-66-86	HA1/c	LST 531 U.S. Navy	3 May 44		Cambridge

Name	Service No.	Rank	Organization	Burial Dy M Yr	ABMC	NARA	Reburied
COWAN, Eugene R.	892-91-68	S1/c	LST 531 U.S. Navy	3 May 44	Cox		Cambridge
SHEPPARD, Thannel V.	534-44-49		LST 531 U.S. Navy	3 May 44	no trace		
SCHIMANSKE, Daniel R.	623-34-49	GM3/c	LST 531 U.S. Navy	3 May 44	no trace		New Albany, IN
CARR, Fredrick C.	627-94-66	Cox	LST 531 U.S. Navy	3 May 44	no trace		
LACEY, Burvil E.	868-18-94	S2/c	LST 531 U.S. Navy	3 May 44	no trace		
PETERS, James D.	819-11-09	Cox	LST 531 U.S. Navy	3 May 44	no trace		
SHOWERS, Lyle F.	312-51-92	PhM3/c	LST 531 U.S. Navy	3 May 44	no trace		
HARRELL, Charles	556-93-72	HA1/c	LST 531 U.S. Navy	3 May 44			Cambridge
WITTEN, Lloyd L.	355-93-60	CPhM	LST 531 U.S. Navy	3 May 44			Cambridge
LEVINE, Harry	812-86-95	Hq1/c	LST 531 U.S. Navy	3 May 44	no trace		
DENTON, H.	807-58-00	SM3/c	LST 531 U.S. Navy	3 May 44	no trace		
CALLAS, Vincent M.	811-88-95	S1/c	LST 531 U.S. Navy	3 May 44	no trace		
BENTON, Elmer C.	601-54-00	S2/c	LST 531 U.S. Navy	3 May 44	no trace		Cedra River, NY
SOCHACKI, Edward A.	312-57-81	PhM2/c	LST 531 U.S. Navy	3 May 44	no trace		
LEEMAN, Hollace H.	846-06-42	HA2/c	LST 531 U.S. Navy	3 May 44			Cambridge
STEMATS, Steve J.	807-54-30	RM3/c	LST 531 U.S. Navy	3 May 44	no trace		
SAUCIER, Henry Q.	188-420	Lt (jg)	LST 507 U.S. Navy	2 May 44	no trace		
KARASINSKI, Louis F.	710-92-02	S1c	LST 507 U.S. Navy	2 May 44	no trace		Beverley, NJ
WOODS, Deward W.	295-80-67	GN1/c	LST 507 U.S. Navy	2 May 44	no trace		
CUSACK, Vincent P.	709-32-53	S2/c	LST 507 U.S. Navy	2 May 44	no trace		
GARLOCK, Charles W.	621-75-50	QM2/c	LST 507 U.S. Navy	2 May 44			Cambridge
LEDBETTER, Alvin L.	834-01-50	S2/c	LST 507 U.S. Navy	2 May 44	no trace		
FIELD, Paul R.	225-40-59	SM3/c	LST 507 U.S. Navy	2 May 44	no trace		Long Island, NY
BAILEY, James	725-84-44	Y2/c	LST 507 U.S. Navy	2 May 44	no trace		Fort Snelling, MS
BENNER, Charles D.	821-05-26	RM2/c	LST 507 U.S. Navy	2 May 44	no trace		
KING, Phillip E.	655-80-45	F2/c	LST 507 U.S. Navy	2 May 44	no trace		
SCHREIBER, William H.	653-88-83	S2/c	LST 507 U.S. Navy	2 May 44	no trace		
MARTIN, Howard A.	819-60-30	S2/c	LST 507 U.S. Navy	2 May 44	no trace		
GRIFFIN, Jimmie W.	892-95-16	SC3/c	LST 507 U.S. Navy	2 May 44	no trace		
MORANCY, Edgar F.	573-28-25	S2/c	LST 507 U.S. Navy	2 May 44	573-28-26		Cambridge
GAMBREL, Jake	856-34-86	S2/c	LST 507 U.S. Navy	2 May 44			Cambridge
MOORE, Joseph M.	818-74-58	S2/c	LST 507 U.S. Navy	2 May 44	no trace		
GOLDSMITH, Leonard	818-30-04	S2/c	LST 507 U.S. Navy	2 May 44	no trace		
HAMPTON, Jerry P.	828-36-37	S2/c	LST 507 U.S. Navy	2 May 44	no trace		Zachary Taylor, KY
DURRAM, J.W.	634-39-33	S1/c	LST 507 U.S. Navy	3 May 44	no trace		
KOSKI, Theodore J.	610-61-07	MoMM2/c	LST 507 U.S. Navy	3 May 44	no trace		
SQUIRES, Lawrence P.	666-98-33	MoMM2/c	LST 507 U.S. Navy	3 May 44	no trace		
GULLEDGE, William T.	833-86-48	S2/c	LST 507 U.S. Navy	3 May 44	no trace		Salisbury, NC
GIBSON, Richard M.	667-20-00	S1/c	LST 507 U.S. Navy	3 May 44	no trace		
CLEARY, James F.	802-34-93	HA2/c	LST 507 U.S. Navy	3 May 44	no trace		
EISENBACH, Harold E.	865-63-87	S2/c	LST 507 U.S. Navy	3 May 44	no trace		
SULLIVAN, George A.	853-87-80	S2/c	LST 507 U.S. Navy	3 May 44	no trace		
GEEHAN, Raymond R.	667-12-94	GM3/c	LST 507 U.S. Navy	3 May 44	no trace		Long Island, NY
SWARTS, J.S.	96231	Lt DVG	LST 507 U.S. Navy	3 May 44	no trace		Fort Bliss, TX
SMITH, Dennan H.	236354	Lt EVS	LST 507 U.S. Navy	3 May 44	no trace		Arlington, VA
COLLINS, Conner D. Jr.	313-728	ENS	LST 507 U.S. Navy	3 May 44	no trace		Hillcrest, MS
HOFMANN, Bruce B.	190-360	Lt (jg)	LST 507 U.S. Navy	3 May 44			Cambridge
CLARK, James J.	211-310	ENS SC VG	LST 507 U.S. Navy	3 May 44	no trace		
WRIGHT, Curtis M.	836-61-51	HA2/c	LST 507 U.S. Navy	2 May 44	no trace		
DINNEEN, Joseph M.	404-73-59	BM1/c	LST 507 U.S. Navy	2 May 44	464-73-59		Cambridge

Name	Service No.	Rank	Organization	Burial Dy M Yr	ABMC	NARA	Reburied
MALOTT, Robert J.	820-99-58	PhM3/c	LST 507 U.S. Navy	2 May 44	no trace		
MATHEWS, John E.	643-19-62	S2/c	LST 507 U.S. Navy	2 May 44			Cambridge
BETTENCOURT, John J.	205-45-89	MoMM3/c	LST 507 U.S. Navy	2 May 44	no trace		
GROWE, James T. Jr.	265-57-39	MoMM2/c	LST 507 U.S. Navy	2 May 44	no trace		
O'CONNELL, Michael J.	338-30-32	MoMM2/c	LST 507 U.S. Navy	2 May 44	no trace		
DICKERSON, William W.	619-15-80	SK2/c	LST 507 U.S. Navy	2 May 44	no trace		
MACKEY, Robert C.	285-04-07	Cox	LST 507 U.S. Navy	2 May 44			Cambridge
STANESIC, John L.	822-89-22	HA2/c	LST 507 U.S. Navy	2 May 44	no trace		
SUTHERLAND, Pete J.	966-13-83	S2/c	LST 507 U.S. Navy	2 May 44			Cambridge
RAGUSO, Paul M.	642-34-34	PhM3/c	LST 507 U.S. Navy	2 May 44	no trace		
STAUDT, Charles J. Jr.	809-02-98	MoMM1/c	LST 507 U.S. Navy	2 May 44			Cambridge
DAILEY, Carl W.	630-82-19	PhM3/c	LST 507 U.S. Navy	2 May 44	no trace		
DELDUCA, Thomas	810-17-78	Cox	LST 507 U.S. Navy	2 May 44	no trace		Long Island, NY
HOFFMAN, Russell W.	819-11-25	S1/c	LST 507 U.S. Navy	2 May 44	Russel		Cambridge
BLACKIE, Henry A.	209-08-71	S2/c	LST 507 U.S. Navy	3 May 44			Cambridge
MILLER, John H.	813-84-35	S2/c	LST 507 U.S. Navy	3 May 44			Cambridge
DOBSON, Henry R.	641-45-73	PhM2/c	LST 507 U.S. Navy	3 May 44			Cambridge
GREECO, Joseph G.	809-42-85	S1/c	LST 507 U.S. Navy	3 May 44	no trace		
RYAN, James P.	601-17-55	SM3/c	LST 507 U.S. Navy	3 May 44		Jr	Cambridge
MAGGARD, Daniel W. Jr.	835-67-34	S2/c	LST 507 U.S. Navy	3 May 44	no trace		
RAPTIS, Charles G.	805-70-65	THM3/c	LST 507 U.S. Navy	3 May 44	no trace		
FITTS, Felton T.	269-12-88	GM2/c	LST 507 U.S. Navy	3 May 44	no trace		
ROGERS, William L.	837-41-73	HA2/c	LST 507 U.S. Navy	3 May 44	no trace		
MEYERS, L.A.	653-83-15	F2/c	LST 507 U.S. Navy	3 May 44	no trace		

ABMC column shows details given by the American Battle Monuments Commission. Therefore "no trace" denotes the ABMC show no record of burial or commemoration as "missing in action" at any of their cemeteries.

NARA column shows enlistment details.

Survivors of Ship 531

U. S. Army Personnel

NAME	RANK	SERIAL NO.	ORGANIZATION
Friley, Olen W.	Pvt	37525021	607 QM
Smith, T. B.	Pfc	37415531	3206 Quarter
Dortch, E. W.	1st Lt	01584149	1st Eng
Solon, M.	Pfc	12134227	35th S. Const Bn.
Wilson, E. G.	Pvt	15372337	35th S. Const Bn.
Metcalf, R. K.	Pvt	37487664	607 Quarter.
Hicker, M. H.	Pfc	32724760	3206 Quarter
Barr, M. C.	Pfc	37659944	3206 Quarter
Carter, B. J.	Pfc	37503087	3206 Quarter.
Picht, Earl	Pfc	37503275	3206 Quarter.
Ferguson, Richard J.	Tec 5	37415582	3206 Quarter.
Nowlin, Robert A. Jr.	Pvt	13121100	531 Engr Shore Rgt.
Verheeche, W. P.	Pvt	37414779	3206 Quarter.
PERRY, John A.	Pfc	33760276	462 ATC.
Hooch, Charles R.	Sgt.	37504362	3206 QM.
Rstoesvich, John C.	Pvt	39236406	531 Engr.
Butt, B. E.	Pfc	37504281	3206 QM.
Samuels, R.	S Sgt	33246074	625 Ord Am.
Longnaker, E. A.	Corp	37191727	531 Engr.
Florence, E. K.	Pvt	35451539	531 Engr
Beaver, Harry E.	Pfc	35290951	531 Engr.
Strilke, Michael J.	Pvt	36728050	531 Engr.
Fitzpatrick, Dale E.	Pvt	37504135	3206 QM.
Stubbe, Raymond T.	Sgt.	32567078	35 Sig. Const Bn.
Piatkowski, L. B.	Pvt	36716883	35 Sig. Const Bn.
McKEE, B.	Pfc	35534357	4144 QM.
Anders, Max	Pfc	32700239	3206 QM Serv Co.
Jones, J. V.	Pvt	36772348	607 QM
Sidenstricker, E. B.	Sgt.	37502557	3206 QM.
Mitchell, Harlen	Pvt	38212608	3206 QM.
Crum, Loyd	Pvt	37504292	3206 QM

Appendix 32

HEADQUARTERS VII CORPS

SHEPLEGH COURT
29 April 1944
MEMORANDUM:

TO: Commanding General or Commanding Officer of Units Participating
In the Exercise.

Regarding enemy activity of night 27 - 28 April during the exercise,
members of this command will not mention the incident to military
personnel not participating in the exercise nor to civilians either orally or
in writing until authorized by this headquarters. Advise all concerned.

By command of Major General COLLINS:

R. G. McKEE,
Colonel, GSC,
Chief of Staff.
DISTRIBUTION:
"Special"

Appendix 33

COPY OF LETTER OF 25 June 1944   200.6 (A)
of 1st Engineer Special Brigade to Com. Gen., Advance section Com. Z

200.6 (A) 4th Ind   CWS/ldt
HEADQUARTERS 1ST ENGINEER SPECIAL BRIGADE, APO 230, U.S .ARMY 25 June '44
      To; Commanding General, Advance Section, Como Z, APO 358, U.S.Army

1. Pursuant to provisions of Par. 12 b (3), Ax 260-10, as amended, and Par 3 of 2nd Ind above, it is recommended that the 3206th QM Sevice Company end the 557th QM Rhd Compnay be given credit for battle participation in connection with an engagement fought in the English Channel off Portland, England, on the night of 27-28 April '44.
2. Casualties suffered by these units in this engagement were as follows:

	Killed	Wounded	Missing
3206th Q,M Sv Co	39	4	156
557th QM Rhd Co	47	2	26

3. LST 507 and 531 on which these companies were embarked were sunk in the engagement which was against E-Boats at about 0130 hours on 28 April 1944.

4. Attached are copies of reports after action against the enemy submitted by troop commanders of other ships in the convoy in compliance with Par 10, AR 345-105, as amended. The company commanders of the two companies herewith recommended were killed in action together with all officers of the 557th.QM Rhd Co and all but one officer of the 3206th QM SV Co. No reports of action against the enemy were submitted for the two LST' s that were sunk.
5. The two companies listed above were scheduled to take part in the landings on the Normandy Coast of France, but due to heavy losses suffered in the engagement they had to be withdrawn.
For the Commanding General,
CHARLES W. SULLIVAN
        Captain, Inf.
        Adjutant.

2 Inc 1.
Incl. 1. Report after action against the enemy submitted
        by Captain Daivid D. Moore.
     2. Report after action against the enemy submitted
        by Captain Theodore E. Wilkinson.

SECRET

RESTRICTED
- - - - - - - - - -

HEADQUARTERS 1ST ENGINEER SPECIAL BRIGADE
GENERAL ORDERS)
A.P.O.562, U.S.ARMY
NUMBER   27)   9
September 1944

1. Under the provisions of Army Regulations 600-45, dated 22 September
1943, the Purple Heart is awarded to the following: ':,..   " ',   ,   ,

Dayton R. Vallicott, First Lieutenant, 01110306, 1605th Engineer   Map Section, for
wounds received in action against the enemy on 28 April 1944, in _____. Entered military
service from Nebraska.

Rollie E. Young, Staff Sergeant, 35121411, 278th Amphibian Truok   Company (TC), for
wounds received in action against the enemy on 28 April 1944, in _____ . Entered military
service from Ohio.
Robert A. Kurz, Sergeant, 31115452, 33rd Chemical Decontamination Company, for wound
received in action against the enemy on 28 April 1944, in _____. Entered military service
from Vermont.

Howard C. Dozier, Technician Fourth Grade, 37064239, 33rd Chemical Decontamination
Company, for eound received in action against the enemy on 28 April 1944, in _____.
Entered military service from Arkansas.

John A. Perry, Technician Fifth Grade, 33760276, 462nd Amphibian Truck Company, for
wounds received in action against the enemy on 28 April 1944, in English Channel. Entered
military service from Pennsylvania.
Paul H. Mueller, Private First Class, 37675782, 1605th Engineer Map Section, for wounds
received in action against the enemy on 28 April 1944, in _____. Entered military
service from Iowa.

Nelson L. Clements, Private, 33636071, 278th Amphibian Truck Company (TC), for wounds
received in action against the enemy on 28 April 1944, in _____. Entered military
service from Virginia.

Charles W. Laverdure,Private, 396053935, _____. Engineer Combat Battalion, for
wounds received in action against the enemy on 21 July 1944, in _____. Entered military
service from Montana.

By order of Colonol MEYER:
CHARLES W. SULLIVAN,
Captain, Inf,
Adjutant.
OFFICIAL:

Appendix 34

PURPLE HEART
Paragraph 2-8, Army Regulation 600-8-22 (Military Awards)
25 February 1995

The Purple Heart was established by General George Washington at Newburgh, New York, on 7 August 1782, during the Revolutionary War. It was reestablished by the President of the United States per War Department General Orders 3, 1932.

a. The Purple Heart is awarded in the name of the President of the United States to any member of an Armed Force or any civilian national of the United States who, while serving under competent authority in any capacity with one of the U.S. Armed Services after 5 April 1917, has been wounded or killed, or who has died or may hereafter die after being wounded-

(1) In any action against an enemy of the United States.
(2) In any action with an opposing armed force of a foreign country in which the Armed Forces of the United States are or have been engaged.
(3) While serving with friendly foreign forces engaged in an armed conflict against an opposing armed force in which the United States is not a belligerent party.
(4) As a result of an act of any such enemy of opposing armed forces.
(5) As the result of an act of any hostile foreign force
   b. While clearly an individual decoration, the Purple Heart differs from all other decorations in that an individual is not "recommended" for the decoration; rather he or she is entitled to it upon meeting specific criteria.
(2) A wound is defined as an injury to any part of the body from an outside force or agent sustained under one or more of the conditions listed above. A physical lesion is not required, however, the wound for which the award is made must have required treatment by a medical officer and records of medical

Appendix 35

COMPANY MORNING REPORT ENDING 250° 4 April 194 4
DATE MONTH YEAR

STATION Bodmin, Cornwall County, England

ORGANIZATION 93rd Chemical Decon Co. C.W.S.

SERIAL NUMBER	NAME	GRADE	CODE
32409916	Bernardo, John	pvt	
99382366	Bertini, Milo V.	pfc	
37408272	Clayton, Kenneth	pvt	
36510674	Mieszkowski, Harry	T/5	
33587420	Rosowski, Anthony J.	pvt	
34443424	Sigman, Charles W.	pvt	
33110688	Stokes, Gris A.	pvt	
35505209	Strapp, John W.	T/4	
34514719	Johnson, Horace	pvt	
Above 9 EM fr dy w/Co to KIA			
	RECORD OF EVENTS		
	----		
28 April 44 ALERTED FOR DEPARTURE			
This morning report recinds consolidated			
morning report covering 22 April 44			
through 2 May 44			

OFFICER STRENGTH	FLD O & CAPT		1ST LT		2D LT		WO		FLT O	
	PRES	ABS'T	PRES	ABS'T	PRES	ABS'T	PRES	ABS'T	PRES	ABS'T
APhD			3	2						
ATCHD GRADES										
ATCHD FR OTHER ORGN										
TOTAL			3	2						

AVN CADET & ENL STRENGTH	AVIATION CADETS		ENLISTED MEN			
	PRESENT	ABSENT	PRESENT FOR DUTY	PRESENT NOT FOR DY	ABSENT	PRESENT AND ABS'T
APhD			76		108	184
ATCHD GRADES						
ATCHD FR OTHER ORGN						
TOTAL	76		76		108	184

RATION	ESTIMATED NUMBER OF RATIONS REQUIRED FOR	DAY OF WEEK Monday		NUMBER
		DATE 1 May 44		180

MESS ATTENDANCE FOR DAY OF THIS REPORT			TOTAL	AVERAGE
BREAKFAST 65	DINNER 65	SUPPER 65	195	65

MEN AUTHORIZED TO MESS SEPARATELY 0   MEN ATCHD FOR RATIONS 0
MEN ATCHD TO OTHER ORGN FOR RATIONS 0   NET 0   O & OTHERS MESSED 0

MEN PRESENT 76	LESS 0	76	PLUS 0	TOTAL 76

PAGE 2 OF 2 PAGES

I CERTIFY THAT THIS MORNING REPORT IS CORRECT AND THAT RATION FIGURES IN FACT IS CORRECTLY AS BEING CORRECT AS REPORTED TO BE.

SIGNATURE _Clayton A. Blomquist_

CLAYTON A. BLOMQUIST, 1st Lt. CWS

Appendix 36

HEADQUARTERS
462ND AMPHIBIAN TRUCK COMPANY (TC)
APO 230, U.S. ARMY

1 May 1944

SUBJECT: Report of Enemy Action, 28 April 1944.

TO   : Commanding General, 1st Engineer Special Brigade, APO 230, U.S. Army.

1. At 0230, Thursday 28 April 1944, during exercise "TIGER", battle
station was sounded on LST 511 and very shortly after, antiaircraft firing
and explosions were heard. I left my room and proceeded to the deck as rapidly
as possible and saw three LST's in flames. Prior to that time the 8 LST's had
been proceeding at approximately 5 mile per hour in single file with one
Corvette as protection. The night was quite dark but clear, no moon was visible.

2. Flares continued to drop but the officers of the LST did not know
whether they were allied or enemy flares. The skipper of the ship, Lt.
Yacevich stated to me that two vessels had been picked up by the Radar prior
to the attack but that he was told that they were other ships in the convoy.
He also stated that we were approximately 15 miles off the French coast and
that we had been struck twice by torpedoes but that they had failed to explode.

3. Two of the LST's were burning for approximately two hours. No life
rafts, vests, or boats were put overboard nor was any attempt at rescue made
despite the fact that LST 613 directly to the stern of us had been exploded.

4. LST 511 suffered 19 casualties among the troops, none from the
462nd Amphibian Truck Company. There were 144 men of the 462nd on board and
45 of the same company on number 613. Three of the forty five returned to the
company for duty. All vehicles and equipment on board the 613 was lost.

THEODORE R. WILKINSON
Captain, TC, Commanding

Appendix 37

HEADQUARTERS
478TH AMPHIBIAN TRUCK COMPANY (TC)
A.P.O. 230, U. S. ARMY

1 May, 1944

SUBJECT: Report of Events Aboard LST 289, 28 April, 1944

TO : Commanding General, 1st Engineer Special Brigade, APO 230, U. S. Army.

General quarters was sounded at approximately 0135 hours. A check was made within five minutes to see that men were awakened, dressed and in their stations All was found to be in good order. A tour was made topside as well. Lt Logan and myself closely scanned the sea on all sides. I was only able to observe one and LST identified as LST 507, approximately 500 yards astern and another LST unidentifed approximately 750 yards ahead. I had just entered the LST amidships when there was an explosion heard and Lt Logan entered and stated very calmly that the LST directly astern had just blown up and that the screams of the men were terrible. This was at approximately 0150 hours. Captain Ashway and Lt Damuck had been stationed to control the movement of the men up the rear hatchway port side in case it became necessary. At approximately 0200 hours another explosion was heard and Lt Logan again reported that the LST directly in front had been hit and was afire.

At approximately 0210 hours when I was up in the chart room we were struck by a torpedo aft. This destroyed the crews quarters, the rudder, and the rear guns. There was also a fire aft and some flooding which was immediately brought under control by the Navy.

The Captain of the ship, Lt Mettler sent word down to me to the effect that if I desired to remove Army personnel by means of Dukws, he would lower the ramp. I went over our approximate position with the ships navigation officer which was 10 to 15 miles east of Exmouth and 20 to 25 miles south. By this time another LST had been torpedoed and was afire. I decided that it would probably be better to evacuate the Army personnel and risk making shore and so informed the Captain. However, by this time the Captain had received word that the ship had quit taking water, that the fires were out and that the engines and propellers were still in working order, and consequently he decided to try to make port. This was at approximately 0230 hours. LCVPs were let over the side and were used to hold the course of the LST straight. A course was set by the North Star and we headed for the British Isles. At approximately 0515 we sighted our first allied craft which apparently was guarding some LCTs and LCVPs. From then on until approximately 1100 hours we were escorted by one or more allied craft. At 1100 hours we were taken in tow by a tug and escorted by a Corvette. We proceeded to Dartmouth where we docked at approximately 1430 hours.

A joint first aid and clearing station was set up by Army and Navy personnel in the Officer's lounge at the time general quarters was sounded. All wounded were brought in there and treated and the bed cases were then placed in the officer's quarters. Captain Humm of the 4th Medical Bn., was aboard with a detachment of that unit and is to be commended for the job that he and his first aid personnel performed.

-1-

-2-

The following Army personnel were wounded in action:

Capt. Elmer B. Ashway	556 QM Rhd Co.
Pfc Raymond A. Brehhe	556 QM RHd Co.
Pvt Stanley A. Morran	556 QM Rhd Co.
1st Lt. Walter E. Damuck	478th Amph Trk Co.
Pvt Samuel E. Stinnett	478th Amph Trk Co.

and all but Pvt Stinnett required hospitalization, being hospitalized at Dartmouth Naval Hospital upon arrival there.

The Naval casualties were as follows:

Number of dead	4
Number of wounded	18
Number of missing	6 (approximately)

The army personnel aboard is to be highly commended for the good order they maintained. There was absolutely no confusion or sign of panic, at any time and any order given was quickly obeyed. The guards all remained at their posts throughout.

A roll call was taken as soon as practicable and all army personnel were accounted for.

All personnel were cautioned before leaving ship not to mention anything that had taken place and were again reminded by myself at a formation upon arrival Stover's Camp.

DAVID D. MOORE,
Captain, Inf.
Commanding

Appendix 38

REPORT OF PROCEEDINGS

S E C R E T

E-BOAT ATTACK ON CONVOY T-4 - EXERCISE TIGER

Sir,

    At 0130B April 28th, 1944, whilst on patrol Dart Buoy to Mewstone under the orders of H.M.S. TANATSIDE, E-boat reports from H.M.S. ONSLOW were received by me on broadcast "CN". On going up to the bridge a signal was in the course of being made from TANATSIDE detaching me to join H.M.S. AZALEA with convoy T.4 in place of H.M.S. SCIMITAR.

    2. At 0137 on completion of receipt of these order, I set a course 080 degrees, 23 knots. Speed was limited to 23 knots maximum owing to the unreliability of No. 1 boiler which was being reserved for emergency high spoeed if in actual contact with enemy E-boats. Course 080 degrees was laid off from Dart Buoy to make the swept channel north of "I" Buoy, intending to proceed up the channel in anticipation of meeting the convoy at 0245 in position 243 degrees Portland Bill 17 miles.

    3. Shortly after detaching from patrol distant starshell were seen in various directions, mainly ahead. At 0215 exchange of tracer was seen in the distance, followed by a sheet of flame as the first LST was hit and caught fire, on bearing 060 degrees. Course was altered towards the burning ship, which was obviously the position of the convoy (AZALEA's first report, T.O.O. 280220B was not received on 2760 kc/s until 0510). At 0225 approximately an exchange of tracer was seen to the Southward of the convoy, and course was altered to starboard to intercept.

    4. At 0230 small radar contact was obtained with Type 291, bearing ahead 4000 yards. The order was given to hold this and the bearing illuminated with starshell, but nothing was seen and no hydrophone effect was obtained by Asdics. The radar operator reported "contact faded" before its movement could be plotted, and he considered it probably a false contact. Starshell was seen shortly afterwards on the probable line of retreat to the South West, but it is considered that H.E. would have been heard at 4000 yards range if the contact had been a fast moving E-boat.

    5. Tracer was again seen in the direction of the convoy, and a second ship was seen to be on fire. Course was therefore altered back to this position. Having no I.F.F. a signal was made to AZALEA stating that I was -ining on a course of 060 degrees in order to avoid possibilities of mis-identification. No contact of the convoy could yet be obtained by radar, though this should be now have been possible if the convoy were in the swept channel. At 0256 the first radar contact of the burning ships was picked up bearing 060 degrees, 12000 yards - which, by plot, was 2 1/2 miles to the Eastward of the swept channel. Scattered contacts of large ships were then obtained on bearings 125 degrees 10,00 yards and 140 degrees 14000 yards, as well as on the bearing 060. Evidently the whole convoy was scattered, as was confirmed by position given by AZALEA in reply to my query (220 degrees Portland Bill, no distance given). As there were destroyer patrols and AZALEA to the Southeast, and numerous E-boat contacts had been reported by the shore plot all over Lyme Bay, I considered the best course of action was to continue in a Northeasterly direction towards the position of attack. Owing to the delay in receiving shore plots on CN broadcast only there was little hope of intercepting individual E-boats except by chance; furthermore, my primary duty was to find and protect the remaining ships of the convoy. As it was, some time had been lost in

searching for the convoy, which had not been reported as scattered, and in altering course towards the various bursts of tracer and starshell that had been seen. It will be appreciated, however, that I could not have reached the convoy in time to assist in preventing the attack, as I was detached at a distance of 30 miles only 40 minutes before the attack took place.

6.   On approaching the position of the burning wrecks at 0315 a small object was seen which, when illuminated by starshell turned out to be the bows of an LST protruding about 15 feet out of the water with about 50 survivors on it. I therefore closed, went alongside, and took them off. There appeared to be a large number of survivors in the water all round, but as there were two or three power boats in the vicinity that had been got away, and the sea was flat calm, I considered it preferable to leave them to carry on with the rescue work and to wait until daylight before working my screws amongst survivors. I continued therefore to make and investigation of the area of attack.

7.   By 0440 reports showed that the E-boats were returning to base, and I requested permission to pick up survivors. This was granted. At 0500 LST 515 returned from the Northeast and lowered all boats to pick up survivors. I therefore considerd it best to leave the job of picking up individuals from the water to the small boats while I screened the LST and searched for outlying groups of survivors. Whilst carrying out this duty the bow of another LST was found protruding out of the water about a mile to the Northward, with two survivors on it. After taking them aboard I sank this wreck with gunfire and depth charges.

8.   At 0600 AZALEA appeared to the Northward escorting the damaged LST 289. I reported to him that I considered 3 LST's had been sunk. ONSLOW and OBEDIENT joined at this time and commenced searching for survivors; BRISSENDEN joined shortly afterwards. I placed myself under the ordrs of Captain (D), Seventeenth Destroyer Flotilla in ONSLOW and was ordered to Portland to land my survivors. I landed 129 survivors from LST's 507 and 531, and reported the situation in person to the Flag Officer in Charge, Portland and by signal to the Commander in Chief, Plymouth. I informed FOIC Portland that tere were a large number of bodies in the position of the sinkings and that some salvageable equipment was adrift there.

9.   Whilst I was in Portland BRISSENDEN found 4 LST's anchored in West Bay and proceeded to escort them. I sailed to overtake, but arrived back in the exercise area shortly before this convoy which, for reasons unknown, came by QZS 462 instead of QZS 461. I reported to TANATSIDE on arrival and resumed patrol.

GENERAL REMARKS.

(1) The statement that 3 L.S.T.'s were sunk was based on the situation found at the position of the attack, namely - one L.S.T. which appeared to be intact was blazing fiercely from end to end. This subsequently turned over and sank.

A second and smaller conflagration appeared to be a section of an LST near which was found the first floating bow with survivors on it - presumably the bows from this burning wreckage.
The bows of what appeared to be a third wrecked LST were about a mile to the Northward of the two wrecks mentioned above.

(2) Most of the corpses seen in the water appeared to be uninjured and were wearing inflatable lifebelts. It is the opinion of this ship that many unnecessary casualties were caused by the troops wearing their lifebelts too low down on the stomach - instead of well up under the armpits - thereby tipping them forward with their faces in the water.

I have the honour to be, Sir,
Your obedient Servant

```
                                    /s/          P.E. KING
                                    LIEUTENANT COMMANDER, R.N.V.R.
                                                      IN COMMAND
```

COMMANDER, FORCE 'U', U.S.S. BAYFIELD.
(Copies to: Commander in Chief, Plymouth;
            Captain(D) Plymouth;
            Commanding Officer, H.M.S. TANATSIDE)

ENCLOSURE Q

Appendix 39

2 May 1944

(60)

From: Commanding Officer LST 531.
To :   Thé Secretary of tho Navy.

Via :   (1) COM LST Gr. 32 (ComTask Unit 125.11.4)
            (2) COM LST Gr. 29 (ComTask Group 125.11)
            (3) COM Task Force 125
            (4) COM Task Force 123
            (5) COM Task Force 122
            (6) COM Twelfth Fleet
            (7) CinC US Fleet

Subject: Loss of Ship - report on.

Reference: (a) Commanding Officer USS LST 531 Secret dispatch 021542B
                of May 1944
            (b) Article 841 (3), U.S. Navy Regulations.

1.   Supplementing reference (a), the following full report on the
loss of the USS LST 531 is submitted as required by reference (b).

2.   This report is submitted by Ens. Douglas G. HARLANDER, D-V(G),
USNR, the senior survivor. Assistance in preparing this report is being furnished by
Commander B. J. SKAHILL, USN, who was the Commander of Convoy T-4 during
this exercise.

3.   No government property was saved.

4.   No publications, records, or accounts were saved.

5.   Narrative of Loss:-

(a) The LST 531 sailed from Plymouth, England at 0945B on
27 April 1944, in company with LSTs 515, 496, 511 and 58 to take part in
Exercise under CTF 125 operation order No. 2-44. The ships were in column
formation, in the following order:- 515, 496, 511, 531 and 58. T-4 convoy
Commander was Commander B. J. SKAHILL, USN, in LST 515.

(b) At approximately 1100B HMS Azelia joined as escort in Lat
50°-13 N, Long. 4° 12' W.

(c) Proceeded at convoy speed of five (5) knots on various
courses to exercise area.

(d) At approximately 1930B on 27 April the Brixham Section
of T-4 Convoy fell in astern of the Plymouth section in the following order,
LSTs 499, 289, and 507. Speed was increased to six (6) knots.

/ 1)

(e) At approximately 2222 B changed course to 090° T in D.R. (61
Lat. 50° - 34' N, Long. 3° - 14.5' W.

(f) At approximately 0029B 28 April changed course to 145°T
in D.R. Lat. 50° -34 N, Long. 2° 55.5' W.

(g) At approximately 0130D general quarters was sounded (X)
when I got to the bridge I was informed that gunfire was heard and tracers
seen. I did not see the tracers nor did I hear any gunfire. I was informed
the gunfire was from the direction of our stern but was not directed at
this ship. The firing did not last over one minute.

(h) Approximately 0150D secured from general quarters. (O)

(i) Approximately 0203 the O.O.D. called to the Q.M. of
the watch to log an underwater explosion. The originator was in the chart
house at the time.

(j) Approximately 0204B a ship was reported afire in the distance
off our starboard quarter. Ens. CANTRELL and the originator of this report
observed the fire and we were puzzled as to its identity. About the time
we decided it was an LST, (Approximately 0218B) this ship was torpedoed
on the starboard side by two torpedoes separated by about one minute of
time. First torpedo hit amidships, the second torpedo hit in the vicinity
of #3 boat. The ship immediately burst into flames and #1-40mm gun
immediately commenced firing to starboard. All electric power failed,
telephones were inoperative, and the engines stopped. Fire fighting was
attempted but was futile, the apparatus used failed to function. It was
apparent the fire could not be controlled and efforts were made to release
#4 boat, these efforts were not successful due to the flames--boats
#5 and #6 were demolished by the explosions.

(k) Approximately 0224B, the ship rolled over and originator
gave the command to abandon ship; it is estimated that not more than 15
men were in the vicinity. Some men had previously jumped overboard.
The personnel observed appeared to be calm and not unduly excited.

6.   Approximately 0700D I was rescued by HMS ONSLOW.

7.   Personnel statistics:-

	NAVY	ARMY
Originally aboard	142	354
Rescued	28 (15 of these are hospital cases)	44 (10 of these are hospital cases)
Dead & missing	114	310

8.   The weather during the night:-
        Sea was calm.
        Wind gentle to zero
        Visibility was fair to good. A quarter moon was out but
        not bright.

D. G. HARLANDER (LST 531)
Ens. D-V(G) USNR

Appendix 40

UNITED STATES SHIP LST #515   FRIDAY 28, 1944

ZONE DESCRIPTION -2   REMARKS

---

0 - 4

    Steaming as before on course 090°(T), 099°(psc) enroute exercise "Tiger", speed 5 knots. 0018 passed unlighted bouy G2 abeam to port, c/c to 144°(T), 153°(psc). 0028 Degausing coils reset for course 144°(T), 153°(psc) on following settings: M+32; Q+26; F-24; A-10. 0135 Gunfire astern believed to be LST #511 firing to port. No target observed by this ship. Sounded General Quarters. Firing one minute duration. 0142 c/c right to 206°(T); Radar turned on. 0153 Secured from General Quarters. 0204 Last ship in column, LST #507, hit. Sounded General Quarters. Gunfire by ships in column to starboard. No target observed. 0208 Ship astern, believed to be LST 531, hit: Large explosion and fire. 0218 Two enemy E Boats crossed column between 3rd and 4th and 4th and 5th ships from starboard to port by radar. 0220 Opened fire with starboard 40 MM guns on radar bearing 351°(T), range 2500 yards. No hits observed. Expended 86 rounds 40 MM ammunition. 0220 c/c left to 170°(T); c/s to 11 knots, taking evasive tactics. 0225 Gun #25 saw target and opened fire. No hits observed. 0232 Advised Radio Portland of E Boat attack acknowledged at 0232. 0235 c/c left to 090°(T) after observing flares to starboard bearing 260°(T) distance about 20,000 yds. Observed fire believed to be burning ship in transport area. 0236 Observed four white flares bearing about 180°(T) distance 4,500 yds. 0237 two LST's which were hit burning fiercely distance 10,000 yds. 0242 Five white flares 180°(T) distance 5,000 yds. 0245 c/c left to 145°(T). 0249 c/c right to 090°(T). Two flares bearing 180°(T) distance 5,000 yds. 0250 c/c left to 080°(T). 0303 Six white flares 170°(T) distance 12,000 yds. 0305 c/c left to 050°(T). Three flares bearing 170°(T), 12,000 yds. 0308 c/c left to 040°(T). 0320 c/c left to 350°(T). 0329 Three flares 035°(T), 6,000 yards. 0358 c/c to 290°(T). 0415 c/c 226°(T) proceeding to scene to pick up survivors.

                                B. W. WAHLBERG
                                ENSIGN USNR

4 - 8

    0435 approaching burning wreckage at various courses and speeds. 0445 Commenced lowering boats to pick up survivors. 0735 all boats returned to ship. Underway various courses and speeds enroute to Portland, England with approximately one hundred and eighteen (118) walking survivors, fourteen (14) litter cases, forty five (45) dead.

                                D. G. DOWNING
Certified to be a true copy   ENSIGN, U.S.N.R.

Appendix 41

H.M.S. "AZALEA"

                                                    28th April 1944.
Sir,
        I have the honour to submit the follwoing Report of Proceedings of
H.M.S. "AZALEA" during the attack by E-Boats on Convoy T4 on the night of
27th.-28th. April 1944.
        2. All times are "B" times. All courses and bearings are true.
        3. There was a slight breeze from the Northward, the sea was calm,
and visibility was good.
        4. "AZALEA" was escorting convoy T4, consisting of nine L.S.Ts. in
line ahead, and was in station 2000 yards ahead of the column.
H2 buoy was abeam at 0135 and course was altered to 206', the speed of the
convoy at this time being 3 1/2 knots.
        5. At approximately 0210 tracer was observed being fired to port by
an L.S.T. "Action stations" was sounded, "AALEA" closed the convoy but
nothing further was observed and no contacts were obtained.
        6. At approximately 0215 an L.S.T. in the rear of the convoy was
torpedoed and set on fire, and tracers were fired by L.S.Ts to starboard.
Within aminute or two a second L.S.T. was torpedoed and set on fire. My
position at this time was 252' Portland Bill 14.
        7. "AZALEA" zig-zagged down the starboard side of the convoy. I was
uncertain from which side the convoy was attacked and did not illuminate,
as I considered that if I illuminated the non-attacking side, the L.S.Ts.
would have been silhouetted.
        8. During the time "AZALEA" ws on the starboard beam tracer was fired
across my bows by an L.S.T., and the convoy was beginning to scatter. Also
at this time a Radar contact, presumably an E-Boat, was obtained close to
and in line with two or three L.S.Ts. This contact was held only for a
short time and was lost among the convoy "echoes" by the time I had altered
towards. No further Radar contacts were made and no E-Boats were sighted.
        9. By this time (approximately 0310), the convoy, although scattered,
was heading in a North-Easterly direction, and I took up station zigzagging to the Southward of them. I did not proceed to the assistance of
the L.S.T.s on fire as, being the only escort present, I considered that my
correct action ws to remain with the convoy. Assistance for the burning
L.S.Ts. was requested by me in my 280410B to H.M.S. "TANATSIDE".
        10. The convoy headed for West Bay. One L.S.T. anchored off Blackner
Point. The remiander closed the land further North and their "echoes" were
lost among the land "echoes".
        11. At 0520 I proceeded to the Westward to search for any further
L.S.Ts. and to pick up survivors if required. L.S.T. 289 was discovered
torpedoed in the stern in position 280 Portlant Bill 12, and as H.M.S.
"SALADIN" was standing by the burning L.S.T.s., I remained with 29 and
escorted this ship to Dartmouth.
        12. H.M.S. "BRISSENDEN" joined at 0750 and I informed him that the main
body of the convoy was in the vicinity of West Bay.

                                        I have the honour to be,
                                                Sir,
                                        Your obedient Servant,

                                        /S/   G/C/ GIDDES
                                        Lieutenant-Commander R.N.R.
                                                In Command.

The Commanding Officer,
H.M.S. "TANATSIDE"

Appendix 42

2Ol - Caffey, Eugene M. (0)

19 July 1951

SUBJECT :   Clarification of Record

TO :   The Adjutant General
                                            Department of the Army
                                            Washington 25, D.C.

1. This letter is inspired by some statements which I saw a few days ago in
"A Soldier's Story" by General of the Army Omar N. Bradley.

2. As it appears in my 201 file, my record in World War II is good.
However, there was an occurrence which I am sure has caused a 1ot of
uncharitable talk and has placed a question mark by my name: Shortly
before the invasion of Normandy I was relieved from command of the
1st Engineer Special Brigade which was to land and support the VII
Corps and the follow up troops coming to Utah Beach. My relief took
place a few days after a full dress amphibious rehearsal on the south
coast of England at Slapton Sands. The exercise was participated in by
the 4th Infantry Division, elements of the 1st Engineer Special Brigade,
the Navy, and the Air Corps. The exercise, held about 28 April 1944,
did not come off at all well. I supposed that those in authority knew the
major reason for the disappointing showing and that they knew that it
had nothing to do with me. Therefore it was a crushing surprise when
my Corps Commander, Major General J. Lawton Collins, informed me
a few days later that I was relieved from my command of my brigade.
He did not say why. I did not ask why. He permitted me to continue on
with the brigade as deputy commander. The new brigade commander
empowered me to run the brigade as I had been doing so I continued to
attend to its operations just as I always had.

3. I went on to Utah Beach with the brigade on 6 June 1944. The record
shows that then and thereafter I did well. However, I have always felt

shamed and discredited because it is a fact that at a crucial time I was relieved from command of an organization destined to play an important part in one of the great undertakings of all warfare. To make the disgrace more bearable, if such a thing could be, there was a complete unawareness on my part of anything I had done or failed to do to deserve it.

4. Concerning the exercise at Slapton Sands, the book referred to in Paragraph 1, above, has this to say toward the bottom of page 248:

" While motoring back to Dartmouth following the rehearsal I checked my findings with Keane, Dickson, Thorson, and Wilson. Like me, they were disturbed on two counts. The beach engineer organization had broken down ... "

" I suggested to Collins that he assign a new commander to Utah Beach engineer brigade.

" Not until four years after the war did I learn that these engineer troubles during the Utah rehearsal had not been caused by a breakdown in command but rather by the S-boat (sic) attack. For what I had been led to believe was a minor brush with the enemy was revealed to have been one of the major tragedies of the European War. Two LST's were sunk in that attack with a loss of more than 700 men. Yet for some unexplained reason the report had been withheld from me ..."

5. Thus, after seven years, the blot on my good name seems to have been erased. I understand now why I was relieved. It is ironic that I was relieved for a reason which it is stated did not exist. I would have been spared seven miserable years had the facts been known and evaluated then instead of later. However, in the hurry and pressures of a big war odd things happen and I have no complaint.

6. I request that this letter be placed with my 201 file so that it may be considered should there be occasion in the future to review my record. I further request that I be advised that the letter has been so filed.

EUGENE M. CAFFEY
Colonel, J.A.G.C.

Appendix 43

"The 507 started from Brixham, England on the afternoon of April the 27th, 1944. She was in company with the LST 499 and LST 289 as the last ship in the group of three. We maneuvered around in the English Channel until approximately 1930 at which time we fell astern of the five ships which made up the balance of the convoy which had come up from Plymouth. We cruised around until late that night on various courses and at various speeds preliminary to going to the assembly point.

At approximately 1:35 on the morning of April the 28th, gunfire was heard and tracers were observed coming from the port quarter. The origin of the fire was never determined, but apparently the fire was not directed at our ship, or at the ships which were ahead of us, our ship being the 8th ship in column, the last in the line. At approximately three minutes afterwards we were torpedoed on the starboard side.

We had noticed two apparently very fast ships on our starboard hand going astern of us probably 20 minutes prior to the time of the torpedoing. These two ships went past us approximately a mile and a half away, turned and came back heading the same way we did. At this time they were about a mile or slightly less away from our ship. We did not know just what they were, assuming that perhaps they were members of our escort. As they came abeam we were suddenly hit by a torpedo on the starboard side which tore through the sides and exploded in the near vicinity of the auxiliary engine room. This immediately knocked out all the lights, the fire main and caused fires to start on both the tank deck, in the engine rooms and topside. At the time we had 282 Army personnel aboard for the exercise, and with the personnel were the necessary trucks, jeeps and DUKWs, as they are called, to be used in the operation. All of the army vehicles naturally were loaded with gasoline, and is was the gasoline which caught fire first. As the gasoline spread on the deck and poured into the fuel oil which was seeping out of the side of the ship, it caused the fire on the water. The bow of the ship entirely separated from the bridge and the stern-most part of the vessel. We on the bridge could not contact the bow at any time.

We went to General Quarters immediately, as soon as we heard gunfire, at approximately 1:35 and were at general quarters until the order to abandon ship was given.

Every effort was made to control the fires which were raging throughout the ship, but due to the explosions the fire main had been rendered inoperative. E tried to fight the fire with the CO_2 containers scattered throughout the ship and with other means which were at hand, but absolutely no progress was made. The ship was sinking by the stern and listing to starboard.

The captain was doing everything in his power to get the fire under control and to keep the ship on an even keel. The captain considered whether to try and contact in some manner if he could, the other ships which apparently had gone ahead, or whether to make preparations to abandon ship. He decided on the latter course and gave the order to stand by to abandon ship. At approximately 2:30 the captain gave the order to abandon ship. Only two of the boats, were gotten into the water. Two of the others had been rendered inoperative due to the explosion and the remaining boats, two in number were afire. Also, since most of the rafts are spread amidships and were in the flame only two of the rafts were gotten over.

The process of abandoning ship was carried out in a very orderly manner. The army personnel was ordered off of the stern and those who were forward left the ship from that point. The army wore lifebelts, and all naval personnel, with the exception of a very few, wore kapok life jackets. The captain was the last man to leave the ship at approximately 2:35 or 2:40. As we left, trying our best to get away from the fire spreading on the water, the ship continued sinking and at approximately 3:15 or thereabouts the stern was down and only the bow was left showing with the fires still burning on the water.

With reference to records and government property. At the time the order to prepare to abandon ship was given, the ship's yeoman, whose battle station was the Captain's helper at the con, came by and asked for the keys to the office inasmuch as he had left his in the quarters. He was given the keys and went into the office, picked up the muster roll and other necessary records, which previously on many occasions he had been cautioned to have accessible for just such an emergency. He picked up his records and left the ship with such records.

However, the yeoman was lost at sea, his body was recovered, but all the records were gone. The leading quartermaster on the ship meanwhile had left the ship with the ship's log and the charts. He also drowned in the water and all records, which he had, were lost. The yeoman was James Bailey, and the quartermaster was Charles Garlock.

Aboard the LST 507 were 165 naval personnel, which included 14 officers. In army personnel we had 282. From this group, 89 of the navy personnel, including 8 officers are listed as survivors; five were picked up and taken to hospitals and being wounded, a total of 94 survivors. Fifty-eight men were picked up as dead, and 13 are still carried as missing. In the army 131 are listed as dead or missing, 151 were picked up as survivors, 19 of whom were hospitalized."

Appendix 44

Battle Casualties Sustained by VII Corps, 6 June–1 July 1944

Unit	Total	Killed	Wounded	Missing	Capture
			Type of Casualty		
All Units	22,119	2,811	13,564	5,665	79
4th Division	5,452	844	3,814	788	6
9th Division	2,438	301	2,061	76	
79th Division	2,376	240	1,896	240	
90th Division	2,399	386	1,979	34	
82d A/B Division	4,480	457	1,440	2,571	12
101st A/B Division	4,670	546	2,217	1,907	
Corps Troops	304	37	157	49	61

Appendix 45

The craft involved in Exercise Tiger and their abbreviated names

As a full-scale rehearsal Exercise Tiger utilized all the craft and ships that would be used by Force "U" on D-Day 6th June 1944.

From flat bottomed LCVPs each loaded with thirty troops, bucking their way to shore in the first assault waves followed by LCIs each carrying sixty combat ready assault troops. Close behind them were LCMs and LCTs carrying tanks, artillery and assault dozers to support the infantry. Slow, lumbering LSTs were each crammed with three to five hundred reinforcements, engineers and transportation troops with their vehicles, DUKWs, jeeps, trailers and cargo trucks. Approximately three thousand reinforcing infantry and specialized troops were carried on the Attack Transport ships.

Explanations of craft – optional for inclusion :-

LCVP = Landing Craft Vehicle / Personnel
LCI   = Landing Craft Infantry
LCM   = Landing Craft Machinery
LCT   = Landing Craft Tank
LST   = Landing Ship Tank

DUKW Amphibious 2½ ton trucks. The designation as a DUKW comes from military terminology where the D indicates a vehicle designed in 1942, the U meant "utility (amphibious)", the K indicated all-wheel drive and the W indicated two powered rear axles. Over 20,000 DUKW's were produced during the war.